AUSTRALIAN BRASS

It is doubtful whether there was another leader in the Australian Army with greater devotion to his job of training and commanding soldiers, or with more military learning or a more complete and carefully worked out doctrine of war.

Gavin Long, official historian of Australia in the war of 1939-45 (1943)

AUSTRALIAN BRASS
THE CAREER OF LIEUTENANT GENERAL SIR HORACE ROBERTSON

JEFFREY GREY

*Department of History, University College,
Australian Defence Force Academy.*

CAMBRIDGE
UNIVERSITY PRESS

CAMBRIDGE UNIVERSITY PRESS
Cambridge, New York, Melbourne, Madrid, Cape Town, Singapore,
São Paulo, Delhi, Dubai, Tokyo

Cambridge University Press
The Edinburgh Building, Cambridge CB2 8RU, UK

Published in the United States of America by Cambridge University Press, New York

www.cambridge.org
Information on this title: www.cambridge.org/9780521122511

© Cambridge University Press 1992

This publication is in copyright. Subject to statutory exception
and to the provisions of relevant collective licensing agreements,
no reproduction of any part may take place without the written
permission of Cambridge University Press.

First published 1992
This digitally printed version 2009

A catalogue record for this publication is available from the British Library

National Library of Australia Cataloguing in Publication data
Grey, Jeffrey
Australian brass: the career of Lieutenant General Sir Horace Robertson.
Bibliographic essay
Includes index.
ISBN 0 521 40157 7.
1. Robertson, Sir Horace, 1894–1960. 2. Australia. Army — Officers —
Biography. 3. Generals — Australia — Biography. 4.
Australia — History, Military — 20th century. I. Title.
355.0092

Library of Congress Cataloguing in Publication data
Grey, Jeffrey.
Australian brass: the career of Lieutenant General
Sir Horace Robertson / Jeffrey Grey.
Includes bibliographical references (p.210) and index.
ISBN 0-521-40157-7 (h/b).
1. Robertson, Horace Clement Hugh, Sir, 1894–1960.
2. Australia. Australian Army — Biography.
3. Generals — Australia — Biography. I. Title.
U55.R53G74 1992
355'.0092–dc20 91-34244 CIP
[B]

ISBN 978-0-521-40157-9 Hardback
ISBN 978-0-521-12251-1 Paperback

Cambridge University Press has no responsibility for the persistence or
accuracy of URLs for external or third-party internet websites referred to in
this publication, and does not guarantee that any content on such websites is,
or will remain, accurate or appropriate.

CONTENTS

Acknowledgments	vii
Illustrations and maps	x
Abbreviations	xiii
Author's note	xv
Introduction	xvii

Part One
1 Foundations: 1894-1915	3
2 A good war: 1916-1919	20
3 Between wars: 1919-1940	47
4 'His crowded hour': 1940-1941	76
5 'A turbulent subordinate': 1942-1946	101

Part Two
6 The occupation of Japan: 1945-1946	125
7 The occupation of Japan: 1946-1947	145
8 The occupation of Japan: 1948-1950	162
9 Robertson, BCOF and the Korean War: 1950-1951	179

Part Three
10 The final years: 1952-1960	195
11 'Red Robbie': a summation	205
Bibliographic essay	210
Notes	214
Index	245

ACKNOWLEDGMENTS

The Scottish novelist Robert Louis Stevenson was asked once whether he enjoyed writing; he said no, but that he enjoyed having written. After five years of living with Red Robbie I might endorse the sentiment. But if writing can be a painful process at times, among a working historian's greatest pleasures is the contact which research brings with all manner of people whose assistance is given so readily. I hope the final product will help to repay the debts I owe them.

Professor Peter Dennis, Alec Hill and my father, Major General R. A. Grey, read the manuscript in its entirety and offered many useful criticisms and corrections. Their different perspectives have greatly strengthened the finished book. Dr Robin Prior was his usual fund of insights into the conduct of the First World War. Dr Peter Edwards and Associate Professor Eric Andrews offered valuable criticisms of early chapters, while Dr Stewart Lone provided some Japanese perspectives on the occupation. All have my thanks; none are responsible for such errors and inconsistencies as remain.

Many others assisted materially in the research for this book, either in the course of their own work or through sharing their recollections of Robertson with me. I wish to thank in particular the staffs of the Australian Archives at Mitchell, Australian Capital Territory, Brighton, Victoria, and Sydney, New South Wales; the Manuscript Room of the National Library of Australia; the Mitchell Library, Sydney; the Royal Military College, Duntroon archives; the Liddell Hart Centre for Military Archives, King's College, London; the Imperial War Museum, especially Roderick Sudderby; the National Army Museum, Chelsea; Peter Liddle of the 1914-18 Personal Experience Archive, University of Leeds; Edward J. Boone, Archivist, MacArthur Memorial, Norfolk, Virginia; the Perkins Library, Duke University, Raleigh, North Carolina. I owe an especial debt to Helen Creagh, Jennifer Davison, and Jane West, all formerly of the Australian War Memorial, Canberra, and to Ron Gilchrist, Jim Stewart and Bronwyn Self, still employed there.

ACKNOWLEDGMENTS

Major General P. R. Phillips, then Assistant Chief of the General Staff — Personnel, Brigadier I. Macinnis, then Military Secretary, and Major General W. O. Rodgers, then Director General, Army Health Services, granted access to Robertson's lengthy personal file, relevant records in the Military Secretary's control, and equally voluminous medical records, which were of great assistance in tying down certain parts of his career. I acknowledge also the help of the staff at the Central Army Records Office in Melbourne in actually supplying the material. Dr David Horner, Chris Coulthard-Clark, Ivan Chapman, Susan Crawford of the Royal Commonwealth Society, Victoria Branch, Betty Krimminger in the United States, and Major General Sir Ivan Dougherty all supplied material in their possession. Walter Scott, of Perth, generously sent me Lieutenant General Sir Charles Gairdner's diary for 1947; I hope he will not feel that his generosity has been abused through the rather critical portrait I provide of Gairdner's position and activities in Japan. Professor Ian Nish of the London School of Economics, Dr Peter Lowe of the University of Manchester, Louis Allen, late of Durham University, and General Sir Anthony Farrar-Hockley, official historian of Britain's part in the Korean War, have discussed the occupation of Japan with me, and my understanding of British policy and British difficulties at this time has benefited accordingly. None however would agree with everything I have said here.

The late Brigadier Tony Hammett had been gathering material in the hope some day of writing something on Robertson; when he heard that I had decided to tackle a full biography he immediately placed this material at my disposal and provided a number of helpful introductions to others who had known my subject. Such selflessness was entirely typical, and his tragic early death in an air crash was a deep personal loss to all who knew and admired him. Scarcely less generous has been the contribution of the late Major General R. N. L. Hopkins. In numerous letters and in a long interview in Adelaide in May 1987, he shared with me his personal knowledge of Robertson acquired through many years of friendship and service together going back to Egypt at the end of the First World War. He long believed that Robbie deserved some greater measure of public recognition, and I hope that this book would have met his expectations. The younger generation of Robertson's family, his siblings' children, helped at an early stage by talking to me about their uncle and, in the case of Mrs R. G. O'Shea and J. H. G. Stevenson of Melbourne, allowed me to take away and copy such photographs and personal papers as they still possessed. I am grateful to them and to Bruce Robertson of Sydney and Mrs Nanette Clutterbuck of Perth accordingly.

The following answered my queries, often by mail at great length and in considerable detail: the late Major General R. N. L. Hopkins; Major General Sir Ivan Dougherty; Colonel Geoff Hollings; General Sir Arthur

ACKNOWLEDGMENTS

MacDonald; Colonel J. P. Buckley; Major General I. R. Campbell; Professor Alan Rix; Ivan Chapman; Major General R. E. Wade; Major General T. F. Cape; Brigadier R. R. Vial; Brigadier Sir Frederick Chilton; H. B. 'Jo' Gullett; the late Field Marshal Lord Harding of Petherton; Colonel C. W. T. Kyngdon; D. W. Rogers; Major Ralph Connor; Lieutenant Colonel Alan Fleming; Major Dudley Braham; the late Professor Gordon Rimmer; Brigadier F. T. Whitelaw; Brigadier L. R. Greville; Professor Christopher Thorne; Professor Alan Powell; Major General J. D. Keldie; Colonel A. A. Argent; B. J. F. Wright; Brigadier Ralph Eldridge; Lieutenant General Sir Thomas Daly; Major General C. H. Finlay; Miss Mavis Lay; Mrs Elyne Mitchell; Major General I. T. Murdoch; Major General R. M. Jerram, RTR; Brian Bond, King's College, London; Major General C. J. Waters, then Commandant of the Staff College, Camberley; Major General David Butler; Professor Roger Buckley; Professor D. Clayton James; Corr and Corr, Solicitors. I was struck repeatedly by the affection and regard in which so many of them held Robertson, even thirty years after his death, although none were blind to his faults.

In the often irksome process of production, I have again been fortunate to call on the assistance of Mrs Elizabeth Greenhalgh for a myriad of supporting tasks without which writing would be that much more difficult, and of Paul Ballard, who once again drew my maps. As always, I am indebted to Professor Alan Gilbert, now Vice-Chancellor of the University of Tasmania, for wise counsel and advice. My thanks also to Janet Bunny, and to Robin Derricourt and all at Cambridge University Press, who have treated me with such solicitude; and to Phil Mayne and the Army Public Relations staff at Headquarters, 2nd Military District in Sydney who came to my aid in procuring a transparency of the official portrait which graces the jacket.

My greatest debt, as always, is to my wife, Gina, and daughter, Victoria, who is still young enough not to begrudge her father his eccentric pursuits.

ILLUSTRATIONS AND MAPS

Illustrations

'No 2 from left, rear half company'. Robertson at Duntroon, 1912. 5

'Old Geelong Collegians' in the Light Horse, Egypt, probably before Gallipoli. Robertson is second from the left in the back row. 8

Robertson outside his dugout on Gallipoli, October 1915. 18

Captain Robertson soon after his return from Gallipoli, Cairo, 1916. *(Author's collection)* 21

Officers of the 10th Light Horse shaving in bivouack after the march from the railhead at Serapeum prior to the battle of Romani. Robertson at left. *(AWM J02972)* 25

Robertson (left) with Major General Sir George Barrow, GOC Yeomanry Mounted Division, and Colonel W. J. Foster, GSO 1, Palestine, 1917. 39

'Yourself and Jessie', soon after the end of the war. 48

Horace and Jessie, Flinders Golf Club, Melbourne, 1920s. 58

Robertson and staff, Headquarters, 7 Military District, 1939. 73

Commanding officers and brigade staff, 19th Infantry Brigade, Burg el Arab, *c.* late 1940. 80

Senior officers of the 6th Australian Division in the Middle East, January 1941. *L to R:* Major Denzil Macarthur-Onslow (divisional cavalry), Squadron-Leader Judge, RAF (air liaison officer), Major Ian Campbell (brigade major, 16 Brigade), Brigadier 'Tubby' Allen (16 Brigade), Major General Iven Mackay (GOC), Robertson (19 Brigade), Colonel George

Vasey (AA&QMG), Brigadier Stan Savige (17 Brigade), Lieutenant Colonel L. C. Lucas (CRE), Lieutenant Colonel C. E. Prior (CO, 2/1 Machine Gun Battalion), Brigadier 'Ned' Herring (CRA), Lieutenant Colonel R. M. Jerram (7 Battalion, Royal Tank Regiment), Colonel Frank Berryman (GSO 1). (AWM 5645) 82

Robertson, Brigadier L. J. Morshead (observer), and Lieutenant Colonel Hogshaw, Royal Northumberland Fusiliers, in the main square of Tobruk after the Italian surrender. 87

'Surrender of Tobruch [sic]. [L to R]: Lt Col Hogshaw, RNF, Robertson, Captain Salventiani, Chief of Staff, Admiral Vietina, General Barberis, Major Key, 2/8 Battalion.' 87

Robertson and Morshead lunching among surrendered Italian soldiers and sailors, Tobruk. 88

Robertson with General Sir Archibald Wavell the day after the capture of Tobruk. 90

Publicity photograph of Robertson as GOC, 1 Australian Armoured Division, probably late 1942. 109

Robertson with Lieutenant General Adachi, Japanese XVIII Army commander, and staff, Wom airstrip, 12 September 1945. 120

Robertson and MacArthur take the salute on the occasion of the arrival of the Australian Minister for External Affairs, Dr H. V. Evatt, Japan, 1947. (AWM 44291) 160

Robertson and Menzies inspect a guard from the BCOF Signals Regiment, accompanied by the commanding officer, Lieutenant Colonel S. J. Greville, Japan, 1950. (Author's collection) 172

Robertson and Air Vice Marshal C. A. Bouchier, Japan, probably 1950. (AWM DUNK 5049) 185

Robertson and General Matthew B. Ridgway take the salute before Robertson's departure from Japan, 1951. (AWM DUNK 5043) 191

Robertson's coffin leaves Scots Church, Melbourne, 3 May 1960. (By permission of the *Age*, Melbourne) 203

Unless otherwise stated all photographs are from the Robertson papers and appear by courtesy of Mrs R. G. O'Shea of Melbourne.

Maps

Positions at Hill 60, August 1915.	15
10th Light Horse attack at Hill 60, 28-29 August 1915. (Based on a sketch by H. C. H. Robertson.)	16
Battle of Magdhaba, 23 December 1916.	32
First Libyan campaign, January-February 1941.	84
British Commonwealth Occupation Force area, January 1947.	132
Japan, showing British Commonwealth Occupation Force area.	132

ABBREVIATIONS

AAMWS	Australian Army Medical Women's Service
AA&QMG	Assistant Adjutant and Quartermaster General
ABDACOM	American British Dutch Australian Command
ACJ	Allied Council for Japan
ADC	Aide de Camp
AFV	Armoured Fighting Vehicle
AG	Adjutant General
AIF	Australian Imperial Force
ALH	Australian Light Horse
AMF	Australian Military Forces
AWAS	Australian Women's Army Service
Bde	Brigade
BEF	British Expeditionary Force
BCAIR	British Commonwealth Air Force [Japan]
BCOF	British Commonwealth Occupation Force [Japan]
BCFK	British Commonwealth Forces, Korea
BGS	Brigadier, General Staff
BRINDIV	British Indian Division
CAS	Chief of the Air Staff
CG	Commanding General [US Army]
CGS	Chief of the General Staff
C-in-C	Commander-in-Chief
CIGS	Chief of the Imperial General Staff
CMF	Citizen Military Forces
CRA	Commander, Royal Artillery
CRE	Commander, Royal Engineers

ABBREVIATIONS

DAQMG	Deputy Assistant Quartermaster General
DDMS	Deputy Director Medical Services
Div	Division
DMA	Director of Military Art
DMF	Darwin Mobile Force
DSO	Distinguished Service Order
EEF	Egyptian Expeditionary Force
GOC	General Officer Commanding
GSO	General Staff Officer
HQ	Headquarters
IDC	Imperial Defence College
JAPC	Joint Administrative Planning Committee
JCOSA	Joint Chiefs of Staff in Australia
MD	Military District
MG	Machine Gun
NAWU	North Australia Workers' Union
NCO	Non-Commissioned Officer
NZEF	New Zealand Expeditionary Force
NZMR	New Zealand Mounted Rifles
OC	Officer Commanding
PMF	Permanent Military Forces
RAA	Royal Australian Artillery
RAAF	Royal Australian Air Force
RAE	Royal Australian Engineers
RAF	Royal Air Force
RAN	Royal Australian Navy
RAR	Royal Australian Regiment
RFC	Royal Flying Corps
RMC	Royal Military College
RNZAF	Royal New Zealand Air Force
ROK	Republic of [South] Korea
SAA	Small Arms Ammunition
SCAP	Supreme Commander for the Allied Powers
UKCOS	United Kingdom Chiefs of Staff
UKLIM	United Kingdom Liaison Mission [Japan]
UKSLS	United Kingdom Services Liaison Staff [Canberra]

AUTHOR'S NOTE

The changing nature and composition of the Australian army between Federation and the 1960s is one of the concerns of this book. A brief explanation of its component parts and their relationship to each other will assist the reader to follow the organisational changes discussed.

Since 1901 the army has consisted of the following components:

The Citizen Military Forces (CMF), often referred to as the militia, was raised at different times by voluntary enlistment or compulsory service on a part-time basis. It has never served as such outside Australian territorial limits. This is the forerunner of the current Army Reserve.

The Permanent Military Forces (PMF), the pre-Second World War regular army, was intended primarily to staff, train and administer the CMF. Before 1939 it had a number of constituent corps, of which the most important for our purposes were the Australian Staff Corps, the Administrative and Instructional Staff (A & I Staff), and the Australian Instructional Corps (AIC), although it included as well small artillery, ordnance, engineer and medical units. The Staff Corps was formed on 1 October 1920, and from that date all officers of the combatant permanent forces, and not just graduates of the Royal Military College, Duntroon, were assigned to it. The A & I Staff, which had fulfilled the administrative and instructional function in the pre-1914 army, was disbanded, and on 14 October 1921 was succeeded by the AIC, which incorporated the majority of permanent non-commissioned officers.

The Australian Imperial Force (AIF), was raised in 1914 and 1939 (the 2nd AIF) on an all-volunteer basis to serve anywhere outside Australia for the duration of hostilities.

The Australian Military Forces (AMF), was the pre-1947 name for the army as a whole. In the Second World War the AMF comprised the CMF, the AIF, and the PMF.

The postwar PMF was reinstituted on 1 August 1947, and on 30 September 1947 became the Australian Regular Army (ARA). It consisted

AUTHOR'S NOTE

of all members of the prewar PMF still serving, and its membership overlapped the Interim Army.

The Interim Army, formed on 1 October 1945, consisted of all members still serving on full-time duty. It carried on where the 2nd AIF left off until a permanent peacetime army was reconstituted. It was disbanded on 14 August 1952, and its members transferred into the Australian Regular Army (ARA) or the Regular Army Supplementary Reserve (RASR).

The Australian Regular Army (ARA) was formed on 30 September 1947 from the postwar PMF. This is the current full-time volunteer force.

INTRODUCTION

The Australian Regular Army possesses a relatively short history, although it has spent a considerable part of it at war. Until 1945, however, the major influence on Australian military policy was not the regular army but the Citizen Military Forces: part-time, amateur soldiers whose main interest, and means of earning a living, lay elsewhere than in the military profession. The struggle of the regular officer corps to assert their role as the principal source of military advice to government was protracted and lasted until after the Second World War. As elsewhere, in Canada and the United States for example, it was ultimately successful not least because of the reputation which regular officers earned in two world wars, but also because the increasing complexity of modern industrial warfare made it essential that those who were charged with the defence of the nation should devote themselves full-time to the task. Involved here too was the parallel development of ideas about the importance of professionalism, not only in the military but in many civilian spheres as well. At the end of the twentieth century the form which Australian defence policy has taken is a legacy of the gradual ascendancy of the regulars in the first fifty years after Federation.

If it now seems to have a certain inevitability about it, this was not readily apparent to the generation of Australians who soldiered through the interwar years. Australians have long possessed a peculiar conceit about their prowess as 'natural' soldiers and redoubtable fighters and, for many in government, the experience of the First World War seemed to confirm an idea which had its genesis in the Boer War at the century's turn. Regulars existed to train and administer, but not to command, the citizen soldiers who formed the nation's first line of continental defence. Imbued with this notion, and driven by that desire to economise in matters of national defence which is the most consistent thread in twentieth-century Australian defence policy-making, successive governments presided over the running-down of an army which, whatever claims are made for its contribution to victory in Europe in 1918, was by 1939 less effective militarily than the old Australian Imperial Force of whose traditions it was allegedly the guardian and inheritor.

War is an exacting school, never more so than in a century littered with individual and national reputations for military effectiveness. Whatever claims might be made for it in the cheery home-front propaganda, in the Second World War the Australian army, volunteer and conscript alike, evolved many of the characteristics of a long-term, regular force in the course of six years of war; this evolution could not have been accomplished without the stiffening of professional soldiers who helped instil in both the AIF and the militia the sense and standards of military professionalism which stood them in such good stead against the Italians, Germans, French and Japanese. The changes in the international order in consequence of the war, coupled in Australia with a tentative endorsement of the recommendations of the Squires report in 1939, led to the creation of a small regular army after 1945. This placed the professional military in charge of the military profession, and enabled Australia to fight a succession of small and medium wars in the thirty years thereafter without resort to the raising of expeditionary forces or mass armies.

Lieutenant General Sir Horace Robertson, as he eventually became, was a central figure in the maturation of the army which he joined as a staff cadet in 1912. His military career spanned more than forty years and two world wars, as well as a lengthy period as the Commander-in-Chief of the British Commonwealth Occupation Force in Japan from 1946, and non-operational commander of Commonwealth forces in Korea in 1950 and 1951. When he joined the army, the Royal Military College, Duntroon was two years from graduating its first classes and the staff cadets who were intended to provide the leavening of staff officers to the Australian forces numbered just forty-one. By the time he retired in 1954, a second Duntroon graduate had been appointed successively to the post of Chief of the General Staff as professional head of the army, in a succession which has remained unbroken subsequently, and Staff Corps officers held all the positions on the Military Board save only that of Citizen Military Forces Member. In the decade after his death in 1960, the Australian army would field a force in Vietnam which would be officered entirely by regulars, or by national servicemen commissioned for the duration of their obligation. With the exception of a handful of CMF officers recalled to full-time duty for short periods, there were no citizen soldiers in the units of the 1st Australian Task Force. Robertson's career thus provides an excellent vehicle with which to chart the development of the regular army in this period.

Professional historians, especially academic ones, from time to time object that biography is not the proper province of historians. Some of the most eminent, Namier and Elton among them, have asserted that biography is a second-rate calling followed by those who lack the creative imagination to work outside the boundaries provided by a single life. To the counter that a 'life and times' approach overcame these objections, Elton responded that even if a person's death marked the end of an epoch — and this was rarely the case — their birth did not, and the formative years of a subject are no fit concern for an historian of an age which was unaware of them.[1] And no individual dominates an age to that extent. 'Very occasionally a "great man's" life may prove a tool useful for opening a problem of history . . . but even when the tool is useful it is not the best available.' Concentration on a single individual therefore involves the biographer in the distortion of the times which the subject inhabited.

The fact that so many professional historians ignore these injunctions in the pursuit of biography should not blind us to their validity. The pursuit of a subject, like the writing of history more generally, is dependent on the availability of evidence and the lack of that evidence often leads biographers into trivialising either their subject or their times in pursuit of trendy psychological theorising which has little to do with either. As Robert Skidelsky has commented, Freud led the modern biographer to see 'not what was, but the cause of what was. The biographer no longer portrayed life, he explained it . . . The real action took place in the unconscious; or if you were a Marxist, in the class struggle'.[2]

It is not necessary to adopt Skidelsky's view that the real function of biography is 'to hold up lives as examples', although this may indeed form part of its purpose, in order to agree that much modern biography has had little to do with the lives of its subjects. The French historian Jacques Le Goff has noted the recent revival of biography in academic writing while lamenting that it so frequently follows a 'traditional' form; 'superficial and anecdotal, boringly chronological, indulging in an out-of-date psychologising and incapable of revealing the general historical significance of a particular life'.[3] He enjoins us to remember that in the first place a biography is the life of an individual, and that the aim must be 'of presenting and explaining one person's life within history'.

Despite some appearances to the contrary, biographies of generals are not a strong suit in Australian historical writing, and good modern ones are even more scarce. While Geoffrey Serle's magisterial work on Monash dominates the landscape,[4] its very existence points up the problem; there is no really adequate biography of Australia's most senior soldier, Field Marshal Sir Thomas Blamey, and the majority of Monash's own subordinates in the First World War, and Blamey's in the second, lack any form of treatment at all. The same can be said for the years of intense military activity since 1945, which are a desert of critical studies of Australia's leading servicemen. In recent years there has been a tendency to substitute studies of command for full biographical treatment; while these have often gone some way towards an analysis of the central professional concerns of their subjects' lives, they have in general been short and episodic in their treatment and thus are no substitute for full scholarly treatments of the sort which Serle, Hill, Pedersen and Lodge have produced.[5]

Having said this, I must admit that this book is much more a professional study of a senior officer than a full interior life of the man. The reasons are readily explicable; the lack of a body of private papers precludes the reconstruction of Robertson's emotional life, thoughts and feelings to anything like the degree which Serle was able to achieve through the vast corpus of the Monash papers. It is a curious thing that most Australian generals do not write much for publication, nor even privately for their own amusement, and this leads as well to a disinclination to keep diaries, letters and the other minutiae of daily life which would enable military biographers to recapture their subjects in all their dimensions. But to this must be added a particular problem, namely the dispersal of such papers as Robertson had gathered at the time of his death, the existence of which is known with certainty and the fate of which can only be surmised.

While this may be regarded as a disadvantage, it nonetheless carries with it something of virtue, for as a result I have had to trawl through the collections of many public and private figures in the search for glimpses and reflections of a man about whom few of his professional contemporaries held neutral views. I have also avoided the temptation, I hope, to write an 'authorised life', reconstructing the memoirs the subject might have written himself if he had spared the time to do so. But it has meant that this book is in large part a study of the rise to prominence of one of the Australian army's more controversial and colourful senior officers at a time of great change in his nation's history. Boswell believed that 'nobody can write the life of a man, but those who have eaten and drunk and lived in social intercourse with him'. I cannot claim to have done so, but I do not believe that my treatment of his military life and public career suffers much for all that. Treatment of his personal life, and in particular of his marriage, is necessarily much less complete. I have commented on the latter in places, but have avoided the temptation to either speculation or gossip.

This book then attempts to do three things. It seeks to return a little of the considerable public recognition which he enjoyed in his lifetime to a man who rendered distinguished service to his country and to the army in arduous times. To that extent the book meets the justification which Skidelsky advanced for biography. Second, it presents the first detailed account of the Commonwealth occupation of Japan at the command level, from its inception at the end of the Pacific war until Robertson's eventual return to Australia less than a year before the signing of the Treaty of San Francisco which brought formal occupation to an end in

INTRODUCTION

1952. This is an incident in Australia's vitally important modern relationship with Japan which is too little known and even less understood. Finally, it examines the development of the regular officer corps through the experiences and career of one of its members, and in so doing I hope meets the need to set a subject in history as Le Goff enjoins us to do. But above all it remains the story of a distinguished Australian, and of a remarkable life.

PART ONE

A soldier's time is passed in distress and danger or in idleness and corruption.

Samuel Johnson

משלי שלמה

CHAPTER 1

FOUNDATIONS: 1894-1915

Horace Clement Hugh Robertson was born on 29 October 1894, in Warrnambool on the coast of western Victoria. His father, John Robertson, was a state school teacher then aged thirty-six, native-born and a keen member of the local volunteer militia. His mother, Annie, neé Gray, was thirty-three and had already given birth to five children, of whom four had survived, in the ten years since their marriage.

As a boy Horace was the unremarkable son of an ordinary lower middle-class family, born in a decade of economic depression and straitened circumstances. The family moved at the dictates of the education department, and Horace attended a number of schools in the course of his education. Between May 1905 and April 1910 he went to the state school at Outtrim, a small town in Gippsland to the south-east of Melbourne. By 1910 his father was teaching at state school No 1190 in the small coastal resort town of Queenscliff on the mouth of Port Phillip Bay, later the site of the army's Command and General Staff College. In April 1910, Horace was sent to board at the much more exclusive Geelong College. He was fifteen and a half, too young to take the public examinations of the day, but it seems clear that he went to the school in order to prepare himself for entry to the newly-created Royal Military College, Duntroon, which was to open its doors on the site of a resumed sheep property near Canberra in the following year. He took no prizes at Geelong, and 'there was nothing outstanding about him as a student'.[1] He left the school at the end of the year. He was still too young for entry to Duntroon, and so spent 1911 in the workforce, although in what capacity is not clear. There may also have been a schoolboy accident involving a diving platform, from which he took some time to recover. In October he applied to sit the entry examination and was accepted into the new class for 1912.

The Royal Military College had been set up on the recommendation of Field Marshal Lord Kitchener during his tour of inspection of Australia's defences in 1910. It was modelled on the US Military Academy, West

3

Point, and not on the Royal Military Academies Sandhurst or Woolwich in Britain, because Kitchener believed the former was better suited to the needs of an emerging post-colonial society. Colonel William Throsby Bridges, a Scottish-born immigrant who had been commissioned into the New South Wales colonial artillery in 1885, had been appointed its first commandant. The regimen was strict and conditions spartan. Cadets were paid, in order that entry should be open, at least theoretically, to all, although in practice they could not draw on their salary and received five shillings a week pocket money from their families, and they enjoyed the status of private soldiers only. Gambling, liquor and cigarettes were banned, as were pets, and marriage was forbidden while a cadet. Like West Point, Duntroon was to be an educational institution as well, and the course lasted four years. In its foundation years the academy was very small, with an executive staff of four officers and a clerk, ten instructors including three civilian professors, of physics, mathematics and English, and thirty general staff. These were to be responsible for an initial intake of forty-one cadets in 1911, which increased to seventy-nine when Robertson and his class marched in on 7 March 1912.[2]

The course at Duntroon aimed at both education and training. The latter encompassed instruction in infantry and light horse exercises, riding, physical training, signalling and musketry, in all of which Robertson performed consistently well. The academic curriculum added physics, chemistry and mathematics, which an officer was thought to need in order to meet the technological demands of modern war, and which was very much in line with the West Point philosophy, and history, English, foreign languages and drawing, which had practical application to the discharge of his duties. Robertson's results in this side of college life were generally good, although his performance in drawing was judged 'keen and energetic' and foreign languages largely eluded him. On the military side his reports were consistently good. A young man 'of cheerful disposition' and 'good temper', smart in his appearance and on parade, he was judged to possess initiative, tact and the power of command. He was keen, alert, industrious, had 'plenty of common sense', and was seen as a good influence within the Corps of Staff Cadets. He was likely to make a good young officer, making 'the most of his brains and the opportunities offered him'.[3]

The received picture of Robertson as a cadet and subaltern is at variance with the popular later image of the hot-headed, extroverted senior officer. His nickname, 'Red Robbie', owed nothing to this later view of his temperament, and was in fact a family name — his elder brother, John Gray Robertson, was known as 'black' to his intimates throughout his life, again on account of his hair colour.[4] As a rule, young men make few appearances in public records or private correspondence until they become figures of note, and we know nothing of what shaped

'No 2 from left, rear half company'. Robertson at Duntroon, 1912.

Robertson's own character and values in this formative period of his military career. That Duntroon was an important influence upon the early classes of graduates is undeniable. Of the first four classes to enter before the First World War, fifty-one eventually reached the rank of brigadier or above, attesting both to their ability and to the wartime expansions of the army. There seems nothing unusual about Robertson in this early group. He was a Victorian, whose state of origin was heavily over-represented in the early classes (forty-eight per cent), and a Presbyterian (seventeen per cent), who had attended both state and private schools at a time when most successful entrants came from state schools.[5] He graduated ninth in his class, won no prizes, held the rank of corporal in the Corps of Staff Cadets, and had attracted just two charges on his conduct sheet in nearly three years at the Royal Military College.

The first great test of the Duntroon product was provided, of course, by the First World War. If it was the making of many of its graduates, it helped ensure the college's future also. Bridges had been appointed to command the Australian Imperial Force (AIF), and was faced immediately with the problem of selecting suitable officers for a contingent of twenty thousand men, comprising an infantry division, three brigades of artillery and a brigade of light horse. The entire peacetime regular army numbered only 2989 all ranks, and Bridges recommended that the first class, due to be commissioned on 1 January 1915, be graduated early and made available for active service. Curiously, the newly-commissioned lieutenants were not posted to staff positions, in general, but were given regimental appointments, in which a good number of them were killed. The second class, not intended to graduate for another year, looked on their seniors with envy, but on 22 October it was announced that they too would graduate early to provide junior officers for the additional contingent then being raised. On 2 November 1914, Horace Robertson was commissioned into the Staff Corps, and appointed to a commission in the AIF.

Within a week of graduating and before departing for his first posting and overseas service, Robertson did something the truth of which he never publicly admitted for the rest of his life — he got married. It was a necessarily private service in a registry office in Collingwood, Melbourne on 7 November. The bride was Jessie Bonnar, a native of Bendigo but at that time living in Sydney. She gave her profession as nurse and that of her father, Robert Bonnar, as station manager. The witnesses, Emily Williams and Katie Ferguson, presumably were friends of the bride for no colleague of the groom's attended. In those days, a permanent officer required the army's permission to marry and Robertson, barely twenty years old and freshly commissioned, would not have received it.

The oddities do not end there. Robertson lied about his age, giving it as twenty-four. The bride admitted to thirty-one, but was in fact thirty-eight. Publicly they stated always that they were married in Palestine in October 1916 where Jessie went to nurse at the hospital at Heliopolis, and a version of this story was given to Robertson's family upon his return from the war in 1919 with supposedly new bride in tow. The reasons for this hurried and furtive wedding are now lost. It was to be a childless and at times cheerless match, and one can only speculate on the effects it had on the younger man as he progressed slowly in his chosen profession amid the frustrations of the interwar years. It may be that Jessie alleged breach of promise, something which was scarcely unknown and which would have been disastrous professionally had it become known. In the semi-monastic life at Duntroon Robertson can have acquired no very great experience of women, and initial contact may have come through family proximity, since by then Jessie's mother lived near his own parents in East Malvern, a suburb of Melbourne. But the mystery remains.

Seven of the class of 1912 found themselves posted to the 3rd Light Horse Brigade. Robertson was the only Duntroon graduate sent to the 10th Light Horse Regiment, as machine gun officer, having been allotted for service 'to L[ight] H[orse], M[achine] G[uns] and Sig[nals] in this order'.[6] The same post was filled by classmates in the 10th's sister units, the 8th and 9th Light Horse, as were four of the troop commands. Of the seven, three would be killed on Gallipoli by the middle of August. The only other regular in the 10th was the adjutant, Captain R. E. Jackson, a member of the prewar Administrative and Instructional Staff. The 10th was the only mounted unit raised in Western Australia, and Robertson joined it at the light horse camp at Guildford, outside Perth, on 19 November.[7] The unit had been concentrating since the first week in October, and Robertson must have been one of the last arrivals before the regiment embarked for war service.

Much has been made of the mystique and romance of the light horse in subsequent historiography, a product of their involvement in the last great mounted campaign in modern war, conducted in a theatre which lent itself to romantic and inappropriate comparisons with the Crusades, the young Napoleon, and so on. Like most commentary on the nature and composition of the AIF, such writing overlooks the tensions and rivalries which exist in any organisation, civil or military, and ignores the part which class and social position played in the selection of officers and men, especially in the mounted units. Bean noted that a higher proportion of men with private school backgrounds was found in the light horse than in the infantry battalions; he also noted that birth and education were important determinants in being selected for officer training units and a commission from the ranks. After January 1915 the only path to a commission in the AIF, other than for Duntroon graduates and officers of the prewar forces, was enlistment in the ranks, but for the first two contingents to sail this was not the case, and the selection of officers was based on a number of factors, not all of which were conducive to selecting the young, the fit, and the professionally competent.

The 3rd Light Horse Brigade was an excellent case in point. The brigade commander, Colonel F. G. Hughes, had been selected for command owing to his social connections and his pre-war association with the militia in rural Victoria; 'an elderly citizen officer belonging to leading social circles' was Bean's description.[8] The weakness in command which resulted was compensated in part through the appointment of a regular with previous service in South Africa, Lieutenant Colonel J. M. Antill, as brigade major, despite his being too senior in rank for the post. He was 'the main influence in command of the brigade';[9] while Birdwood, the Indian army general who was Bridges' successor in command of the AIF, had little confidence in Hughes, he was unwilling to remove him outright. Whatever his other deficiencies, at fifty-eight Hughes was simply too old for active service. The same could be said of the commanding officer of the 10th Light Horse, Lieutenant Colonel N. M. Brazier. A pastoralist and surveyor with good pre-war militia connections, he was forty-nine years of age on Gallipoli, and unfit for the demands of a rigorous campaign. His limitations did not end there. The 10th had been raised on the framework of the 25th Light Horse Regiment, the militia unit based in Western Australia as part of the pre-war army, and commanded for several

'Old Geelong Collegians' in the Light Horse, Egypt, probably before Gallipoli. Robertson is second from the left in the back row.

years before 1914 by Brazier himself. He attempted to take many of his officers with him into the AIF, regardless of age or competence. Some, like Captain T. J. Todd, proved to be excellent. Brazier's insistence on taking Major A. J. Love as his second in command, over the objections of Headquarters, 5th Military District in Perth, was to have unfortunate consequences on Gallipoli. Brazier did not get on with Antill, either, and their feuding added further strains to an already weakened organisation.[10]

A light horse regiment consisted of a headquarters (six officers and thirty-nine other ranks), three squadrons (each with six officers and approximately 150 other ranks), and a machine gun section (one officer and twenty-six other ranks), for a total strength of twenty-five officers and about 500 other ranks. The light horse were not trained as cavalry, nor intended to be used as such. Like dragoons in the eighteenth century, they relied upon their horses for mobility, not for shock action. They were mounted infantry, a type of soldier believed by many in the British army to be best produced in the colonies. The attachment of a machine gun section to each regiment boosted the firepower of a dismounted unit which was smaller than an equivalent infantry battalion and could not put as many rifles into the line. At this stage, each squadron had two Vickers guns, and guns were not yet grouped into machine gun units. After Romani, in August 1916, the number of guns was increased to twelve and machine gun squadrons were developed for each brigade, in six sections of two guns each, with a total of eight officers and 221 other ranks. This both recognised tactical exigencies and paralleled developments in France.[11]

After concentration at Guildford, the 10th Light Horse moved to Claremont on 18 December and, after Christmas leave, to Rockingham on 6 January. Brazier had noted in his diary that while 'things [are] getting better generally' there was 'a lot to do yet'.[12] The second contingent of the AIF did not embark for Egypt until February, and the intervening time was used in training and gathering equipment and stores, although whether the training regimen went much beyond a basic stage must be doubted. On 2 February 1915 the 3rd Light Horse Brigade, spread over six transports, set sail for Egypt and the war in the Middle East. The bulk of the 10th was aboard the *Mashobra*.

Contrary to much popular and some military expectation, the war undertaken so confidently in August 1914 was not over by Christmas, and indeed before the end of the year had widened with Turkey's entry on the German side in November. A belligerent Turkey posed a threat to Britain's Middle Eastern possessions, and the prospect of Turkish-fomented Muslim insurrection in its colonial territories alarmed Britain's leaders. In the course of the war the Turks were to fight on five different fronts, and lost on all save one, the Dardanelles, in direct defence of Turkish soil. But the campaigns in the Middle East demonstrated as well the weaknesses which empire could bring for the British: the need to safeguard India and the Suez Canal was a constant drain on men and material which could have been utilised in France against Germany, the main enemy.

The 10th was the first unit to reach Egypt, the transports arriving at Port Said on 8 March. The brigade disembarked at Alexandria and was allocated quarters at Mena Camp, recently vacated by the 3rd Infantry Brigade which had sailed for Lemnos preparatory to leading the assault on the Turkish positions at Gallipoli. On 29 April the newly arrived light horse moved to Heliopolis racecourse, and continued to train. Nearly all the training in Egypt was in infantry work; there was very little mounted training before embarkation for Gallipoli.[13] The training syllabus emphasised dismounted action: for the week ending 8 May the 10th

Australian Light Horse was to practice reconnaissance for the attack, the advance under shell fire, and the attack, retirement and counter-attack at regimental level. On another day the three regiments of the brigade were detailed for training as follows: '8th — entrenchments; 9th — field firing practice with ball [ie, live] ammunition; 10th — squadrons in attack, dismounted'.[14] All such training was based on the pre-1914 British training syllabus, and took no account of the changes in modern war revealed by early experience in France. With a lack of modern training went deficiencies in equipment, especially artillery, and a lack of the trench stores necessary for positional warfare. When the Dardanelles campaign bogged down into trench warfare after the first few days of fighting, the Australians and New Zealanders were woefully under-prepared for what followed.

News, and casualties, from Gallipoli had begun to filter through, and with them the pressing demand for reinforcements. The 1st Australian Division had lost half its infantry strength in the first week of fighting, and Generals Bridges and Birdwood wanted the light horse regiments broken up and used as drafts of reinforcements for the infantry, a view with which the Commander-in-Chief of the Mediterranean Expeditionary Force, General Sir Ian Hamilton, concurred. General Sir John Maxwell, who commanded the mounted brigades for the defence of Egypt, refused to allow this, and in this he mirrored exactly the views of the officers and men concerned. When approached by their commanding officers, the 2nd and 3rd Brigades volunteered to serve on Gallipoli dismounted, although some commanding officers still wanted to take the horses. Maxwell cabled Hamilton that 'the men are entraining full of enthusiasm. I think you had better take this lot as it is.'[15]

The first to go were the machine gun sections, which left their units on 8 May. The sections from the 2nd and 3rd Brigades were brought together under the command of Captain W. H. Hastings, an Indian army officer, and sailed from Alexandria on the night of 9-10 May, leaving their horses behind.[16] The remainder of the regiments embarked on 16 May, again leaving their horses behind although, in the case of the 10th at least, they did not receive the necessary infantry webbing and equipment until July.[17] They also left a quarter of their strength to act as horse handlers, and this served to emphasise Bridges' concern that the units sent as reinforcements might prove too weak to be effective tactically. The 10th arrived on Gallipoli late on 21 May and dug in for their first night on active service behind Plugge's Plateau. They were commanded by Major Love; Colonel Brazier had stayed behind in Egypt for no adequately explained reason. The latter confided to his diary on the day his regiment marched out: 'Oh Lord. How rotten are things in general. Nothing looks right. Some men have left but should not. We are all short of officers and the muddle is awful. Preparatory details and to see they are carried out are lessons to be learnt from this.' And in July, just before himself embarking for the peninsula, he noted dolefully that 'Egypt is a rotten place'.[18] The shortcomings in some of the command appointments were increasingly clear.

For the rest of May, the 10th Light Horse Regiment was detached and served with the 1st Light Horse Brigade under Colonel H.G. Chauvel, occupying positions on Quinn's Post, one of the most dangerous and exposed positions on Anzac. The machine guns were not with them. As the infantry training manual noted, 'by employing several sections under the control of one commander a brigade commander is able to keep a powerful reserve of fire in hand to be used for any special purpose'.[19] The brigading of the machine guns and their liberal use in providing fire support for the infantry compensated for the weakness of the positions on Gallipoli in the first two months. 'The feature of difference between night and day most marked', wrote one trooper from the 10th Light Horse, was 'the artillery fire during the day and rifle and machine gun fire at night. Turkish guns and our own guns ashore rarely fired at night owing to the danger of exposing their positions ... Rifle fire and machine guns on the other hand rattled briskly and continuously all night.'[20] We may be sure that Robertson and his men were kept busy. Instructions from Headquarters, New Zealand and Australian Division, directed that 'our machine gunners ... must be constantly on the lookout for fresh positions from which to open, when the time comes, effective fire, which should come as a surprise to the enemy. Several alternative positions for each gun must be prepared.'[21] On 1 June the regiment moved to new positions on Walker's Ridge, which they occupied until the end of July, and the machine gun section was posted back to its parent unit, at least temporarily.

After the failure of the major Turkish attack on 19 May, both sides had settled down to positional warfare while building up their reserves and planning new offensives which, it was hoped, would break the stalemate and end the campaign. Despite the absence of major attacks, casualties were incurred continuously, and this was especially serious in the smaller light horse regiments. The shortage of officers and men was felt as early as the beginning of July. Because of the number of officers who had been left behind in Egypt to supervise the care of the horses, selected non-commissioned officers were commissioned in the field 'under special exigencies of active service'. But this could not make up for the losses among the other ranks. Such losses were incurred not only through enemy action, but as a result of disease, poor diet and the hard conditions under which the men laboured and lived. 'The men, for the most part, were far below their normal standard of fighting efficiency. Physically they were weakened and wasted. The intense summer, the ever-lasting racket of digging, the long front-line vigils with the necessary standing to arms, the contaminated fly-ridden food with its accompaniment of dysentery and diarrhoea, and the shortage of water, had left their marks upon most of them.'[22] By 28 July, less than a fortnight before the brigade was to take part in the August offensive, it reported 421 men away in hospital, twenty-one per cent of those who landed in May, or twenty-five per cent less those killed and wounded.[23]

The story of the August offensive and the charge of the 3rd Light Horse Brigade at The Nek is well known. For the 10th Light Horse it was a disaster. Seven officers and seventy-four other ranks were killed and two officers and forty-nine men wounded. The 8th Light Horse, which charged before them, lost even more heavily, suffering 210 casualties, including its colonel. The brigade lost over 350 men in little more than half an hour. Robertson's machine gun section had been returned to its parent unit for the attack, but seems to have played no part in the disastrous events of the morning of 7 August. Lieutenant Colonel Brazier had arrived to take command of his unit at the end of July, and attempted to prevent the slaughter of the third and fourth lines of the charge, without success, being over-ruled by the brigade major, Antill. The antipathy between the two can only have been heightened by this incident. The remnants of the brigade remained in the trenches, expecting a Turkish counter-attack which never came. The men were exhausted and emotionally overwrought after the trials of the day, and when Major Love came around the forward trenches that night — supposedly the first such occasion on which he had been seen forward of regimental headquarters — one trooper attempted to kill him with a bayonet.[24] The men remained in the trenches around Russell's Top for the next three weeks.

The loss of so many officers and NCOs at The Nek meant a rash of promotions in the units affected. Robertson was promoted to captain, effective from 7 August, and posted to A Squadron as second-in-command to Major Todd, who was evacuated to hospital in any case. Good luck, which can play such a large role in war, had not only preserved Robertson but had brought him early advancement. Had he been posted to a troop instead of the machine guns, there is every likelihood that he would have been killed, since the regiment had seven subalterns killed that day. Although reinforcements arrived, August brought little respite for the brigade. 'There is little rest and no relief and it badly after 13 weeks incessant and most arduous work requires rest and change: numbers are down and a good deal of sickness resulting from weakness and weariness'.[25] On 20 August Antill noted that 2170 men had landed, losses stood at 1263, the brigade had received just 498 replacements and could field an effective strength of 907 all ranks.[26]

The weakness and confusion in command continued. Major Love was evacuated sick from the peninsula soon after the August offensive, although he returned to the unit later in the campaign. He was eventually relieved and sent home at Antill's recommendation in November.[27] On 23 August, Brigadier Hughes relieved Brazier of his command following an extraordinary interview in which he told Brazier of his dissatisfaction with his general performance, and Brazier complained that brigade headquarters 'had been hitting him up', and that 'he would sooner be out of it and transferred, and his manner was such that combined with other matters which had led to the Brigadier speaking to him on several occasions', he was relieved of his command. Hughes then informed his own superior, General Godley, at Headquarters, New Zealand and Australian Division. When Hughes sent for Brazier again later that evening, the latter sent an orderly with an insolent note requesting that future communications be in writing! Lack of confidence in Hughes himself, however, resulted in Godley's headquarters declining to endorse the action he had taken, although paradoxically they concurred in its wisdom. The upshot was that on 26 August, Brazier was reinstated in command of his unit after further communications between Hughes and Godley.[28] Behind it all, Brazier was convinced, lay Antill who, he charged, was trying to get rid of both Brazier and Hughes in order to attain command of the brigade himself.[29] The matter was resolved, more or less, by the Turks two days later, when Brazier was lightly wounded and evacuated to Egypt. He did not return. His place was taken by Major J.B. Scott, and Robertson found himself placed in command of C Squadron. In less than a month he had gone from subaltern in command of a section to become one of the regiment's senior officers.

The 10th Light Horse fought one more major engagement on Gallipoli, at the end of August. The failure of the August offensive necessitated some straightening of the line to the north of Anzac to ensure safety of communications between that position and the those of IX Corps around Suvla. This required the capture of Turkish positions at Hill 60. Like so much else in the Gallipoli campaign, the intelligence and staff work associated with this attack were deficient. The high command believed that a network of Turkish trenches occupied the summit of the hill, and that the capture of these would bring with them possession of the hill and command of the approaches to the north. In fact, the Turkish defences occupied the forward slope of the hill, and were connected by communications trenches to further Turkish positions to the rear. It would be necessary to take these also if the attack's objectives were to be attained. Some 2500 casualties would be expended for the partial attainment of the objective.

The initial attacks were made on 21 August by a mixed force of British, Indian, Australian and New Zealand troops under Major General H.V. Cox. After strong efforts, the summit was still in Turkish hands on 23 August. On 26 August Birdwood received permission to try again.

Going in on the afternoon of the following day, a foothold was gained on the southern slopes of the hill, but at considerable cost. The 9th Light Horse was sent up as reinforcements that night and in the ensuing attack their colonel and one entire squadron were killed.

The 10th Light Horse then moved forward to renew the attack.[30] Unit strength had declined to such an extent that A and B Squadrons had been amalgamated under the command of Captain Fry, while Robertson commanded C Squadron, the regiment totalling about 200 all ranks. Brazier was wounded during the reconnaissance on the afternoon of 28 August, and his position was taken by Major Scott, leaving no second in command. The machine gun section was still detached, and positioned on Walker's Ridge. About 160 men thus were available for the attack, which went in at one a.m. on the morning of 29 August. The idea was to mount a converging assault upon the Turkish positions, with the 10th Light Horse assaulting on two axes to the north from positions captured in previous attacks, while the remnants of the 9th Light Horse pushed bombing parties along the line of trenches to the left of the main assault. The attack was a surprise 'and the trench was captured fairly easily', although Turkish machine guns caught the second assault line from C Squadron in the open and killed or wounded thirteen men including the squadron sergeant major who was leading them. Captain Fry was killed a short time after the attack commenced, leaving Robertson as the senior officer in command of the whole force.

The 10th's attack was so quick and successful that it reached its objectives ahead of the bombing parties from the 9th, and a triangular fight ensued briefly between the Turks and the two assaulting parties of light horse. A Squadron reached its objectives, but most of its officers were killed or wounded in clearing the Turks from the trenches, and a party under Lieutenant H. V. H. Throssell barricaded the position and beat off inevitable Turkish counter-attacks. The enemy made three such attempts to oust the attackers over the ensuing three and a half hours. Most of the defenders were wounded in the course of the fighting, including Robertson, whose face was peppered with metal fragments when a Turkish bullet shattered a bayonet, but the Turks were held at bay until they called off their attacks after dawn. At about seven a.m. the remaining members of the assaulting squadrons were relieved and evacuated to the dressing stations.

The 10th Light Horse suffered heavily at Hill 60, losing three officers and eleven men killed, twelve men missing and three officers and fifty-six men wounded. Just eighty-three all ranks remained on the evening of 30 August. Throssell was awarded the Victoria Cross, on Robertson's recommendation, and there were five awards of the Distinguished Conduct Medal, attesting to the severity of the fighting. For all that, the attack failed as the Turks reinforced and fortified the communications trenches

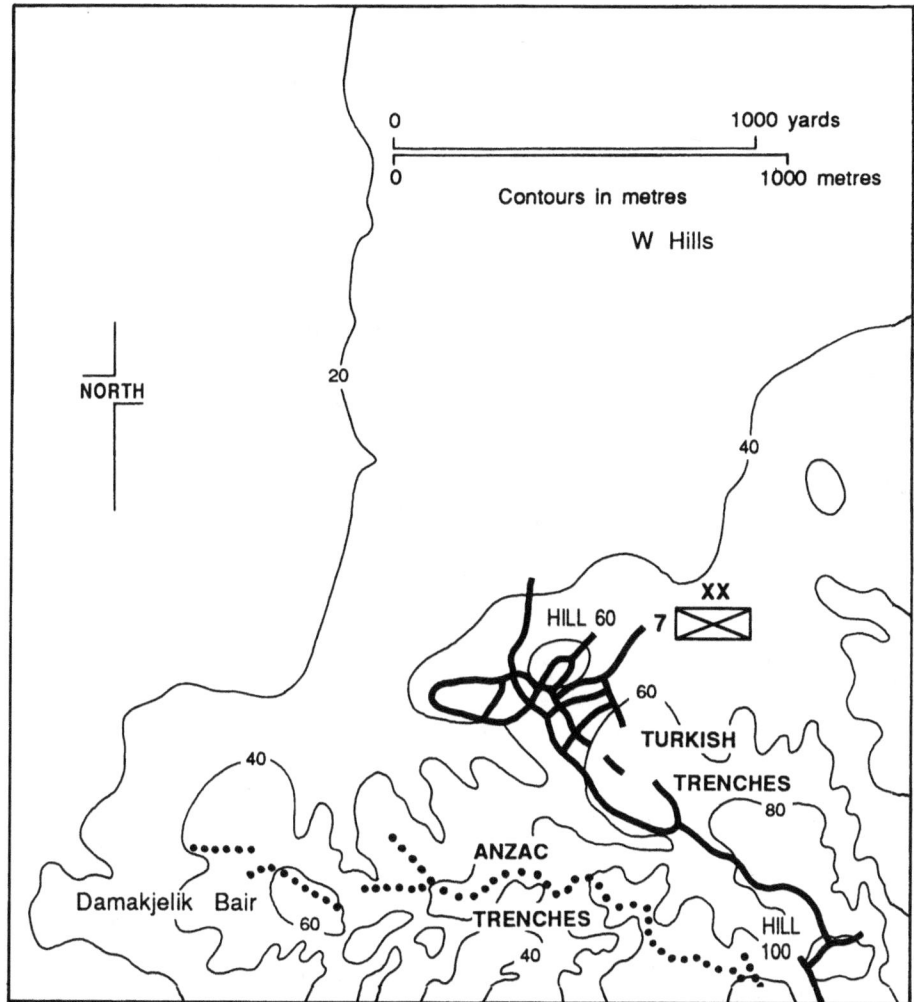

Positions at Hill 60, August 1915.

which led back from their positions on Hill 60, and the Anzacs now lacked the strength for further offensive action against them. Robertson later wrote that 'another fifty yards to the eastwards would have given us all the commanding ground, as well as the main Turkish trench running across to Chocolate Hill'.[31] And to Bean he wrote of his conviction that 'had we followed up the 10th LH attack by another and larger one within the next 24 to 48 hours, the whole hill would have been in our hands and the Turkish line must have fallen back some distance. We were on the brink of a considerable success and one more push must have obtained the Eastern end with its dominating position.' He may be forgiven for

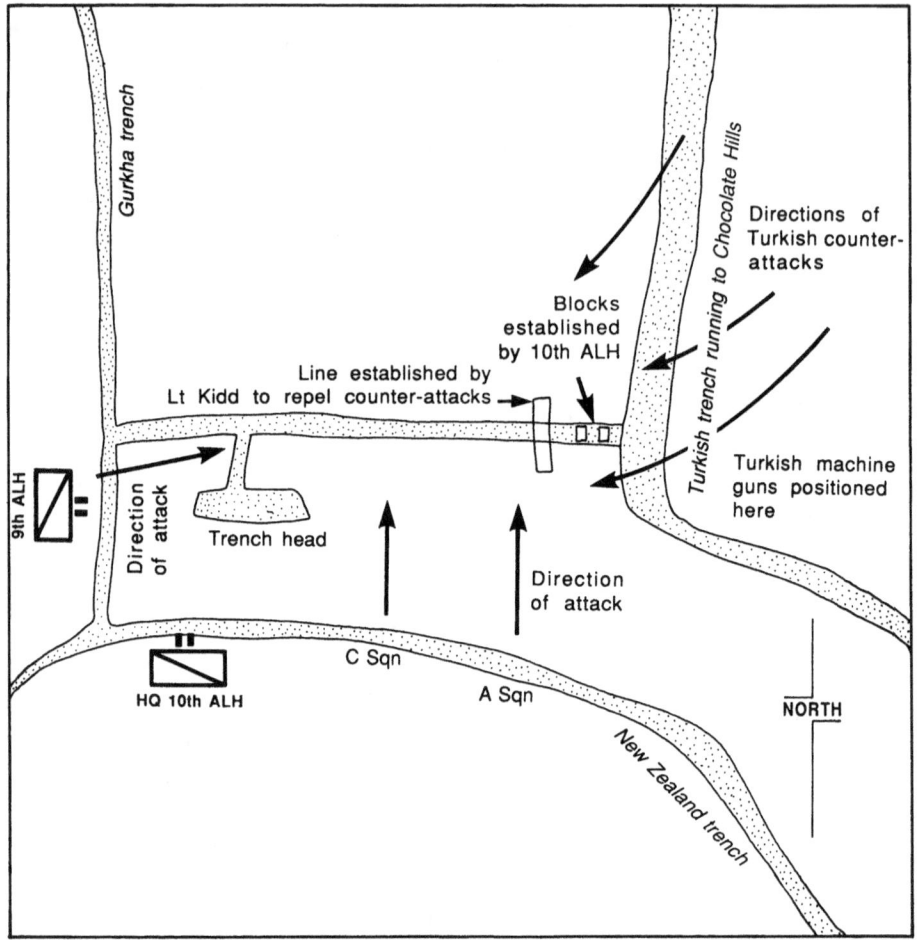

10th Light Horse attack at Hill 60, 28-29 August 1915. (Based on a sketch by H. C. H. Robertson.)

perhaps over-rating the importance of his first significant action, but at the same time he observed the reason why this follow-up attack could not occur: 'The troops taking part in the operations ... had a very bad time, and I well remember meeting many NZ officers whom I knew, and noting the weariness and strained faces as compared with their looks a fortnight before.'[32]

The Anzacs' capacity for offensive action was now exhausted. After their exertions in August the 10th Light Horse were sent from Hill 60 to positions around Table Top and Rhododendron Spur, where they were destined to remain until the evacuation. The regiment desperately needed some respite, and their new camp was the closest thing to it on the peninsula. 'The new camp was safe from shrapnel and snipers, and there was plenty of firewood and water handy, so was a pretty good spot', wrote Foss.[33] But it was not a rest camp, and the men were kept hard at work in the trenches. Foss described how:

> *the regular order of things was to go into the trenches early at night with full equipment up, after standing to arms till 8 o'clock, half turn in, the rest sap till 12 o'clock, when they would camp and the other shift replace them. All would stand to arms from about 4 o'clock to 6 o'clock. During the day a portion remained in the trenches, the rest going back to camp. They came back to do three hours work during the day through sapping, either in the morning or afternoon. This left very little time for sleep or cooking, and as the men were terribly weak and shaky, a big proportion drifted away to hospital. At night a couple of patrols were placed some little distance in front to cover the sapping parties, and were usually on duty from 8 o'clock to 4.*

Casualties were light, but they continued to occur; on 8 October Major Scott, the CO, was killed by a shell burst. Antill calculated that of those officers who had embarked with their units from Australia, only two in the 8th Light Horse, just one in the 9th Light Horse, and three in the 10th Light Horse remained, together with twelve of the thirty-one replacements. On 8 September the brigade had just twelve officers on duty, twenty-three having been wounded, twenty-four evacuated sick, and thirty-one killed. There was one machine gun officer left, with just six worn guns under his command. The situation in the ranks was no better. The brigade held 550-600 yards (500-550 metres) of trench with fewer than 400 men; 'if a serious attack is made we cannot hold our trenches'.[34]

This situation could not continue, and in September some of the men who had served longest were withdrawn for rest and refitting on the island of Mudros. The 3rd Light Horse Brigade's turn came in November, and Robertson was sent to the rest camp on Mudros on 28 November, together with 282 other men from this brigade. The 3rd Brigade remained chronically under-strength, largely because of the chaos in the rear areas in Egypt which saw men evacuated and then not returned to their units, and Antill noted at the end of November that he remained the only original officer in the brigade, and that only some 130 other ranks remained, of the 1900 who had landed in May.[35] On 13 December the 10th Light Horse, now commanded by Major T. J. Todd, received orders to leave Gallipoli. At 11.15 p.m. the following night the remains of the regiment, approximately 150 men, boarded the lighters for the steamer *Abassia*, and sailed for Mudros. The machine gun section and the scouts remained behind, and were evacuated a few days later.

After regrouping on Lemnos, what was left of the light horse brigades was shipped back to Egypt, spending Christmas on board the transports 'with plenty of food and drink and cosy lounges', at least for the officers.

Robertson outside his dugout on Gallipoli, October 1915.

'After the way we had been forced to "pig it" on Gallipoli, we felt we were in the lap of luxury.'[36] For Robertson personally, the campaign had been something of a success. Although wounded lightly in the face during the fighting at Hill 60, he missed the awful slaughter at The Nek in which so many young troop and section leaders were killed or seriously wounded, and by the end of the campaign was commanding a squadron of the regiment in which he served. Many of his friends had been killed, and the casualties among Duntroon graduates had been heavy, but both personally and professionally the experience had been valuable. He had come to the favourable notice of his seniors, and had had the opportunity to observe the pitfalls which attended the appointment of officers too old or otherwise unfit for their positions — a lesson he would act upon when selecting his own subordinates at the beginning of the next war. For the Australian Imperial Force as a whole, Gallipoli had exposed many of the weaknesses which existed in personnel, organisation and leadership. It was a heavy price to pay in order that such shortcomings might be exposed.

CHAPTER 2

A GOOD WAR: 1916-1919

The 10th Light Horse under Lieutenant Colonel 'Tom' Todd returned from Gallipoli with about 150 men. With the new year the regiment began at once to absorb replacements and rebuild the unit. Men of the 9th, 10th, 11th, and 12th Reinforcements from Australia were incorporated and the regiment brought up to establishment. The light horse were back where they had started, full of fit, keen men with practically no experience of war. Antill noted that his brigade started the year 'with very few old officers or senior officers but plenty of reinforcements. Old men are to be used as a nucleus for troops and squadrons.'[1] This was a sensible decision, since it not only spread the experienced men among their newly-joined comrades but also spread the strain. The New Zealanders were to leave their Gallipoli veterans concentrated in the 1st Infantry Brigade, and were to rectify the mistake only later in France when the brigade showed signs of breaking down under the effects of prolonged exposure to battle.

Antill, now confirmed in command of the brigade, wasted no time in getting the men down to work, and training programmes commenced on 3 January. There were shortages of horses and saddlery, and riding tests had to be implemented since the riding skills of the reinforcements were 'not up to [the] standard of [the] old Brigade'. By 20 January the horse strength had improved thanks to the efforts of the remount depot, and the men had progressed to dismounted drills at troop level, but there were still shortages of equipment because the ordnance branch was dealing with requisitions in the order in which it had been decided that brigades would be needed in the field, and the 1st Light Horse Brigade had priority. By the end of the month the reinforcements were showing the benefits of extended preliminary training and by early February it proved possible to commence regimental training.[2] But it was hard work for the tiny group of experienced officers and non-commissioned officers who remained, and Antill wrote in January that he was 'right up to my neck reorganising and retraining this brigade, having to start

Captain Robertson soon after his return from Gallipoli, Cairo, 1916. *(Author's collection)*

practically *denovo,* [sic] and have therefore very little time for my meals, not to say correspondence'.[3]

Robertson found himself in command of B Squadron, although substantively he still held the rank of captain, and that only as an Australian Imperial Force rank. The system of ranks and promotions which operated in the First World War was markedly discriminatory in the case of officers of the Staff Corps and the Permanent Military Forces. During that war there was a prohibition against Staff Corps officers being promoted above the rank of major, regardless of ability, which meant effectively that they were to be denied unit commands. Such promotions as they did obtain were to AIF ranks only and, at the cessation of hostilities, they would revert to their substantive ranks in the peacetime regular forces. Thus Robertson who, as we shall see, was the senior major in his regiment by the end of 1916, was only promoted substantively to captain in the permanent forces in September 1920, and that only because he had been awarded a brevet major's rank for distinguished service in Palestine. He was not promoted substantively to major in the Staff Corps until 1932, although he held the AIF rank from May 1916. Not only was such a system unfair, but it carried considerable financial penalties in an age when army officers were anything but well paid.

The instructions limiting the promotion of Duntroon graduates are now lost, and indeed even during the war members of the parliament were unclear as to the basis on which a ceiling was placed on promotion, although there was agreement that such a barrier did exist.[4] The Minister for Defence, Senator George Pearce, stated in 1920 that neither he nor his predecessor in 1914 had issued such an instruction. 'No such order was issued by the Department [of Defence] in Australia', he stated. It originated at AIF headquarters, and Pearce argued that the motivation behind it was to give young regular officers as wide a range of experience as possible to better fit them for their postwar role of training and administering the militia. It has been suggested equally that the authorities did not wish to be faced with the problem of employing young officers of relatively senior rank in equivalent positions in an inevitably reduced peacetime establishment.[5] Whatever the merits, it created resentment and a sense of grievance which additional interwar inequalities were to compound.

On 29 January the regiment moved to the Canal Zone and on 8 February relieved the 3rd Infantry Brigade in positions ten miles (sixteen kilometres) forward of the Suez Canal in what was designated the No 2 Section of the defences. Based on the camp at Serapeum Railhead, the 10th Light Horse was to occupy a line of trenches and outposts stretching some six miles (ten kilometres) against a possible renewal of Turkish attempts to capture the Canal defences. The Suez Canal, which was to bedevil thinking on imperial strategy for half a century, was the lifeline to India and the Asian and Pacific colonies, and Turkish disruption, much less capture, of this artery of communications would not only interfere with the flow of reinforcements from India and the Pacific dominions, but might threaten Britain's hold on Egypt and the Middle East.

The next five weeks were spent in digging trenches and improving the defences, with constant patrolling to a distance several miles (three or four kilometres) forward of the lines and with strong standing patrols mounted at night. Trench digging in sand was made possible only by the use of frames, constructed from timber and grass matting strutted with wire. Revetments and fire steps were made from sand bags but the trenches, dug to a depth of seven feet (two metres), tended to fill up with sand as quickly as they were dug and keeping them clear was a constant task. In mid-April the regiment were relieved by a battalion of the 54th Division and returned to Serapeum. 'They had seen little or nothing of the enemy, but their task had been heavy and exacting.'[6]

Their first opportunity for offensive mounted action came in June. It was clear that the Turks were preparing a further advance upon the

British defences in the Canal Zone, and were busily pushing forward supply dumps and surveying the wells and water supplies on the central inland route which they had used in their previous attack in February 1915. Alive to the possibilities, and wishing to restrict the possible axes of advance open to them, General Sir Archibald Murray, Commander-in-Chief, Egyptian Expeditionary Force, ordered that the water supplies along the inland route should be destroyed. The task was entrusted to Todd, regarded by his superiors as 'a soldier of conspicuous energy and organising capacity'.[7] He led a raiding column comprising A and B Squadrons of his own regiment, two squadrons of the 9th Light Horse, the machine gun sections from the 8th and 10th Light Horse and detachments of Royal Engineers and supporting troops, backed up by a supply and water column of 903 camels. The objectives of the raid comprised a large freshwater lake at Khabrit-el-Habbal some fourteen miles (twenty-two kilometres) from the Canal, a group of cisterns at Wadi Mukhsheib some forty miles (sixty-four kilometres) south-east of Serapeum which dated from Roman times and which had a capacity of half a million gallons (two million litres), and the cisterns at Mubashia. They reached these first on 11 June, and pumped them out over a continuous twenty-four hour period. With aerial reconnaissance reporting that a large Turkish force was gathering a few miles distant at Jif-Jaffa, Todd's column then retired towards Er-Rigum and Khabrit, where they drained further pools. The column returned to camp at dusk on 14 June, but mounted a further raid four days later to finish the destruction of the water supplies. If the Turks intended to attack the Canal, they were committed now to the coastal route.

At Serapeum, the 10th Light Horse resumed its programme of drill and training, and for most of July maintained a general routine. Stables had to be built for the horses, who were suffering severely in the summer heat, and the men were moved into tents. On 27 July the brigade moved north via Ismailia to a position in the front line on the northern sector east of Ballah, and here began preparations for the operations which, it was felt, were not far distant.

Much has been written about the war in the Middle East, but the real difficulties of campaigning in such an environment are not generally appreciated. For both sides the climate and terrain determined strategy and tactics. The vital importance of securing water supplies for any advance has already been noted. Wheeled vehicles had an impossible time in the sands of Sinai, and all resupply of allied forces was by camel, thousands of which were pressed into service with the Egyptian Labour Corps. The horses found movement over the sands difficult, and in January 1916 companies of the Imperial Camel Corps had been formed from available British, Australian and New Zealand soldiers. Movement for the infantry and artillery was equally problematic, and wire netting tracks were laid in order to facilitate the march forward while the mounted units secured the flanks and covered the advance to the front. In addition, the Turks were tough and skilful soldiers, tenacious and hardy and capable of surprising feats of mobility on foot. The Turkish army's great weakness was at the top, and in the quality of its officer corps, which in general was poor. Both the Germans and Austro-Hungarians sent expeditionary forces to fight alongside their Turkish allies, but the influence of these should not be over-rated although they did provide some important technical support and often proved as hardy and determined in defence as their allies.

In intensity of operations, the experience of the light horse pales by comparison with that of the infantry on the Western Front. But as Robertson himself noted, 'if the Australian troops in Egypt and Sinai missed something of artillery barrages, they found equivalents in the long years of sand, heat and natives'. Troops in France could get leave in England and in the rear areas in France which provided a pleasant contrast with conditions at the front, but in Egypt 'there was scant comfort, even when away from the line'.[8] Medical evacuation in Sinai was fraught with problems, and wounded or sick men were faced with a long and debilitating journey by camel to the medical facilities perhaps some hundred miles (kilometres) to the rear. The climate was unhealthy, and as many Australians were to die of disease as of wounds. The British pushed a light railway and water pipeline forward behind their advance, and with it moved various depots and support facilities, but progress was slow and throughout 1916 the majority of base units and higher headquarters remained in Egypt.

The Turks had resumed their advance against the Canal, and the evening of 3 August found them occupying a line forward of Katia running from Bir Nagid to the sea. The Anzac Mounted Division was entrenched around Romani, then the terminus of the military railway and pipeline. Early on the morning of 4 August the 3rd Light Horse Brigade moved to a position astride Hill 70, some six miles (ten kilometres) north-east of Kantara and well to the rear of the front line, where they remained for the rest of the day while the opening stages of the battle of Romani unfolded. At 6.45 p.m. the following morning the brigade moved out in pursuit of the Turks, making contact with the enemy at Bir Hamisah at a range of 500 yards (460 metres). Enemy machine gun fire held up the 9th Light Horse in the van, who were reinforced by A Squadron of the 10th Light Horse and soon after by the rest of the regiment. After about two hours' fighting, during which the light horse sustained few casualties, the enemy hoisted the white flag when they perceived that their left flank was threatened by an encircling movement mounted by the 10th Light Horse. Three machine guns and 439 prisoners were taken, and the brigade returned to Nagid.[9]

Officers of the 10th Light Horse shaving in bivouack after the march from the railhead at Serapeum prior to the battle of Romani. Robertson at left. *(AWM J02972)*

The pursuit was resumed the next day; towards dusk contact was made again with an entrenched enemy at Hod es Sagia. The 8th Light Horse attacked the next morning, with the 9th in support and the 10th in reserve. The Turks resisted strongly until evening, then withdrew towards the next line of positions at Mushalfat where the the 8th Light Horse again came into contact on 9 August. A two-regiment attack was launched with supporting fire from the Inverness Battery of the Royal Horse Artillery, but the Turks were present in force and towards evening counter-attacked with the bayonet. The 9th ALH were having a rough time of it, but the situation was saved by the prompt arrival of B Squadron of the 10th under Major Robertson, whose intervention helped throw the enemy back with heavy losses. The following two days saw continuous shelling and sniping while the New Zealand Mounted Rifles pressed their assault against Bir-el-Abd to the north. The Turks evacuated their positions opposite the 3rd Light Horse Brigade on the night of 11 August; El-Abd fell the following day, and the enemy began a wholesale withdrawal on Mazar. Thus the first phase of the Sinai campaign ended, with the Australians taking some 3500 prisoners and considerable amounts of material, and with an area roughly sixty miles (ninety-seven kilometres) east of the Canal cleared of the enemy.[10]

Romani was decisive, in that the Turks lost the initiative in Sinai and never regained it. The higher direction of the battle left much to be desired, however. The Anzac Mounted Division under Chauvel had received little or no support from other formations available and a chance to destroy the Turkish force was lost. Chauvel had excelled in his first major battle as a divisional commander, and the victory was owed to the quality of his mounted units. The light horse had shown that they had recovered fully after the heavy losses and unaccustomed role as infantry on Gallipoli, and were now highly proficient as a mobile arm — although the assaults were carried out dismounted. Casualties in the division were around 700 all ranks, although officer casualties represented over ten per cent of the total.

The 3rd Light Horse Brigade was to lose Antill, although not through enemy action. Birdwood had requested that he be made available to command the 2nd Infantry Brigade, part of the 1st Division in France. Antill elected to accept and, on the evening of 9 August, he handed over command of the brigade to Brigadier General J. R. 'Galloping Jack' Royston. Antill had held the brigade together through its severe tests on Gallipoli, when its commander had proved inadequate and some of his subordinates were equally lacking. He had then rebuilt it upon its return to Egypt. A severe and in some ways unappealing figure who neither courted, nor attracted, much personal popularity, his professional skills had served his light horse units well at a time when such skills were in desperately short supply throughout the Australian army, although it should be added that as an operational commander, both on Gallipoli and at Romani, his performance was not above criticism.[11] His successor was a South African-born farmer with considerable service against Boers and Zulus behind him, who came to the brigade fresh from command of the 12th Light Horse. Born in 1860, he was old for an active field command, but 'despite his years and his weight he appeared as insensible to fatigue as he was utterly careless of danger'.[12] He commanded the brigade with distinction until the eve of Beersheba in October 1917, when he returned to South Africa for personal reasons.

There now followed a period of reorganisation in preparation for the next stage of the campaign to clear Sinai of the Turks. The 10th Light Horse spent three weeks at Hod-Fatir while supplies were moved forward, and on 3 September advanced to new positions on the line running through Hod-el-Hisha, Bir-el-Abd and Hod-el-Bada. Robertson and B Squadron were camped in outposts around Bada with regimental headquarters and, like the other squadrons, were occupied in patrol and outpost work although the line was left unmolested by the enemy. Units of the brigade were involved in several large reconnaissances in force, 'chiefly productive of long rides, sleepless nights, and extreme fatigue of both men and horses without much actual achievement to show for it'.[13] On 16 and 17 September the 2nd and 3rd Brigades were involved in an abortive attempt to take the Turkish positions at Mazar, but were not seriously engaged before the planned attack was called off because of the poor prospects of success.

A month later the 3rd Light Horse Brigade moved back to Romani for a month to prepare for the next phase of operations, including the incorporation of the new Lewis guns, which had been adapted to a mounted role and which were introduced on an establishment of three guns per regiment, replacing the Vickers guns used on Gallipoli. In the interim the Turks fell back from Mazar to new positions on a line running through El Arish, intending to deny the British entry into southern Palestine. It was towards the enemy positions on this new line that the advance would now be directed, and on 23 November 1916 the 10th Light Horse, along with the rest of the Anzac Mounted Division, received orders to move again to the front.

It was during this period of rest and refitting that Horace and Jessie allegedly married, in October. She was nursing at Heliopolis, although in what capacity is not clear. She was not serving with the AIF; there is no record of her on the nominal role of the force. All nursing sisters were officers (and therefore traceable by virtue of their commissions), and in any case there was a policy that Australian nursing sisters were to be discharged from the Australian Army Nursing Service upon marriage. No such provision applied to nurses in the British service. There were also civilian hospitals supporting the military medical effort in Egypt. It seems most likely that she served in either a British military or British civilian hospital, but the details are now lost.

The Australian mounted units were once more at full strength, and were never again to fall disastrously under establishment as they had done on Gallipoli. This was largely due to the nature of the war they fought, since despite some stiff fighting at various stages the casualty level overall was low, certainly by comparison with the Western Front. This was as well, because already after Romani Birdwood had tried to get all reinforcements destined for the light horse remustered as infantry and sent to France in order to make up the awful losses suffered on the Somme. He was unsuccessful, but the mounted units were to come under threat on various occasions for the rest of the war. By mid-1917 Australia was having great difficulty maintaining its army in the field, as voluntary enlistment declined and the electorate rejected conscription as a means of providing reinforcements. The replacement manpower demands of the Australian units in the Middle East remained low, as did the availability of fresh drafts for that theatre, and gaps in the light horse were often made up through the return of wounded or sick men following convalescence. But this was in the future, though not too distant, and the 3rd Light Horse Brigade still mustered ninety-four officers, 1997 other ranks, 2013 horses and 340 camels at the end of November 1916 as its units moved out for the final operations to clear Sinai.[14]

To date, the light horse had been used entirely in the dismounted role when in action, as dictated by standard mounted infantry doctrine. There had been little opportunity to deploy the units of cavalry proper, since the desert sands of Sinai made the use of mounted men in shock action very difficult. At this time the cavalry was represented by the 5th Mounted Brigade (British Yeomanry) under the command of Brigadier General E. A. Wiggin, but their strength was to be increased fourfold early in 1917, with the arrival of three additional Yeomanry brigades in the Palestine theatre.

Now that it was evident that operations were moving out of the desert sands and into 'hard' country more suited to horses and mounted action, a wider role was envisaged for the cavalry units. To this end, there was agitation for the Yeomanry to retain their swords, which had been of little use so far in the campaign. As Wiggin wrote to the commander of the Desert Column, General Sir Philip Chetwode, 'the ANZAC troopers do not carry swords, and as I consider it of vital importance that at least one brigade of the Desert Column be so armed, I beg to represent in the strongest possible manner that my Brigade should retain these weapons, in the use of which they have received a very thorough training. Furthermore, I am convinced, from the point of view of morale, that the knowledge that they have a sword and know how to use it adds greatly to the confidence and dash of mounted troops.' His superior in command of the Australian and New Zealand Mounted Division, Brigadier General E.W.C. Chaytor, concurred in this, making representations also to the effect that 'it is quite conceivable that the most far-reaching effects will be produced by being able to launch a body of mounted troops, trained as the Yeomanry have been, to mounted action on a retreating enemy ... I am strongly against taking the sword away, just at the time opportunities may occur to use it'.[15] In fact, much later, in August 1918 the 3rd, 4th and 5th Light Horse Brigades were issued with swords and given some instruction in their use, and the 10th Light Horse made a mounted charge with drawn swords against a Turkish position at Jenin on 20 September that year. But there was no suggestion of adapting the light horse generally to a cavalry role in 1916.

The role and effectiveness of cavalry in the Middle East was to become a vexed question in the interwar period. The sentiments noted above were an expression, in part at least, of the understandable desire of cavalry officers to see their arm of service prove its usefulness despite the changes in modern warfare which had finally and irrevocably rendered the cavalry obsolete in France. Sinai and Palestine offered opportunities long gone on the Western Front, and some very able cavalrymen played a significant and distinguished part in the campaign which led to the Turkish defeat in 1918. The lesson which many commentators after the war missed altogether was not that cavalry still had a major role in war, for it did not, but rather that mobility was still an important factor on the open battlefield. The primitive state of the internal combustion engine in the period 1914-18 meant of necessity that mobility was equated with horseflesh. As the petrol engine became more reliable, the vehicles which it powered would take the place of horses, although this was a lesson firmly resisted in some quarters of both the British and Australian armies until after the outbreak of the Second World War. By the same token, it would be unwise to dismiss the cavalry school entirely, for on a number of occasions offensive shock action by mounted men prevailed against fixed Turkish positions. The earliest example of this phenomenon was provided by the 10th Light Horse, and in circumstances which allowed Horace Robertson to shine.

General Headquarters assumed that the Turks intended to hold El Arish in order to deny the British entry into Palestine, the defences of which were in a rudimentary state. At this stage the Turks disposed about 16,000 men in Sinai and Palestine, with a further three divisions far to the north in Syria. Chetwode decided to capture the Turkish position at El Arish, garrisoned by about 1600 Turks, and then destroy the surrounding garrisons in villages like Abu Aweigila and El Magdhaba. The railway and pipeline could then be pushed forward to Rafa and the British would stand poised to enter Palestine and take the war to the enemy. Before the British could strike, however, the Turks evacuated their force from El Arish and the Australian and New Zealand Mounted Division took over a town empty of the enemy on the morning of 21 December 1916. Measures were put in hand at once for the pursuit of the retreating Turks.

The enemy's movements were uncertain. Two lines of retreat suggested themselves: along the coast towards Rafa, or along the Wadi El Arish towards the camp at Magdhaba. Aerial reconnaissance reported heavy tracks heading in both directions, and Chauvel was ordered to move his forces towards Magdhaba while a detachment of the Camel Corps operated towards Rafa. When it became clear on the afternoon of 22 December that a considerable force was encamped at Magdhaba the Camel Corps was recalled, and Chauvel was ordered to proceed with all haste.[16]

The 3rd Light Horse Brigade marched out at 5.30 p.m. that evening on a night approach march. 'Our idea was only a vague one as to where we were marching to' wrote Major L. C. Timperley, now commanding

B Squadron of the 10th Light Horse. 'We had our greatcoats on throughout the night, but the wind had a keen edge on it, and unless moving about, we could not get any warmth out of our coats.'[17] The men carried three days' rations for themselves and their horses, and as much water as they could manage, for there were no supplies between El Arish and Magdhaba and it was assumed that the Turks had mined the wells in the village. The men also carried 230 rounds of small arms ammunition.[18] The march was terribly cold and many of the men fell asleep in their saddles. 'About 11 p.m. all the officers were called up by the Brigadier, who told us where we were going, anticipated time of arrival at our destination, the approximate number of troops there, time of attack etc. He said he thought it would be a nice little show, and that we were to clean the place up, and *quickly too*.'[19] At 12.45 a.m. on the morning of 23 December, Chauvel's forces reached the concentration point to the northwest of Magdhaba, and continued their approach. The going was good, with the men riding for forty minutes, leading for ten, and resting for ten; 'as the night was very cold the leading was a great benefit to all'.[20]

The 10th Light Horse, placed to the rear of the column, had a more difficult time, reinforcing the need for march discipline. 'The pace varied from that of a snail to a hand gallop', wrote Robertson later, 'and was punctuated by sudden checks — the rear of the column ... was performing a continual concertina motion. The main trouble was caused by dust. Thousands of horses' hoofs pounded the fine clay of the wadi bed, so that it rose in clouds, and obscured the units in front. This started those behind hurrying for fear of losing the column, and the haste multiplied towards the rear.'[21] At 3.50 a.m. they saw the bivouac fires of the enemy and an hour later the force halted about four miles (six kilometres) from the Turkish camp.

Aerial reconnaissance early that morning revealed a strong enemy force and a pilot from 67 (Australian) Squadron Royal Flying Corps, which had worked closely with the 10th Light Horse before, passed this information on to Robertson, who was now senior major and second-in-command of the unit. 'Dear Robbie. How are things? The bastards are there all right in the redoubt N[orth] of the camp and in the wadi south of the camp. Party there is about 300 strong. Christ knows what is in the redoubt but something passed through the air close to me ... Hope you get the place. Best love to you all and heaps of luck.'[22] At 8.22 a.m. Chauvel issued a signal to all brigades: 'From its appearance Magdhaba is held by from 2000 to 3000 men. The GOC intends to attack.'[23]

The Turkish positions comprised two strong redoubts on the left bank of the wadi, connected by communications trenches and linked back to the buildings in the village on the right bank. There were further redoubts on this bank, as well as numerous rifle pits and posts, and the enemy had a number of field guns available. To the south-west were rough foothills, while to the north there were sand dunes and sparse low scrub. The ground in front of the redoubts was absolutely exposed and the Turkish positions were well sited to give mutual support and good fields of fire all round. The 3rd Light Horse Brigade was pushed out several miles (kilometres) to the east of the main allied position, and deployed facing south towards the right flank of the Turkish positions with the 10th Light Horse in reserve. Placed in command of part of his regiment on the left of the brigade position, Robertson pushed some patrols out still further to the east to screen the brigade, and there the regiment waited while the whole division deployed for the attack.

The main attack commenced at 9.55 a.m., while Royston's brigade was still deploying to the east. With the artillery laying a good covering fire the Camel Brigade moved directly on Magdhaba from the north-west, across two miles (over three kilometres) of open country devoid of cover. A little after 10 a.m. Cox and the 1st Light Horse Brigade were sent forward in response to a report that the Turks were abandoning their positions and withdrawing. They drew heavy, though inaccurate, enemy fire, which disproved the report, and Cox moved his units to the right and into the cover of the wadi and proceeded to support the attack of the Camel Brigade. Although out of the attack, the 10th Light Horse were taking casualties and Lieutenant Colonel Todd was wounded. This placed Robertson in command of the unit.

The attack was held all along the line, and at 1 p.m. Chauvel received a message that the engineers had failed to find water in the vicinity. This placed the attacking force in a precarious situation, since if Magdhaba was not taken that day the horses, which had not been watered since the previous afternoon, would begin to die. Chauvel was forced to consider withdrawal, but as he did so the situation improved. Cox had managed to gain a foothold in the wadi and the 2nd Light Horse was closing on the left of the enemy's No 2 Redoubt, south of the wadi.

By now the 10th Light Horse was drawn into the battle, although the sequence and timing of events is confused. At 9.30 a.m., General Chaytor had ordered that the 10th, together with two sections of the brigade's machine gun squadron, should make a wide flanking march through Aulad Ali and around Hill 345 to take the enemy in the right rear. By midday, however, the unit was still in place to the north-east, where it had been all morning. Robertson recalled that Royston instructed him at about 12.30 p.m. 'to push forward whenever I got the chance, in cooperation with [the renewed] advance'.[24] Realising the opportunity which presented itself, and seeing that a considerable expanse of open ground must be crossed, Robertson ordered up the horses and resolved on a mounted attack. 'I mounted the regiment, extended it, and led it over the sand dunes down into the river bed, riding with my trumpeter about one hundred yards ahead, so that all could see my signals'. About halfway

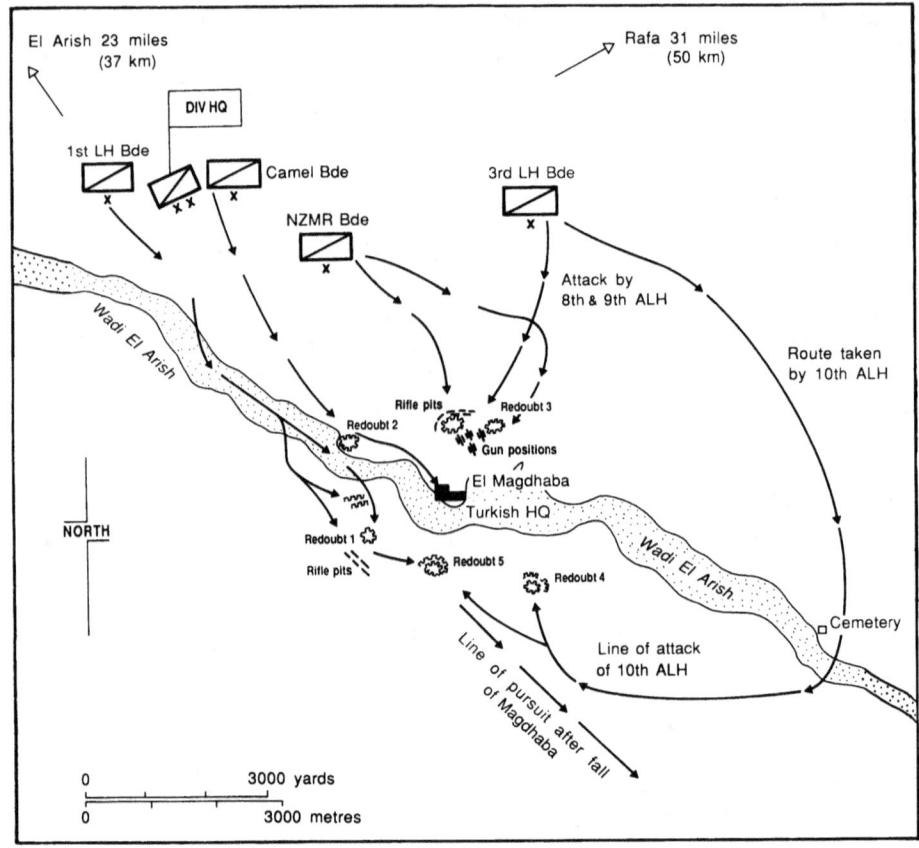

Battle of Magdhaba, 23 December 1916.

across the plain the regiment came under heavy rifle fire but the men pushed on and occupied the wadi, taking prisoner six officers and 290 men. The regiment then swung round and faced west and pushed on towards a series of entrenchments around the enemy's Nos 3 and 4 Redoubts.

'I realised that I had the luckiest cavalry role of the whole attack, and I was young enough to be rather elated at my chance, so I decided to risk everything on it.' Leaving a small force to block the wadi and cut off the escape of any Turks who came that way, Robertson pushed a squadron against each of the redoubts. The squadrons 'advanced at the gallop but were met by very heavy fire. 2 troops charged right through the enemy and joined up with the 1st Brigade who were facing east. Lewis and M[achine] Guns were brought into action and the regiment attacked again mounted.'[25] The men had fixed their bayonets to their rifles and some carried them lance-like. Some men dismounted once they entered the redoubt and proceeded to clear the Turks from the position. Casualties, especially among the horses, were growing, but the all-round pressure began to tell. 'The moral effect of the galloping horsemen assisted by the covering enfilade fire of the dismounted troop had the desired effect on the redoubt', and by 4.15 p.m. the enemy was surrendering in large numbers.[26] The 10th Light Horse alone took 722 prisoners as well as fifty-seven camels loaded with stores and ammunition. All organised resistance ceased by 4.40 p.m., and the men were able to water their horses in the village wells, which turned out not to have been mined by the Turks after all. The total haul of prisoners was 1210 unwounded, including a regimental and two battalion commanders, forty wounded, four mountain guns, 1200 rifles and over 100,000 rounds of small arms ammunition. The division had suffered five officers and seventeen other ranks killed, seven officers and 117 men wounded, and fifty-nine casualties among the horses.[27] The light casualties were explained by the poor shooting of the Turks, although the threefold superiority in artillery which Chauvel enjoyed probably played a part. After the prisoners had been concentrated and the wounded attended to the division returned to camp at El Arish, arriving on the following morning.

Magdhaba 'will be remembered as a notable instance of the effective employment of mounted troops against isolated fortifications in open country'.[28] For Robertson, it was his first independent command in action, a dashing and highly successful, as well as slightly unorthodox, action. Both the British and Australian official histories state that Royston led the charge of the 10th Light Horse, which Robertson vigorously refuted. 'I am equally emphatic that from the time General Royston spoke to me near Katib-el-Teir, I neither set eyes on him, nor received an order from him, until after 4 p.m. when I found him at his Bde HQ in the deep channel behind the 8th LH. At the time of the attack I would have welcomed his presence, as I was only 22 years of age, and the responsibility of a regimental mounted attack across a mile of flat river bed . . . against enemy fire, was weighing heavily on me. I was not even sure of the main enemy dispositions when General Royston left me to ride off towards the other regiments, after giving me the orders.'[29]

There is no doubt that Royston was in the thick of the fighting — his temperament would not have permitted him to be anywhere else. He was not with the 10th, however, but almost certainly went in with the 8th and 9th Light Horse, who attacked with the Wellington Mounted Rifles to the left of the Camel Brigade at about 2 p.m., and in support of whose renewed assault Royston had ordered Robertson to act. Certainly neither Lieutenant Colonel Todd, back at his post late in the afternoon, nor Royston himself, were in any doubt as to Robertson's part in the battle. In the recommendation for the Distinguished Service Order which he wrote the next day, Todd described how Robertson had shown 'conspicuous ability and initiative throughout the whole action both in the preliminary taking of the high ground overlooking the enemy's right and later in the mounted charge around the positions ... Having a very extended front I placed Major Robertson in charge of the left and to his resource and dash I attribute greatly the successful result of the whole operation in our sector.'[30] To add to the enjoyment of the moment, Robertson had taken the surrender of a senior Turkish officer who had been on an inspection tour of the Sinai defences and had been caught up in the fight. The sword which was surrendered to him was a prized possession for many years.

Magdhaba was a resounding success, and demonstrated both the tenacity and skill of the light horse and the coolness and decision of their commander, Chauvel. Some weaknesses were shown up also. It seems clear that Chauvel was unaware of the flanking movement of the 10th Light Horse until the unit was in among the Turkish positions, and at times he was unclear as to the locations of some of his units through breakdowns in communications between divisional and brigade headquarters.[31] The enemy's shooting had been poor, but they had shown no inclination to surrender quickly even when surrounded, and 'in future we must be prepared for any enemy holding on and meeting us with the bayonet'. The precarious supply situation was a warning of things to come, and would result in the failure before Gaza in March the following year.

The mounted charge of the 10th Light Horse created something of a stir, and Robertson believed that it paved the way for Grant's attack at Beersheba in October 1917, and that together these two actions demonstrated 'finally to the light horse that they must become cavalry if they wished to reap the full harvest of mounted action'.[32] In fact the 10th's 'charge' was less a full-blown cavalry movement than a series of mounted rushes from position to position, 'galloping, dismounting, firing, remounting, and galloping to the next ridge, while other troops would remain and put in covering fire'.[33] But at this stage of the campaign such action was still unusual, and showed the potential for decisive mounted action in the right circumstances.

After Christmas spent at El Arish, the light horse moved out on 8 January for the attack on Rafa. The Turks again were in strongly fortified positions forward of Rafa in the village of El Magruntein. Their redoubts covered all the high ground and the approaches were devoid of cover. The New Zealand Mounted Rifles Brigade swung around to the east and then invested Rafa from the north. The 1st and 3rd Light Horse Brigades were put to the assault from the left, with the Imperial Camel Corps Brigade to their left attacking from the south and the 5th Mounted Brigade, in an independent role, attacking from the south-west. Thus a ring of troops was gradually drawn around the defenders. As at Magdhaba, however, the Turks showed no signs of surrendering when cut off, and hard fighting ensued in which ammunition expenditure was high and the dismounted attacks of the forces to the south and east were held up by strong Turkish fire. Once again, the Australian and New Zealand Mounted Division was operating at the end of its supply lines and a decision was vital before dark or else the attacking forces would be forced to retreat towards El Arish. Just when it seemed that the order to retire would have to be given, the New Zealanders poured over the high ground to the north of the Turkish positions and captured the northernmost redoubt. 'Our men leapt up and rushed straight at the Turkish trenches in front of them. There were bursts of fire from some redoubts, but as we closed, white flags and raised arms proclaimed a general surrender, and, except for odd shots, fighting had practically ceased by 4.30 p.m., truly one of the most dramatic five minutes I have ever experienced', wrote Robertson later.[34] Another brilliant short action, it resulted in the capture of 1600 Turkish soldiers and thirty-five officers, including ten Germans, together with quantities of stores and weapons. Of still greater importance, it marked the final clearing of the enemy from Sinai and heralded the opportunity for the British to go over fully to the offensive with the invasion of southern Palestine. The Turks withdrew to begin strengthening the defensive line between Gaza and Beersheba while the allies pulled back to El Arish to build up their forces for the renewed offensive, to begin in March.

The mounted units underwent reorganisation in this period. The Anzac Mounted Division remained, but now comprised the 1st and 2nd Light Horse Brigades, the New Zealand Mounted Rifles and the newly arrived 22nd Yeomanry Mounted Brigade. A new division, the Imperial Mounted, was formed from the 3rd and recreated 4th Light Horse Brigades, the 5th Yeomanry and new 6th Yeomanry Brigades.[35] Robertson too found himself posted to new surroundings. Todd placed on record his appreciation of 'the manner in which the duties of senior major were carried out' by Robertson, and had given a fuller assessment of the latter's service in his DSO recommendation: 'This officer has been with the Regiment for over two years having joined us from Duntroon as MG officer and has through consistent good work risen to his present position. He has never been away from the Regiment since joining and I consider he is worthy of the highest recognition. He has fine military ability with determination and I predict a very successful career.'[36] In addition to his DSO for Magdhaba he was awarded a mention in dispatches in March for his work overall with the 10th Light Horse. But as a Staff Corps officer with a postwar career in prospect it was important that he broaden his experience and, as one of the most able young officers in the theatre, he was now posted to the staff. On 17 February he was attached to the headquarters of the Desert Column for staff duties.

The appointment of Australians to the higher staff organisations had a chequered history and was the cause of disagreement between the Australian Imperial Force and the British high command, both in Palestine and France. The issue demonstrated the problems posed by the shortage of prewar regulars with staff training, the high casualties among young officers, and the disinclination of some British senior officers to believe that colonial soldiers enlisted for the war's duration could fill the higher staff appointments without a regular army background and prewar staff training. For the first two years of the war a large proportion of the staff jobs on Australian divisional headquarters were filled by officers of the British and Indian armies. The same was true in the Canadian and New Zealand divisions. After Gallipoli, General Murray had attached young officers to higher divisional and corps staffs for brief periods as staff 'learners', and a number of the Duntroon graduates who had survived the campaign were promoted and posted to Australian brigade and divisional headquarters. By 1917, the staff of I Anzac Corps in France, under Birdwood, was largely Australian but Godley's II Anzac Corps never had any Australian or New Zealand representation except at the most junior levels. In Palestine the staffs of the Desert Mounted Corps and the Australian Mounted Division remained largely British in composition for the whole of the war.

This was not through any lack of suitable Australian officers, nor was it by Chauvel's design. When the Australian Mounted Division, originally designated the Imperial Mounted Division, had been formed early in 1917, Chauvel recommended Australians for the divisional staff, but only two out of nineteen posts went to Australians.[37] Every staff position on the Camel Brigade headquarters, three-quarters of whose strength was ANZAC, was occupied by a British officer. The army in Palestine at the beginning of 1917 'was staffed by officers of whom many were low in capacity', wrote the Australian official historian H. S. Gullett.[38] After the war, he put his view even more bluntly. 'It is, I think, beyond all question that the British professional soldier blundered frightfully in the degree in which he endeavoured to keep every job worth having in this great war in professional hands. There was also the folly amounting to crime of continuing to employ men who had failed . . . I personally met lots of British officers at Palestine formation . . . each of whose positions could have been filled by incomparably capable men from the Light Horse. This and our staff representation was far from all it should have been.'[39]

In large part the problem of adequate staff representation was Birdwood's fault, since he insisted that Australian officers might only be appointed to Australian staffs, and although situated in France he kept a tight grip on staff appointments in the Middle East. In the course of 1917 Birdwood relented, not least under pressure from the British themselves. General Sir Hubert Gough, who as commander of Fifth Army in France was not greatly liked by the Australians he commanded, inquired whether it would be possible to exchange officers in both command and staff positions. 'I may add that this is a matter which the Commander-in-Chief [ie, Haig] has very much at heart, and that he is always anxious to appoint Australian officers to the staffs of British formations if they can be spared.' In reply, Birdwood stressed the shortage of suitable officers and the requirement for Australian troops to be commanded by Australians, but conceded that 'a trial might be made of the principle of interchange by exchanging a few staff officers. As conditions improve, and as our resources develop, it may be possible further to extend this system until an ideal is more nearly reached.'[40]

It is difficult to account for Birdwood's attitude. While protesting the lack of suitable officers for staff postings he was able to write to his divisional commanders on the subject of promotion of junior officers and NCOs that 'we have enlisted men of intelligence, initiative and resource, and it therefore behoves us to make full and ample use of these, and to satisfy ourselves that our resources in this respect are not allowed to lie fallow'.[41] At about the same time the War Office made it clear that there was no objection in principle to the appointment of dominion officers to imperial staffs.

> *The policy of the Army Council has always been to regard the Staff as an Imperial organisation in which officers of the Dominion forces equally with those of the British service shall be considered interchangeable... The only obstacle to the fulfilment of this principle hitherto has been the paucity of officers of the Dominion forces with the necessary training and experience, but now that we are entering the fourth year of the war and with the increased facilities... for acquiring this experience there should be little difficulty in providing a representative proportion of Australian officers for staff appointments both inside and outside the Australian Imperial Force.* [42]

It was against this background that Robertson found himself at Headquarters, Desert Column whence, on 25 February, he was sent to the staff school at Mena in Egypt.

His initial enrolment proved abortive, for on 7 March he sustained a compound fracture of the left leg in a riding accident and was hospitalised for over two months.[43] Discharged in late May, he started on the third course at Mena and graduated on 17 June, judged suitable for appointment to a low-level staff position as General Staff Officer 3, a result which nonetheless does not appear to have carried the connotations of bare competence which would be the case in a later war. On 26 June he joined the headquarters of the Yeomanry Mounted Division at Khan Yunis on the border of southern Palestine. This new division, formed through the bringing together of the Yeomanry mounted brigades, was commanded by Major General Sir George de Symons Barrow, 'a forceful cavalry soldier of the old, hard-riding school ... perhaps the greatest leader of cavalry proper on this front'.[44] Barrow had served in France with a cavalry brigade during the retreat from Mons in 1914 and, like the new Commander-in-Chief of the Egyptian Expeditionary Force, General Sir Edmund Allenby, had been sent out from France to take a grip of the situation in Palestine after the costly reverses suffered before Gaza in March and April. The general reorganisation which followed Allenby's arrival saw the 1st and 2nd Light Horse and New Zealand Mounted Rifles Brigades sent to form the Anzac Mounted Division under Chaytor, the 3rd and 4th Light Horse and the 5th Mounted Brigades comprising the Australian Mounted Division under a British officer, Hodgson, and the Yeomanry Mounted made up of the 6th, 8th, and 22nd Mounted Brigades. The whole comprised the Desert Mounted Corps, command of which was given to Chauvel. The 6th and 8th Brigades were being returned to Palestine from the Salonika front, and when Robertson joined the division it was scarcely formed, with units concentrating around Khan Yunis through the first half of July and the division kept in reserve by Chauvel as a result.[45] In line with the changes in staff appointment policy, Robertson was not the only Australian on the Yeomanry Division's headquarters. The new General Staff Officer 1 (the principal operations staff officer in the division) was a prewar Australian regular, Colonel W. J. Foster, aged thirty-six, 'a first rate staff officer and a very fine soldier'.[46] Foster remained with the division until after the war's end; he went to the staff college and was then given command of the Cavalry Brigade at Tidworth, the first dominion officer to hold a regular command in the British army.

Robertson remained with the division some nine months, until March 1918. During this period British forces were involved in the Third Battle of Gaza, which unlocked the defences of southern Palestine, and in the pursuit of the Turks which followed and which culminated in the capture of Jerusalem on 9 December. This was followed by preparations for operations in and beyond the Jordan Valley which themselves led to the last great offensive of September and October 1918 and the climactic battle of Megiddo. While Robertson was serving with them, the Yeomanry Mounted Division was involved in a series of significant operations which alternated hard fighting with strategic manoeuvre over considerable distances — the sort of open, mobile warfare which had disappeared entirely on the Western Front at this time.

The activities of the brigades and regiments of the Yeomanry Mounted Division at this time are not, in detail, the story of a young staff officer on divisional headquarters. Despite his staff training at Duntroon and the considerable regimental experience which he brought to the post, Robertson was a very junior cog in the headquarters wheel and, at least for the first month or two, was as much novice as practitioner in the arcane world of the headquarters staff.[47] His duties varied. Apart from

A GOOD WAR: 1916-1919

Robertson (left) with Major General Sir George Barrow, GOC Yeomanry Mounted Division, and Colonel W. J. Foster, GSO 1, Palestine, 1917.

a subordinate role in operational planning and administration, Robertson was frequently used as a liaison officer and courier between the general officer commanding and his subordinate units and formations. This entailed long hours in the saddle in all weathers and at all times of the day and night, and on occasions was dangerous work, since enemy cavalry patrols were often active.

A little of Robertson's life and activities at this time may be gleaned from episodes during the preparation and pursuit phases of the Third Battle of Gaza. The first occurred in September 1917, while the Yeomanry Mounted Division was engaged in pushing in the Turkish cavalry screens around Beersheba on the left of the enemy's defensive line. The division was to be held in reserve during the first phase of the attack — the capture of Beersheba — and was thus involved in preliminary reconnaissance and screening work to spare the men and horses of the other mounted formations which would take part. The right flank of the British position 'although relatively well secured by waterless and difficult country, needed outposts and patrolling to prevent any surprise from that quarter'.[48] Desert Mounted Corps HQ maintained contact with its three mounted divisions by telephone line and, during the days in which the Yeomanry units were thrown forward to hinder the Turks' reconnaissance Robertson found himself left behind to mount a 'radio watch', maintaining the link between the division in the field and higher headquarters, and to deal with any sudden emergencies. It was routine, uneventful duty although occasionally it brought its surprises, as when Robertson chanced across a German officer disguised as a British lieutenant colonel, engaged in a little spying-out of British positions.[49]

The officer aroused no suspicions, at least initially, but his accompanying 'Australian' orderly immediately attracted Robertson's interest. 'The orderly was dressed in a rather crumpled Australian uniform, which was much too big for him; he was dark complexioned and he avoided my eye.' Knowing that only British officers attached to Australian units would have Australian orderlies, Robertson became thoroughly suspicious. It was an interesting comment on the enemy's perceptions of the Australians they fought that, as he noted, 'The orderly was . . . *too* untidy. The Australian dresses for comfort, but he does it by leaving off unnecessary clothes when the weather is hot — his uniform is not several sizes too big for him, nor does it look as if it has been stuffed in a bag for weeks.' And it was an odd Australian who, on meeting a fellow countryman in strange surroundings, did not give some sign of recognition; 'he might even salute!' Without a horse to hand, and with the divisional camp largely deserted, Robertson rang headquarters at once to alert them to the strangers' presence, but the German officer escaped detection. It transpired that he had been sighted a number of times in the area, but he was never caught: 'a very brave and quick witted man' in Robertson's view.

Once the offensive began, however, it was a different matter. In the initial phase of the Third Battle of Gaza Allenby had kept the Yeomanry Mounted Division in the gap between XXI Corps on the left, which mounted a demonstration before Gaza itself, and XX and Desert

Mounted Corps on the right, charged with the capture of Beersheba and then turning the enemy's left flank. Following the success of this first phase, the Yeomanry Mounted Division was pushed across to the right and on 6 November supported infantry assaults against the Turkish positions at Khuweilfe. While XX Corps cleaned up the Turkish defensive line running to the east of Beersheba, the Yeomanry threw out a strong screen to protect the British flank. Within three days it was clear that the Turks were retreating in some disorganisation, and the division was pushed forward towards Huj. On 10 November, elements of the 6th Mounted Brigade encountered the Turkish rearguard, which did not stand. Over the next two days the mounted brigades continued to advance in company with the infantry, engaged in reconnaissance, intelligence, attacking the enemy's communications and safeguarding its own, as well as in the tactical shock role which Wiggins and Chaytor had foreseen.

Several things can be said about these operations. The first is that they were highly mobile, the mounted units covering considerable distances over periods of days at a time. The second is that the operations made great use of combined arms; they were never simply or even mainly mounted actions. The mounted brigades had artillery attached to them, and acted in concert with the infantry in the various phases of the operation. The last thing to note is the very considerable logistic difficulties which faced the British advance. Any period of rapid forward movement led the forces involved to outstrip their supply lines. During the operations around Khuweilfe, the Yeomanry Mounted Division had experienced great difficulty watering its horses in the arid country in which it found itself, and units had to return between twelve and fourteen miles (nineteen and twenty-two kilometres) to Beersheba to water men and animals, and this on average only once every forty-eight hours. When the division transferred from the right flank to the coastal front on 10 and 11 November, the brigades had to spend a day watering the horses and collecting rations before resuming the offensive. Mounted units had to limit strictly what they could carry in order to remain mobile; limiting their supply train meant that they could remain mobile only for short periods of time.

The division's activities on 13, 14 and 15 November illustrate some of these features well, and involved Robertson in an active role. Having taken up a position on the coast behind the Anzac Mounted Division, Barrow's division was poised to resume forward movement on 13 November, aiming for a line between 'Aquir and a bridgehead across the Wadi Jamus east of Yibna. Communications between Desert Mounted Corps and Barrow's headquarters had broken down, however, and when Barrow issued his orders for the next day's activity at 7 p.m. on 12 November, he was unaware of the coordinated attack which the brigades of the 52nd

Infantry Division were to mount to his right. Robertson had been sent off to Advanced Headquarters, Desert Mounted Corps to obtain the orders for his division, only to find that they had been sent on to Headquarters, Anzac Mounted Division earlier in the day, and that there were no spare copies. Returning to his own headquarters about 5.30 p.m., he was then ordered up to Anzac Mounted Division to establish personal liaison and obtain the necessary orders. Departing about half an hour later, 'it was then dark, there was no road, a thunderstorm was gathering, the country was intersected by trenches prepared by the Turks as a defensive position [and] I did not know the position of Anzac Mtd Div HQ'. Arriving about 7.30 p.m., Robertson was then faced with attempting to establish links with the 52nd Division, since this had not yet been done either. At this point, the thunderstorm arrived and put out the telephone lines between the two headquarters. After waiting vainly for contact to be re-established, Robertson set off once more at 11.30 p.m. to deliver his orders to his own general.

'I made for the railway as it was a pitch black night and raining. I hit the railway but got into such a maze of trenches and when I thought I had passed them struck back again to the railway. I imagined I had come too far so turned North collecting in my passage a complete Brigade staff who were lost.' Finally making it back at about 1 a.m. the following morning, 'I then had some food while the Div Cmdr and GSO1 considered the orders. At about 1.30 a.m. we commenced to write orders (they had all to be hand-written and on account of the number of copies it generally required about four of us).'[50] Little could be done by that stage to effect the takeover from the Anzac Mounted Division, with the result that the Yeomanry Mounted Division was some distance behind the advance when the 52nd Division began its assault next morning.

Robertson spent much of that day in the saddle again, riding between divisional headquarters, the various mounted brigades, and the formations they were supporting. At about 3 p.m. a request came from the 52nd Division for assistance as the infantry was held up by strong Turkish forces around El Mughar. Robertson was sent off by Barrow with orders for the 6th Mounted Brigade. The brigade commander resolved on a mounted attack, across nearly two miles (three kilometres) of open ground, through 'a belt of enemy machine guns and a battery of artillery'.[51] The brigade major of the 6th Mounted Brigade invited Robertson to stay and observe the action, but the latter had to report back to headquarters that the orders had been received, 'so I rode back and reported and then slipped away towards 6th Mtd Bde HQ to the top of a hill from which I observed the actual attack'. After dark, he was sent out again to renew contact with the brigade, communications having broken down again, and 'after falling into numerous wadis and nearly killing my horse' he eventually found it'.[52]

For the next ten days this pattern of activity repeated itself, with Robertson keeping his commander appraised of the division's activities as the rapid series of advances and mounted actions unfolded. The mounted brigades again charged Turkish positions at Abu Shushe on 15 November, killing over 400 Turks and taking more than 1000 prisoners. When the division came to rest around Foka on 23 November it had been on the move and in action continuously for nearly three weeks. 'Owing to the lack of water and great difficulty in getting up supplies it became imperative for the division to either go forward, if possible, or send back all horses which could be spared.'[53] Once again, mobile operations in the desert demonstrated the need for the forces to free themselves from dependence on their lines of supply. But freedom of movement was limited in time by the amount which could be carried with the units, supplemented by such foraging as the terrain would permit.

The division was involved in holding the Turkish counter-attacks, launched on 24 and 25 November, and in the fierce enemy defence of the approaches to Jerusalem, before going into reserve around Akir on 2 December. The Yeomanry thus played no direct part in the final capture of Jerusalem, which Allenby entered personally on foot on 11 December. Operations largely ceased at the end of the month, and preparations were placed in hand for the capture of Jericho and the advance into northern Palestine and Syria which would begin in February.[54]

Much of Robertson's activities with the Yeomanry Mounted Division in this period differed little if at all in kind from those of other young staff officers in Palestine. The pace had been hard, and it appears likely that the leg which he had broken early in 1917 was giving him trouble by the time the allied offensive ran out of steam at the end of that year. With the end of the active phase of operations, at least for the time being, Robertson looked for a quiet posting in order to nurse his injury without fear of being invalided home to Australia — the fate of several Duntroon graduates wounded early in the war. This was potentially disastrous professionally while the war was still going on since, once returned, a regular officer was precluded from further service overseas. No doubt with the help of his seniors, he was posted as General Staff Officer 3, Headquarters Delta Force at Abbassia, in Egypt, taking up duty on 3 March 1918. Formerly Western Force, it had been involved in operations against the Senussi revolt in the Western Desert in 1915 and 1916, and had then assumed general security duties in the rear of the Egyptian Expeditionary Force's advance. Robertson's duties were minor and involved maintaining the headquarters' war diary and making inspection visits to the handful of units under its command.[55] On 8 April Delta Force was disbanded, its functions being assumed by Headquarters, the Force in Egypt. With detachments at Sollum, Abbassia and Tel el-Kebir, the Force in Egypt was charged with security and monitoring the activities of the Bedouins and others in the Western Desert and the Canal Zone (although responsibilities for the latter were transferred to Palestine Line of Communications Headquarters in July), and with some liaison with Britain's Italian allies in Libya.

Robertson's duties again were light: responsibility for contingency plans to meet any threat in the rear areas from dissident tribes or rioting allied troops, and policy and supervision of the training of such units as the force had under command. At this time these amounted to some armoured car batteries, eight garrison battalions of infantry, two companies of the Camel Corps, and some transport and supply details. The most useful aspect of his experience in the rear, apart from the opportunity which it provided to recuperate, was the chance to work with Lieutenant Colonel A. P. Wavell, General Staff Officer 1 of the Force in Egypt when Robertson marched in and under whom Australians would serve in the same theatre in 1940.[56] On 1 September he was posted again, this time back to the Australian Imperial Force as Deputy Assistant Adjutant General (DAAG) AIF Headquarters, Cairo.

By now his leg had improved, and the spell in Egypt meant that he knew the organisations and personalities on the headquarters there. He had amassed useful staff experience, and with the war now virtually over AIF Headquarters in Cairo was charged with the demobilisation and repatriation of the Australians in the Middle East. Nominally, the task was given to Chauvel, but his many other duties meant that the bulk of the work was done by the small number of staff on his headquarters and, with his further appointment as Assistant Adjutant General (AAG) of the AIF in Egypt just four days after arrival, the planning and administration fell largely to Robertson. Unlike in France, the AIF in Egypt was repatriated in units, not occupational groupings, which meant also that it was available for use in putting down the Egyptian revolt which broke out early in 1919. Repatriation was suspended while light horse units helped with internal security duties, but by May the situation had eased and, under pressure from the Minister for Defence, Senator George Pearce, repatriation by units was resumed. By the end of July only a small number of headquarters and base troops remained.[57]

Chauvel had returned to Australia via England in April, and Robertson finally left Egypt for home on board the transport *Morvada*, which departed Kantara on 22 July. After an uneventful voyage he reached Melbourne on 25 August. Following a month's welcome leave, he was to resume peacetime duties on the instructional staff of the 3rd Military District, based on the state of Victoria.

By any measure he had had a good war. As well as the DSO, he had received two mentions in dispatches, the second for his work with the Yeomanry Mounted Division, and was to receive an Egyptian decoration, the Order of the Nile, 4th Class, the following year for his services in Egypt itself. Clearly he had played a part in the suppression of the revolt, although the details have not survived. Like the other Australians involved, doubtless he had few if any problems with his role as an 'enforcer of Empire'. Lightly wounded on Gallipoli at Hill 60, he escaped major injury in Palestine although his left leg was to cause him trouble periodically for the rest of his active service. He had led his regiment in a significant action, earning the plaudits and admiration of AIF officers not easily impressed by what many still thought of as 'tyro' officers from Duntroon, and he had come favourably to the notice of one of the regular army's most senior generals, Chauvel, for his able staff work in Cairo.

Young Staff Corps officers would appear to have had an impact out of proportion to their numbers, which in truth were very small. The first graduating class in August 1914 represented just 3.4 per cent of the total number of officers present in the first contingent, while the thirty graduates of Robertson's class in November the same year constituted 5.3 per cent of the officers in their contingent. There were 133 Australian and twenty-five New Zealand graduates between August 1914 and November 1918, and the Australian graduates who served in the AIF came to just 1.2 per cent of the officer corps of 12,335. Of the 158 graduates who served, forty-two were killed (thirty-seven of them Australians) and sixty-six wounded (fifty-three Australians wounded once, nine twice, and four three times). The death rate was higher among Staff Corps officers than for the AIF generally (twenty-eight per cent as opposed to twenty-three per cent),[58] but as noted already promotion was retarded artificially, so that while fully a third of Staff Corps officers had reached the rank of major by the war's end none had progressed beyond it despite the fact that some, like Robertson, had commanded their units in action and had held the rank of major for two years or more.

Their impact in a qualitative sense was evident. Chauvel noted the importance of Duntroon graduates in supporting the largely militia commanders at battalion, brigade and divisional level.[59] Recommending that the Royal Military College be retained in its existing form in the face of financial stringencies in 1923, Brudenell White drew on his observations of the Duntroon product during the war when noting that 'adequate and efficient training is now an essential in the production of leaders. Efficient colleges are therefore a vital factor in national insurance which takes the form of preparation against war.'[60] The frustration of career expectations in the interwar years would seem a poor reward for such distinguished service, collectively and individually.

On another level, Robertson's war service stood him in excellent stead professionally for what was to follow. Despite the fact that in certain respects Palestine was a strategic sideshow to the main effort of Britain and the empire, the war in Palestine held greater benefits for the thinking soldier. Apart from the trite but necessary observation that a young officer had a far higher chance of survival there than on the Western Front, there were important military lessons in the Middle East campaign which service in France did not provide. Through extensive regimental and staff experience, Robertson had been in a position to observe the continuing importance of mobility in modern warfare in the right circumstances, and the virtue of shock action at the tactical level. His own charge at Magdhaba had demonstrated this, as had the Yeomanry's charges at El-Mughar, Abu Shushe and in the pursuit to Jerusalem which followed. No one arm dominated the fighting in Palestine, as arguably the artillery did in France, and especially on the staff a young officer could come to appreciate the importance of the combined arms approach in circumstances other than trench warfare, which was unlikely to be repeated.

Finally, the nature of climate and terrain coupled with the mobile nature of operations instilled an awareness of the vital part which logistics played in modern war — a lesson which was lost on many of those Australians whose service was confined to the static warfare of the Western Front. All in all then, Robertson's war service brought both personal benefits, in the form of decorations and recognition, and professional benefits, if he cared to apply himself to the lessons drawn from his own experience. In the coming years, a process of professional education and a naturally reflective character would develop the virtues shown as a junior officer, and would prepare him for the challenges brought by senior rank in war.

CHAPTER 3

BETWEEN WARS: 1919-1940

The Australia to which Robertson returned in August 1919 was warweary, bitterly divided on political and sectarian lines as a result of the conscription referenda of 1916 and 1917, and reeling under the effects of the Spanish influenza pandemic which, worldwide, killed more people than had the Great War so recently concluded. In the course of the 1920s Australia, like much of the rest of the world, sought only to put behind it the memories of the casualties and suffering of the war. Great hopes were held for international disarmament, pioneered at the Washington conference in 1921 and 1922, and the armed services suffered financial stringencies as people convinced themselves that the war fought to end wars had achieved exactly that. Attitudes did not change much in Australia in the course of the 1930s either, although by then the rise of fascism in Europe and the aggressive militarism of an expansionary Japan sent warning signals to the few in the western democracies who were prepared to note them. When Australia went to war again in 1939, its forces in some respects were less prepared perhaps than at any other time in the nation's history.

Robertson's initial appointment upon his return was to the instructional staff of the 3rd Military District, which encompassed the state of Victoria. This was little more than a holding post, for within a few months he was appointed brigade major of the 7th Light Horse Brigade, commanded by Colonel F. G. Hughes, his first brigade commander on Gallipoli. (One might ponder a system which regarded failure in the field as no barrier to continuing employment in command of troops.) The brigade comprised three militia regiments, the 4th, 19th and 21st Light Horse, based at Colac, Ballarat and Ararat respectively.

The army was undergoing considerable reorganisation and after nine months with this brigade Robertson found himself posted back to Headquarters, 3rd Military District in September 1920 as a staff officer. His tasks were routine, including the usual support functions of a district headquarters but involving also the administrative backlog arising from

'Yourself and Jessie', soon after the end of the war.

the demobilisation of the Australian Imperial Force. Once again, he spent only a few months in the job before being sent to the headquarters of the 2nd Cavalry Division as a staff officer in the 'G', or Operations Branch in May the following year. He stayed there until July 1922, when he was posted to a similar position on the headquarters of the 3rd Infantry Division, with units based around Melbourne. From there, he was nominated to attend the Staff College, Camberley, in Britain, and departed at the end of November. He was not to return to Australia for three years.

The years immediately after the First World War saw both considerable change and continuity in army policy. Very little has been written on the army in the interwar period, and most of that has dealt with its relationship to interwar considerations of imperial defence. As a result, we know very little about the domestic activities of the army in the decades between the world wars. As in Britain, and indeed elsewhere, the army remained very much the poor relation in terms of defence budgets and planning during this period, largely as a result of the Singapore strategy on the one hand, which emphasised the role of naval forces in Australia's defence, and the infatuation with flight and the military applications of air power on the other, which led to a misplaced emphasis on the defensive capabilities of the air force, a theme taken up by the Australian Labor Party during the mid-1930s. The army was reduced to a coastal defence role, planning counter-measures in the face of enemy raiding parties and the protection of shore installations, ports and cities.

With the end of the war the existing scheme of compulsory training was revived and once more made the basis of Australian territorial defence. But the lessons of the war were not ignored, and in January 1920 the Minister for Defence, Senator George Pearce, convened a committee comprising some of the leading figures of the AIF to advise the government on the future direction of army policy. Chaired by Chauvel, and consisting of Monash, McCay, Hobbs, White and Legge, it delivered its report on 6 February after little more than a fortnight's continuous deliberation. Whilst advising on the establishment of a munitions supply branch, the provision of fixed defences, and providing a lengthy survey of the political and strategic considerations governing Australia's defence, its most important recommendations concerned the organisation, establishment and training of the ground forces which would make up the field force for the defence of Australian territory.

The conference of senior officers recommended a force of two cavalry and four infantry divisions, troops for local defence amounting to a fifth division, personnel for coastal defence establishments and a proper proportion of corps and army staffs and troops for a total of 130,000 men in peacetime boosted to 270,000 in the event of war, when units and formations would be manned at war establishment levels. The army was to be organised on a divisional structure in peacetime in order that the component units and the higher staffs would get used to the basis on which they would find themselves operating in war. Divisions would be controlled from Army Headquarters in Melbourne, and not by the headquarters in the military districts in which they were based. The latter were to be reorganised as 'district bases', responsible for supplies, logistic support of the field force, and controlling the coastal defence establishments of the major ports. The divisions would be numbered after the divisions of the AIF, as would the component units 'in a way which will carry to them the traditions of the Australian Imperial Force, [so that] there should exist and continue that regimental pride which goes far to make successful fighters'.[1] The report recognised that certain extra-divisional and line of communications organisations could not be provided by the army given existing financial stringencies and lack of materiel: medium and heavy artillery, air defence, tanks, and mechanical transport would all be deferred to some period not specified. These were precisely the areas in which the greatest advances would be made in military doctrine elsewhere in the ensuing two decades.

Nonetheless, given the ministerial instruction that 'proposals which were too ambitious could not be accepted', and that 'not counsels of perfection, but counsels of practicability were required',[2] the report laid a reasonable basis for the territorial defence of Australia in the immediate aftermath of the war. It was never given a chance. Within a year of its implementation the government of William Morris Hughes, seized by the advances in disarmament agreed to in Washington in the field of naval armaments, chose to reduce the army also, primarily as a financial measure and confident that such a step would prove popular electorally. Chauvel fought hard, and successfully, for the retention of the divisional structure, but virtually every other recommendation was scaled down or dispensed with such that the army became little more than a cadre organisation, involved in recruit training of citizen soldiers under the compulsory training scheme but lacking the capability to put a force in the field should the need arise. The Permanent Military Force was reduced by 460, the navy by a smaller number, and seventy civilian employees were retrenched also.[3] In his report as Inspector-General of the Australian Military Forces Chauvel noted the consequences of this change. 'Owing to the constant changes and curtailment in the approved programmes necessitated by financial considerations, it cannot be said that, except in organisation and the training of officers and non-commissioned officers, any progress has been made during the past year.' And noting the reduction of the army's overall strength from 118,000 to 30,000 in a single year, he commented that this 'will still enable the provision of an organised force for the defence of Australia, provided always *there will be time after the outbreak of war* to train the rank and file'.[4]

The drastic reduction in the size of the army meant not only that the opportunities for regular officers were seriously curtailed, but that many suffered a reduction in rank and pay as a result of the smaller establishments to which they returned following their war service. Thus in the 3rd Military District, at the time that Robertson was serving with the 7th Light Horse Brigade, the Staff Officer for Engineers on the headquarters was Major V.A.H. Sturdee, who had been chief engineer on the staff of the 5th Division in France with the acting rank of lieutenant colonel, and who was later twice Chief of the General Staff; George Vasey, who had served with the artillery in France and had been brigade major to the 11th Infantry Brigade, now reverted to the rank of lieutenant while serving as adjutant of the 8th Field Artillery Brigade in Victoria; Lieutenant R.N.L. Hopkins, a captain with the light horse in Palestine, was also reduced in rank when adjutant to an infantry brigade in the 3rd Military District; likewise Lieutenant William Bridgeford was brigade major to the 18th Light Horse Brigade, despite having held a major's rank for two and a half years in France. Such examples could be multiplied endlessly. As noted earlier, progress in rank was desperately slow for regulars with the result that able officers with distinguished war records languished in junior postings for years. No such restrictions applied to officers of the citizen forces, since the size of the militia, while reduced, was still greater than that of the permanent forces and thus permitted a greater number of more senior postings. All this built a measure of unfairness into the system and helped to foster resentments and hostilities between the two groups which would be played out in full during the Second World War.

Although the situation which faced the regulars was a dispiriting one, it should not be assumed that the militia had things all their own way. Militia units suffered from recruitment and retention problems throughout the interwar period, and peacetime soldiering generally, whether regular or citizen, lacked appeal. As Gavin Long noted, 'it conferred little prestige; indeed, an Australian who made the militia a hobby was likely to be regarded by his acquaintances as a peculiar fellow with an eccentric taste for uniforms and the exercise of petty authority'.[5]

The militia found it difficult to attract and keep members, especially after the abolition of compulsory military training in November 1929. Turnover in units was often high, and the militia commanders who met in early 1932 identified poor rates of pay, failure to attend parades, the poor quality of recruits, the small amount of time spent on training and the quality of the training actually done as factors requiring attention. Since they were also factors which required additional funds they were unlikely to be dealt with by a federal government in the depths of the worst depression of the century. But even before then, the Military Board had noted that little progress had been made in improving the duration of training 'owing to financial stringency'.[6]

The strength and composition of militia units could, and did, fluctuate widely, and a regular officer sent as adjutant or brigade major to a militia unit or formation might find himself administering a sizeable or greatly attenuated body. Following the abolition of compulsory training, five infantry battalions, two light horse regiments and two batteries of field artillery were disbanded; only 1500 personnel were involved, but the reduction represented one-twelfth of the militia infantry establishment, and all the units concerned were rural ones. In July 1930 a further two light horse regiments and nine battalions disappeared from the order of battle.[7] In recognition of manpower deficiencies, the Military Board formally varied the peacetime establishments of units in November 1929, such that an infantry battalion at the lower establishment would muster nineteen officers and 212 other ranks, as against a normal establishment of twenty-five and 310 respectively. Even then, the anti-tank platoon and two of the four machine gun platoons were not maintained due to shortages of equipment. This divergence between peacetime training establishments and war establishment was common to all arms, as the following table shows.

Unit	War establishment		Training establishment	
	Officers	*Other ranks*	*Officers*	*Other ranks*
Infantry battalion	32	795	25	384
Light horse regiment	26	624	19	253
Field artillery battery	23	677	19	312[8]

Important in any discussion of the state of the army in the interwar years is the question of command and control of the peacetime forces. The two terms are not always well understood, and are sometimes held to be interchangeable. Control involves the design, monitoring, management and direction of the system which implements policy; command is the management and direction of the operations and activities of the service.[9]

Both the control and administration of the army resided at two levels in the interwar period, the Defence Committee and the Military Board of Administration. The former was founded in May 1926 and regularised in March 1929; it comprised the three chiefs of staff — all regular officers — and a member of the secretariat of the Department of Defence, over time a position taken by the secretary of the department. The Military Board was made up of the heads of the principal branches of the service: the chief of the general staff, adjutant general, master general of the ordnance, quartermaster general, and a business member and a finance member, both of whom were civilian officials of the Department of the Army. The secretary of the board was provided by the department also. The Military Board was charged with 'the control and administration of all matters relating to the Military Forces, in accordance with the policy directed by the Minister'.[10] The point worth noting is that the first full representative of the Citizen Military Forces to sit on the Military Board was Major General George Wootten, whose appointment dated from 4 February 1948.

After 1922 the command of the six district bases, the organisational headquarters based on each state and which provided the administrative and logistic support to the militia, was vested in Staff Corps officers on the recommendation of Brudenell White, then Chief of the General Staff. In conjunction with the running of the Military Board, the regulars thus largely monopolised the senior administrative posts of the army throughout the interwar period. The command of the forces was a slightly different matter, although even here the picture varied. From the late 1920s the command of certain of the mixed brigades, responsible for local defence only, passed to the commanders of the relevant district bases in the interests of economy. For most of the period most of the field formations, two cavalry and four infantry divisions, were commanded by citizen soldiers, although in 1937 two of the infantry divisional commands were held by regulars. Against this it should be noted that in 1926 militia officers were posted to staff positions in district base headquarters, and that in January 1939 the minister for defence approved the creation of more than a dozen additional militia staff officer positions.[11] Thus the situation was less that the militia controlled all the posts of any worth in the army than that they largely monopolised those from which the commanders of any expeditionary force might be drawn. And if one drops below the highest levels to the command of units and sub-units — the level which affected the majority of younger regular officers — the citizen force monopoly here was complete.

The effect this had on the generation of regular officers who would command Australia's army in the next war is an open question. Formerly outgoing and gregarious as a young officer, Vasey became moody and introspective in the face of years of professional neglect.[12] Some, like Major S.F. Rowell, later Chief of the General Staff, thought about resigning their commissions but stayed through devotion to duty and a lack of civilian skills or opportunities; others, like George Wootten, later to command the 9th Division in New Guinea, did leave, in his case setting up practice as a solicitor. Chauvel's own sons transferred to the Indian army and made careers there; still others, like John Wilton, another future Chief of the General Staff, went to the British army direct upon graduation from Duntroon but returned to the Australian service at the outbreak of war. Like countless other Staff Corps officers, Robertson soldiered on through the interwar years, driven by devotion to his chosen profession and the sure and certain knowledge that, should another war break out, his carefully honed professional skills would be desperately needed in a rapidly expanding army which would be short of everything. Urged at one stage by his father to resign his commission and study law, he refused; 'the Army is my chosen profession', he replied, 'as long as there is an Army I'll stick to it'.[13] But years of stunted career prospects and professional and personal frustration left their mark. By the 1930s Robertson was demonstrating those attributes of egotism, arrogance and vanity which increasingly would be remarked on by contemporaries, juniors, and casual observers, some of whom would mistake these surface characteristics for the substance of the man. Psychohistorical interpretations are best avoided, in general, but it seems reasonable to speculate that the shift in personality which Robertson underwent owed something at least to the situations in which he found himself professionally as part of the tiny regular officer corps, and personally, in a marriage which whilst it never broke down seems to have offered fewer and fewer comforts and which, because of Jessie's age, denied him the family life he undoubtedly sought.

In April 1922 Robertson sat for the Staff College, Camberley entrance examination, gaining 6056 marks and securing nomination as an Australian student to the two-year course, to commence in January 1923. The examination involved eight three-hour papers, and included three optional subjects drawn from a diverse list which included foreign languages, political economy, chemistry and physics, the history of British India, and movements by road and rail, as well as the basic subject areas of 'training for war' (largely strategy and the principles of war), organisation and administration, and imperial organisation. Preparation for the latter, candidates were advised, involved such texts as Dr Cornish's *Naval and Military Geography of the British Empire* and MacDonnell's *Outlines of Military Geography*, together with the injunction to 'get the *Times* daily, and read all the important articles'.[14] 'Training for war' required a 'more or less detailed study' of assorted campaigns, both from the Western Front, Mesopotamia and Palestine in the recent war, but including also the Napoleonic battles of Ulm, Jena and Waterloo and the Shenandoah Valley campaign from the American Civil War. Examinees were able to refer to the annual report on previous examinations and the relevant examination notes, both issued by the War Office, and we may be sure that in keeping with the demands of the syllabus and the importance of gaining the nomination, Robertson spent most of the preceding twelve months working towards the examination.

The Imperial General Staff which emerged after the war was a British staff with dominion officers occasionally attached. The Canadians, in keeping with their generally more robust attitude towards the imperial relationship, had formed their own general staff. Both Australia and New Zealand spoke of theirs as 'sections of the Imperial General Staff', although in practice these were as separate as the Canadian. All three, together with the British Indian army, sent students to the British military education system. As well as short professional courses in the arms and services schools, dominion officers attended the Staff Colleges at Camberley, in Surrey, and Quetta, in India, and for senior officers the Imperial Defence College, London. The Imperial General Staff was the central policy-making organ of the army, and attendance at staff college courses was a vital and necessary step for those regular officers marked out for future advancement.

Camberley had reopened in March 1919, with the first three courses specially picked because of their war experience rather than entering by examination. These were 'enlivened by the fact that the pupils knew as much as the instructors, and more in certain areas, and that many colonels present had been brigadier-generals or higher in the thick of the fighting'.[15] Among those who attended the first two postwar courses were twenty such officers, as well as five VCs and no fewer than 170 DSOs.[16] The same situation had pertained in the early postwar courses at Quetta.[17] Entry to the staff college was contested keenly, since progress through the general staff was a necessary career step for any ambitious officer, and the staff colleges could cater for at most ten per cent of the officers of appropriate rank.[18] But like much else in the interwar Commonwealth armies, the military education system in the staff colleges was less than it might have been. There were some inspired members of the directing staff, including the future Field Marshals Sir John Dill, Lord Gort, Lord Alanbrooke, and Viscount Montgomery, all of whom would become Chief of the Imperial General Staff; some original thinkers like J. F. C. Fuller; and future senior generals like General Sir Ronald Adam, Adjutant General 1941-46, Lieutenant General Sir Philip Neame, who commanded in the Western Desert against Rommel in 1941, General Sir Andrew Thorne, commander of XI Corps 1940-41 and of Scottish Command 1941-45, and General Sir Bernard Paget, Commander-in-Chief Home Forces 1941-43 and in the Middle East 1944-46. But there remained a proportion of drones and hacks concerned only with returning to 'real soldiering' and with fighting the last war rather than preparing for the next one. The good ones were very good indeed, but 'their influence over the next fifteen years was uneven'.[19]

The course which Robertson attended illustrated the tensions inherent in an army which had fought and won a great industrial war, but many of whose members hankered after the peacetime regime of the small, long-service prewar regular army, and which was faced with financial stringencies and doctrinal confusion in the face of that same war experience. The course lasted two years and the students were divided into a junior and senior division, corresponding to their year of entry. In the first year the instruction was taken up with organisation, staff duties and tactics in a division, and was strongly practical in orientation. In the second year studies progressed to a higher level and dealt with inter-service cooperation and staff duties at corps and army level.[20] Instruction was (and still is) based on the syndicate of around ten students who tackle the problems presented, supervised by a member of the directing staff. There were plenty of lectures as well, and those to the senior division in 1923 covered a diverse range of subjects: international law, the organisation of a base port in an overseas theatre of war, higher artillery organisation (these from Lieutenant Colonel A.F. Brooke), a number of lectures on the tactical and administrative practices of the French, the engineering industry with emphasis upon munitions production and the creation of prototype equipment (delivered by Major Giffard le Q. Martel, another important figure in the mechanisation of the British army), and a single lecture entitled 'tank battalion (small war)'.[21]

There was plenty of military history and study of specific campaigns as well. Although there were four lectures on the Dardanelles and a lecture on the operations against Tanga in German East Africa in November 1914, the majority of the campaign study was devoted to the war against Germany on the Western Front and, at least while Major General Sir Edmund Ironside was commandant, a substantial series of lectures on the war on the Eastern Front. In general, 'study was concentrated on the static Western Front operations to the neglect of the brilliant campaign in Palestine which pointed to the value of surprise, mobility, and speed in movement'.[22] Imperial strategy was discussed, but usually in relation to the Middle East or even Afghanistan which, in 1923, was at least topical. Only one lecture was devoted to imperial strategy in the Pacific, and no attention was paid to the Japanese armed forces. Students were required to lecture to the course in their senior year, but the choice of topic was left to them and produced a disconnected, and sometimes bizarre and eclectic collection of subject matter, ranging from grand historical themes to tactical and operational problems. Like many before him, in his senior year Robertson drew on his war experiences to lecture on the attack at Hill 60 as an example of the dangers of a night attack on converging lines.

Two Australians were sent to Camberley each year. In 1922 the nominations had gone to Lieutenant Colonel R.E. Jackson of the Staff Corps (whom Robertson had known from the 10th Light Horse in 1914 and 1915), and Wing Commander Richard Williams, Chief of Staff of the infant Royal Australian Air Force, who only joined the course for the senior year. With Robertson in 1923 went Major J.H.F. Pain, also of the Staff Corps, while in 1924 the Australian nominations were Major

A.J. Boase and Major John Northcott, whose career would overlap with Robertson's on a number of subsequent occasions. The divisions were not large; Robertson's senior year numbered fifty-five. It included Major A.E. Percival, later to command tragically against the Japanese in Malaya, Captain J.G. Smyth, VC, who would lead a division against the Japanese in Burma during the retreat of 1942, and Lieutenant Colonel H.D.G. Crerar and Major G.P. Vanier of the Canadian army, the former destined to lead the First Canadian Army in 1944 and 1945.

The junior division that year included Major Vyvyan Pope, a leading exponent of armoured forces killed in the Western Desert in 1941, Major C.W.M. Norrie, who commanded a formation in the CRUSADER offensive in the Western Desert in the same year, and Captain A.E. Nye, later Vice-Chief of the Imperial General Staff, to name but three. In the year above Robertson were Major H.R. Pownall, later VCIGS and Commander-in-Chief, Far East 1941-42, and Lieutenant Colonel F.A. Pile, another early exponent of armour and modernisation and General Officer Commanding Britain's anti-aircraft command from 1939 to 1945. The stars were not only among the directing staff and, as has long been recognised, one of the key benefits of staff college attendance lay (and continues to lie) in the friendships formed between the generation of young officers likely to rise to the top of their profession. It was useful also, as S.F. Rowell noted of his own attendance at staff college, to get to know the strengths and weaknesses of men with whom one would deal in war before one was called on to cooperate on the battlefield. Berryman likewise noted the value of prewar contacts: 'with 6 Div in the Middle East, I knew most of the key officers in the British forces, while Vasey [who had attended Quetta] knew them in the Indian divisions, so through personal contact the doors of cooperation opened easily'.[23]

The Camberley interlude was undoubtedly a pleasant one also. The Robertsons had a bungalow in Camberley, converted from two army huts joined by a covered walkway, and living was made more affordable through the system of allowances paid additional to his army salary. The social life was active, at least for the officers on the course, and Robertson no doubt found many opportunities for tennis and golf, both of which he played very well. The great social activity of the Camberley year was the Drag Hunt, riding in which was compulsory for all officers. The horse was still the centre of much of the daily routine at Camberley, officers being required to ride daily in order 'to shake up the livers of [the] chairborne'.[24] This can have been no hardship for a light horse officer, but provided one further small example of the tension between the traditional and the modern which was played out in the British army at this time.

During the summer vacation parties of officers visited armies on the continent. This provided an enjoyable interlude of foreign travel which may, on occasions, have proved instructive as well. There was a series of

Horace and Jessie, Flinders Golf Club, Melbourne, 1920s.

battlefield tours during which the students walked over the sites of the opening engagements in 1914 and discussed the possible course of future actions over the same ground. All in all, attendance at the staff college had limited utility for officers of the dominions if one concentrated solely on the content of the syllabus, but the opportunity to meet and study with potential leaders of several empire armies was a valuable process for young officers from the tiny and rather inward-looking dominion services.

Robertson did spectacularly well at Camberley, becoming the first Australian to graduate with an 'A' pass. In his report, Ironside wrote that he was 'an officer of strong character and high ability. He is hard-working, quick and keen, [and] possesses shrewd common sense. His work throughout has been good, showing sound judgement and common sense. Takes a great interest in his profession. Has the makings of a commander. Suited for all staff. I recommend that his promotion be accelerated.'[25] This was high praise from one of the British army's rising stars, at one time the youngest major general in the army and a future Chief of the Imperial General Staff, a man of intellect who believed that too many officers became caught up in their daily work and did not take the time to read widely, either within their profession or outside it, and who deplored the 'barrack square mentality' which was creeping back into the peacetime service. Aged just thirty, Robertson's performance at staff college, on top of his war record, marked him as one of the coming men in the Australian regular army.

He was to attend a further variety of short courses and service schools in Britain. When Brudenell White had handed over as CGS to Chauvel in 1923 he had noted the need to upgrade the instructional facilities at the Small Arms School, then based at Randwick in Sydney. 'A warrant officer of the AIC [Australian Instructional Corps] is in command (under the Base Commandant) of the Small Arms School. A Staff Corps officer should be trained for the work.'[26] The school had been developed from the old School of Musketry in 1922, but in his report for that year the inspector-general noted several deficiencies: 'Instruction in light mortars and grenades is not at present undertaken', he wrote. 'This is mainly due to the state of training of the Australian Military Forces and to lack of equipment ... The need for an instructor of the Small Arms School staff to do a tour of duty at Hythe and Seaford, with an object of being generally "Refreshed" in all Small Arms School work ... is realised but has not yet been finalised.'[27]

Thus Robertson spent an extra year in Britain qualifying for his next posting in Australia as senior instructor at the Small Arms School. Between January and May he attended the long qualifying course at the School of Musketry at Hythe and the Machine Gun School at Netheravon, graduating as 'distinguished' in both.[28] As part of the intended modernising of the Australian system of instruction, he spent the rest of the year on various other attachments. In May he attended the Range Finding (Instructors) course at the Artillery College, Woolwich, the senior officers' course at the Anti-Gas School at Porton, and the short course at the School of Anti-Aircraft Defence at Westerham. In June he was back at Netheravon to qualify on the senior officers' course, spent a fortnight at the Royal Tank Corps Central School at Woolwich, and did another senior officers' course at Hythe, where he spent July qualifying on the Hotchkiss machine gun. August found him back at Netheravon again, where he did another long qualifying course until the middle of October. A planned attachment at the War Office in December was cancelled, and he returned to Australia on board the *Orama*, arriving in Melbourne just before Christmas 1925.[29] He had passed every course he had attended, had gained invaluable experience on which to build in his new posting, and had been 'fully occupied during the whole period'.[30] The assistant commandant at Hythe wrote that he possessed 'zeal and smartness to a marked degree and his professional attainments are excellent'.[31]

After Christmas leave, Robertson took over officially as Chief Instructor on 12 January 1926. To that time, the Small Arms School had conducted qualifying and refresher courses in rifle and bayonet, light automatic weapons and the Vickers machine gun for officers and NCOs of the permanent forces, and had run short courses for the citizen forces and the senior cadets in the military districts. In 1925 twenty-six officers and 177 warrant officers had attended the first, which were of thirteen weeks' duration, and forty-nine officers and forty-one warrant officers of the CMF and thirty-six officers of the senior cadets had qualified as instructors in the 1st, 2nd and 3rd Military Districts. The facilities of the school were inadequate, as Chauvel noted on a number of occasions in his reports, and the closing of the Central Training Depot in 1922, as a cost-cutting measure, meant that much of the elementary work in small arms training had to be done at the Small Arms School, limiting the scope of the syllabuses.[32] In Robertson's time as Chief Instructor the numbers attending courses actually declined — in 1927 and 1928 138 officers and NCOs of the permanent force and ninety-six officers and NCOs from the CMF attended courses — but the standards rose gradually and consistently as units sent better prepared men to undertake the courses. The staff, led by Robertson, attended the annual militia camps to assist in weapons training, and in 1929 he threw open the long instructors' course, formerly restricted to regulars, to the Citizen Military Forces. By 1930, 270 officers and NCOs of the CMF were attending small arms courses, and the inspector-general noted that year that results at the school 'can be considered as quite satisfactory'.

In 1926 and 1927 the army had sent a single officer and one NCO to Britain to observe the trials conducted with tanks (armoured fighting vehicles as they were then known) by the Experimental Mechanised Force, formed in May 1927, and to attend a number of courses. Four Vickers medium tanks Mark II were ordered, with spare parts and 250 rounds of ammunition, at a cost of £72,000, but these did not arrive until September 1929. A tank cadre was formed and based at the Small Arms School, and became Robertson's responsibility. A CMF light horse unit, the 19th Australian Light Horse, was converted to an armoured car role in the early 1930s, but the unit never received the appropriate vehicles. Little more was done until 1938 and 1939, apart from some useful training by the small armoured instructional unit, the so-called regular army tank cadre.[33] Doctrinal conservatism was as prevalent in Australia as in Britain and the light horse ethos was as strong and inhibiting a factor as the cavalry spirit. But Robertson was given an opportunity to become familiar with tank organisation, if only briefly with the armoured vehicles themselves, and with his experience in Palestine drew appropriate conclusions about the contribution such weapons might make to mobility and shock on the battlefield.

His four years as Chief Instructor laid the foundation for his later reputation as a formidable trainer of troops. More immediately, his success at the Small Arms School brought him to the attention of his seniors once again. In his confidential report for 1929 Brigadier General C.H. Brand, Second Chief of the General Staff, wrote that 'the efficiency in small arms training throughout the Citizen Forces is traceable to the sound and complete instruction imparted by the S.A. School under this officer'. The report noted his 'sound tactical knowledge', 'strong personality', 'self-reliance and initiative', and that 'he has kept himself up to date'. Brand recommended him for a 'G appointment with a formation'. In an unusual step, the Chief of the General Staff, his old chief, Chauvel, wrote on the report that he was 'a staff officer of outstanding capabilities, suitable to be GSO 1 of a Cavalry Division, but would fill almost any staff appointment requiring initiative with credit'.[34] Chauvel in fact appointed him to the Inspector-General's Branch at Army Headquarters from 1 February 1930, based in Sydney. His duties involved standing in for officers who were absent from their units on leave or in attending courses, assisting in the running of courses and schools, sitting on boards, courts of inquiry and committees, and 'in such other capacity as the Base Commandant may employ him'.[35] None of this was new to him, since he had acted for the Inspector-General's Branch on previous occasions, reporting on the efficiency of the units he helped train at annual camps.[36]

The office of Inspector-General of the Australian Military Forces had been revived in 1920, and Chauvel had filled this post as well as that of Chief of the General Staff following White's retirement in 1923. He reported annually to parliament, and he and the small staff of the Inspector-General's Branch were responsible for overseeing the training, equipment and general efficiency of both the permanent force and the CMF. Chauvel used his reports to comment on the drifts in government policy; for example, in his final report in April 1930 he made a number of observations on the effects on the forces of the latest round of disarmament talks in Washington. His was an important and influential position, as he himself noted, 'in a partially trained army such as ours where formations are so widely separated as to be liable to reach different standards of training'.[37]

Chauvel retired in April 1930. An army is like any large organisation, in which seniors foster their able juniors and opportunities are created so that the talented may shine. Chauvel had been instrumental in assisting Robertson's career on several occasions, and we have seen that he rated him very highly indeed. His retirement, however, left Robertson open to the jealousies and intrigues of lesser men and within a few months he was posted again, this time to be brigade major of the 7th Infantry Brigade in Brisbane. It was a demotion, and a calculated slap, and Robertson took it as such. The circumstances surrounding the incident are now lost, but Robertson was in no doubt that there were 'unnamed people who had it in for him'.[38] One contemporary commented many years later that 'there were one or two people on the old A&I [Administrative and Instructional] Staff, more than one or two, who really were pretty poor types ... whatever trouble there was in the IG Department was serious ... and made him suspicious and hostile to a degree'.[39] It was certainly through no professional failing; his annual report spoke of his 'great ability and considerable professional knowledge', and rated him 'much above the average ... he can be relied upon to do anything he undertakes'.[40] The 7th Brigade was a militia formation, part of the 1st Division, the rest of which was based in New South Wales and, with the recent abolition of compulsory training by the incoming Labor government of J.H. Scullin, semi-moribund. The setback did not last long; in February 1931 he was appointed brigade major of the 1st Cavalry Brigade, although still based in Queensland. But the episode undoubtedly soured his outlook, and contributed to that tendency to egotism and boastfulness already noted. The lesson he may have derived was that talent alone was not always sufficient, and that one had both to be good, and to let others know of it.

The 1st Cavalry Division, of which his brigade was a part, was commanded by Colonel L.C. Wilson who had served in Palestine also, and once back with a mounted formation Robertson thrived again. 'Despite the fact that "Robbie" has worked 1 Cav Bde up to 100 per cent strength, he has still found time to annex most of the golf trophies about the place', noted the *RMC Journal*.[41] Wilson recommended him for a staff appointment, and he had passed the promotion exam for lieutenant colonel at the end of 1933 (although the promotion itself would not follow for several years. By 1933 four Staff Corps officers wore the rank of lieutenant colonel but were still paid as majors.)[42] In February 1934 he returned to Sydney and the position of General Staff Officer 2, Operations, Intelligence and Training, Headquarters 2nd District Base, 'striking terror into the hearts of many "nineteenth holers" in the Mother state. He still lies as fluently as ever about his car and dog.'[43]

The services had suffered severely in the Depression, the army especially undergoing reductions as a consequence of government austerity. In 1935 the new Chief of the General Staff, Colonel J. D. Lavarack, wrote of the 'many grave deficiencies in the armament and equipment, strength, training and organisation of the Australian Military Forces'.[44] It was a lean period for many militia units as well as for the regular force.[45] Financial stringency had seen the closure of Duntroon and the transfer of an attenuated Royal Military College to Victoria Barracks, Sydney, in 1931. From June 1934 Robertson was appointed to instruct part-time in tactics and, in the following year, as Director of Military Art, the senior instructional post in the college, and Commanding Officer of the Corps of Staff Cadets. He was the first Staff Corps officer to hold the post.[46] The commandant, Colonel J. D. Lavarack, tried to block his appointment on the grounds that he lacked 'the balance and tact, and the happy temperament, which are required of an officer who is to serve ... as a model for Staff Corps officers in the making', although he was forced to admit that Robertson 'is not very well known to me personally, particularly as regards his capacity to perform the duties'.[47] The college moved back to Canberra only in 1937, and Robertson returned to Duntroon with it.

It was appropriate that he should find himself in the military educational system again, for in the course of the 1930s he devoted much of his time to thinking and writing about military and defence problems. In March 1929 he had been appointed honorary sub-editor for Australasia for *The Cavalry Journal,* a British service publication founded before the First World War, and for which he wrote half a dozen articles between 1929 and 1935. These were short pieces, mostly anecdotal and narrative in nature and dealing with episodes of his war service or with matters equine which were calculated to interest a horse-minded readership. He wrote a string of articles on his war service for the Returned Services League journal, *Reveille,* in this period also. Of more importance were the pieces published in the British professional journal, *The Army Quarterly,* dealing with tactical, operational and strategic issues. The earliest of these, 'Simplicity in Fire-Plans', grew out of his period at the Small Arms School and stressed the necessity of adapting fireplans for the conditions of open warfare which the latest edition of the Field Service

Regulations stressed as the most likely type to be faced by the British armies.[48] He emphasised also the importance of disseminating new doctrine to territorial and militia officers.

His other writings were more radical in tone, and concerned Australia's place in empire defence in the event of war. 'The Empire and Modern War' took as its starting point a Saki short story, 'Alice in Pall Mall', and quoted the exchange between Alice and the knight to the effect that, having read somewhere that 'warfare under modern conditions was impossible', the knight then went to war, 'but NOT UNDER MODERN CONDITIONS'. From there, he argued that the defence relationship between Britain and the dominions was not suited to the likely demands of another modern war, and suggested that while the component parts were sound enough there was little or no imperial organisation and that the emphasis in imperial defence planning on local defence was strategically unsound. He concluded with the observation that Britain, the dominions and the allies (unspecified) should plan in peace for their wartime roles and bind themselves by written agreements.[49]

The longest and best known of his writings was 'The Defence of Australia'.[50] This was the text of his entry for the Australian Military Forces Gold Medal Essay competition in 1934, which he won against six other entries, but which had not been published by Army Headquarters due to lack of funds.[51] The article followed on those published by H.D. Wynter (1927) and J. D. Lavarack (1932) which had argued against the belief that the Royal Navy was strong enough to guarantee the defence of the Pacific dominions. By implication, all three authors argued for a re-examination of the whole basis of Imperial cooperation and strategy. In his own contribution to the debate, Robertson first surveyed the state of empire defence machinery before turning to Australia's special problems. These he saw as caused by geography, the smallness of the population and vulnerability of the industrial base and trade routes, the potential provocation supplied by the White Australia policy, and the inadequacy of defence spending: 'No country which spends £2 per head on old age and invalid pensions and 10s. per head on defence can have any conception of the dangers to which inadequate defence leaves it open', he wrote. He then examined a number of the proposals advanced for the defence of Australia, mostly based on airpower and navalist solutions although he dismissed also the 'freak armies' proposal for special forces of small mobile units 'to dart about from place to place and ward off an enemy's blows wherever they may fall'. He concluded with a suggested organisation which placed emphasis upon a modern, well-equipped army acting in conjunction with a submarine force and sufficient air assets to provide anti-aircraft defence and air-ground cooperation, while stressing as well the need for development of war industry and the stockpiling of strategic materiel. 'Since the very nature of the problem makes the Army the predominant partner', he concluded, 'Australia's local defence should be organised on an army basis, the other Services conforming to the needs of the Army.'

All this was highly contentious at a time when British authorities, conscious of the inadequacy of their own arrangements for the defence of their world-wide commitments, were desperate to maintain dominion commitments to the demands of empire — and not merely local — defence. Robertson's summary paragraphs flatly contradicted official policy:

> *The only condition under which Australia would be expected to make an Imperial contribution in war would be that she was not herself in danger, and the form of defence suggested would enable her to make a very good contribution of army and air units. It therefore fulfils her implied Imperial duties. The organisation, moreover, would fulfil Australia's allotted tasks in Imperial Defence, ie, local defence, and would ensure that she did not throw unnecessary tasks on the rest of the Empire through her own unpreparedness.*

To which the editor of the *Army Quarterly* responded in his editorial comments that 'this doctrine of local defence . . . carries with it an element of danger to Imperial unity in defence . . . local interests are likely to have a disintegrating effect and to make it more difficult, if not impossible, to devise a sound and effective cooperation in time of war'. And although he quoted with approval the judgement of Admiral Sir Herbert Richmond, commandant of the Imperial Defence College and a leading theorist of Imperial Defence, that 'no localisation of defence can ensure those [Empire lines of] communications, whose interruption . . . would be the greatest calamity which could befall the Empire', he conceded that Robertson's view 'is generally shared by his countrymen, and is not an unreasonable one in view of the present weakness of the British Navy'.

As Paul Hasluck concluded, the Australian discussion of defence needs 'tended at times to develop into a Navy *v.* Army controversy'.[52] It also came down to an argument between those who stressed the primacy of defending the metropolitan centre (ie, Britain) first and foremost, and those, entirely in the dominions, who believed that the dominions increasingly must look to themselves. Despite the efforts of the Australian government to stifle criticism of defence policy, including the celebrated occasion on which Lavarack, as Chief of the General Staff, was informed that defence policy was none of his concern, the views advanced by Robertson and others gained wider currency as war approached.[53] Preparedness was another theme of Robertson's writings, and he concluded an address to the Institute of Engineers in 1938 with the observation that 'when war does come to us, if you expect your soldiers to win it, then you must give them proper organisation and proper equipment'.[54]

Robertson was an excellent choice as Director of Military Art. Keen, energetic and diligent as always, he was also an inspired instructor capable of gaining and maintaining the interest of his audience on virtually any subject. A good golfer and tennis player, he took a full part in the social and sporting life of the college, although his vanity and ego could at times get the better of him, as when he was worsted at tennis by a couple of new and very junior officer cadets. Not everyone responded to his mixture of ability, charm and egotism; one officer cadet wrote caustically later that 'there was no bushel large enough to hide [his] light. If one had been found he would have been astonished and dismayed ... Vain, self-centred and arrogant, he looked and acted the part which he had written for himself.'[55] Another has written of his 'active and supremely confident mind'. 'He carried off all his undertakings with flair and panache and I have not before or since seen ego so masterly displayed. At the end of the year the graduating class presented him with a picture of the greatest living commander. It was a mirror which he accepted with full and courteous control.' But he was an excellent instructor in military history and tactics, and a field exercise which he took over at short notice when the tactics instructor responsible fell seriously ill 'was a talking point of the classes involved for years. I have not experienced quicker and better grasp and control.'[56] Others more senior saw the quality of mind present also, including the commandant, Brigadier C.G.N. Miles, who recommended that Robertson be sent to the Imperial Defence College at the end of his four year term as Director of Military Art. Attendance was reserved for those intended for the highest positions in the service, but the outbreak of war put paid to any such proposals.

If Robertson was inordinately ambitious, there were good reasons for it. As he wrote later, Duntroon had filled 'a very important role in that all the senior officers of the regular forces are graduates of it, but they have to thank two wars for their progress'. (This was almost, but not quite, true; by 1939 eighty-five per cent of regular officers were RMC graduates.) The unfairness of the regulation which had restricted the promotions of Staff Corps officers in the First World War still rankled, as no doubt did his feeling of grievance over his treatment in 1930. He thought that in the First World War 'a few of the senior officers were sincerely interested in the progress of RMC graduates', but that 'to the great majority of the regular officers of the A&I [Administrative and Instructional] Staff the graduates were regarded as dangerous competitors whose training had been so much more complete than their predecessors. They had consequently to be kept down and not allowed to get ahead'.[57]

A revealing incident, which he wrote down later, exemplifies his ambitions at this time. Soon after the Munich crisis Robertson was invited to dine in Canberra with the newspaper magnate Keith Murdoch. To his surprise, he found himself part of a gathering of a dozen which included not only the commandant of Duntroon, himself and Murdoch, but Prime Minister Joseph Lyons, and two previous prime ministers, J. H. Scullin and W. M. Hughes. In such prominent company the conversation centred mostly on Munich and the possibility of war. When the party broke up, Murdoch asked him to remain and, over a drink, discussed with him the likely choices for command of the next Australian Imperial Force. Robertson declined to be drawn on the relative merits of Blamey and Lavarack, but asked 'what was the use of training regular soldiers if when war comes you then passed them over for command'. He then wrote that:

> *looking back now I assume KM was putting me forward as Chief of Staff AIF, a post in which I was not interested. I had done 2 years Staff College . . . and got a very high report "A" with recommendation for accelerated promotion and as suitable for command, and it was command that I had from then on concentrated on. I felt that if I prepared myself specially for command I could easily outpace the Citizen Force commanders and could thus restore to the Regular soldiers their rightful place as commanders of the forces as they are in every country except Australia. Not only was I not interested in being C of S AIF but I assumed since Rowell had been appointed staff officer to Squires the IG he would probably become COS AIF and I was quite content to let him have it while I pursued my aim of command. So Murdoch must have thought me a rather uncooperative guest . . .*[58]

Aside from the light which it throws on Robertson's own ambitions, the wider context of these remarks deserves comment. The financial meanness and lack of understanding of successive governments between the wars had led to a situation in which many Staff Corps and militia officers came to view each other with bitterness and suspicion. The prominent CMF officer Major General Henry Gordon Bennett wrote a series of inflammatory newspaper articles in 1937 in which he attacked the capacity and competence of the Staff Corps. 'Experience has proved', he claimed, 'that citizen soldiers can handle our citizen army more efficiently than permanent officers.' He was censured by the Military Board, but the incident merely exacerbated existing tensions. (Gordon Bennett's attack on the Staff Corps was not based on any detestation of elite privilege or belief in the virtues of commissioning from the ranks; indeed he opposed the latter strongly, arguing that the 'Australian working man has more respect for a "sahib" who is a true gentleman and has education and breeding'.)[59] As well as mistrust between CMF and Staff Corps, there were definite rifts within the Staff Corps itself, especially between members of the first two classes to graduate from Duntroon in 1914. This was one of the consequences of a tiny military establishment in a long period of peace during which professional jealousies and personal animosities could and did fester. Not all militia and Staff Corps officers disliked each other by any means, and there were strong lines of friendship and alliance in the Staff Corps itself, both within individual classes and across class lines. But the feuding between senior officers which would continue for the whole of the Second World War had its origins not in the 'two armies' policy adopted in 1939, disastrous though that was, but in the interwar period and, for some, further back even than that.

In 1938 the post of Inspector-General, unfilled since Chauvel's retirement, was revived and was offered to a British officer, Lieutenant General E. K. Squires. His first report to the government, delivered in 1939, was concerned particularly with the organisation of the army in the face of another war, with the state of the regular forces, and with the condition of the Staff Corps, on all of which he made various recommendations. His comments on the Staff Corps went to the heart of much that was wrong with interwar military policy:

> *I cannot speak too highly of the keenness, devotion and efficiency with which the majority of the Staff Corps officers carry out their duties. But the present conditions of service are such that not only do they fail to attract in sufficient numbers, candidates of the type that is needed, but owing to the slowness of advancement under the present system, they have created among the officers now serving — and particularly among those who are now approaching the higher ranks — a feeling of despondency which cannot but be detrimental to the best interests of the service.*[60]

He recommended revisions to the retirement ages and pension rights of various ranks, an upgrading of ranks against certain positions, increases in pay, and promotion above the rank of major to be by selection, not seniority.[61]

The need for such reform is demonstrated by the structure of age/rank retirement then pertaining. By 1938 Australian officers were distinctly older on average than their British counterparts. Retirement age for a colonel in the Staff Corps was sixty, in the militia fifty-eight, and in the British Army fifty-five; at the other end of the scale, a regular lieutenant might serve till he reached fifty-five, his militia counterpart forty-eight but his British equivalent left at forty-five.[62]

Squires' principal recommendation, and the one which held out real hope for the existence of a viable professional army, urged the creation of a regular force of two brigades with a peacetime establishment of 7500 men. It implied a command role in peacetime for regular officers which would lead logically to a command role in wartime and the end of any monopoly on such positions exercised by officers of the Citizen Military Forces. It went in hand with the recommendation for the reorganisation of the existing force structure and base organisation. The system of district bases located in each state was to be abolished, to be replaced with four regional commands together with an independent garrison at

Darwin, and each would be responsible for the forces in its region. The need for reform here too was pressing. By 1938 Army Headquarters in Melbourne dealt with no fewer than thirteen subordinate formation headquarters (6 divisions, 6 district bases and one independent command) and four permanent and three temporary educational establishments. There was no peacetime command appointment higher than a division — the corps structure which must develop, and quickly, in the event of war did not exist in Australia's peacetime organisation, which meant that no senior Australian officer, or any of their staffs, had any experience at this level of command. The reorganisation proceeded in October 1939. The creation of a regular army lapsed, but a foretaste of what would come after 1945 lay in the creation of a regular garrison force for the 7th Military District, the newly-created command based on the Northern Territory. On 13 March 1939, Lieutenant Colonel H.C.H. Robertson was appointed Commandant of the 7th Military District.

Characteristically, he was involved in the affairs of his new command even before his appointment was announced. In early January 1939 he was sent to Liverpool Camp to inspect the training and organisation of the Darwin Mobile Force and to report on its progress.[63] The force was activated in November 1938 and numbered 245 men. In keeping with Squires' recommendations, the officers of the unit were drawn from recent Duntroon graduates, thus maintaining the entirely regular nature of the DMF. Apart from providing command experience for Staff Corps officers, the DMF's roles were to provide a mobile force to guard against possible sporadic raids in the Darwin area, to provide basic training for all members of the force, and to give its members the necessary experience prior to transfer to the Australian Instructional Corps, in which the majority of regular NCOs were employed. Its force structure emphasised its dual role as a unit of the field force and as a proving ground for young officers and future NCOs. Ninety infantry were supported by four 18-pounder field guns, four 3-inch mortars, four Vickers medium machine guns, and intelligence, signals and pioneer elements. Although the unit was not intended as an officer training establishment for other ranks, over 100 of its members would receive commissions in the 2nd AIF and as many again rose to senior NCO and warrant officer rank, evidence of the quality of soldier recruited from the more than 3000 applications to enlist.[64]

The DMF was not the only force available for the defence of Darwin. The 9th Heavy Battery, Royal Australian Garrison Artillery, the 7th Fortress Engineers, Royal Australian Engineers, the 2nd Anti-Aircraft cadre, Royal Australian Artillery, and Service Corps and Ordnance base workshop details were located there, quartered at Larrakeyah Barracks and responsible for the installation and manning of defensive works in the port. As part of the government's rearmament programme a militia unit was raised in January 1939. The 7th Garrison Company, Australian Army Medical Corps, it would be of little direct use should the Northern Territory come under attack, but it trained regularly and enthusiastically since, as Robertson told its members shortly after his arrival, its services would be required 'before very long'.[65] The Darwin Mobile Force was accommodated in barracks converted from the old meat works abandoned by Vestey's after the First World War and located twenty miles (thirty-two kilometres) outside Darwin itself. As well as training and field exercises, the unit built tactical roads and erected defences in the area and stood guard over the naval refuelling facilities and flying boat station in the port.

The reorganisation which had led to the strengthening of the Northern Territory was in response to fears of raids against northern Australia at the outbreak of any hostilities, and Robertson was concerned that the new military district should be brought to as high a state of readiness as possible short of war conditions. He instituted training programmes for the troops in his command, and when ordered to despatch fifty men south for training as NCOs complained that this would disrupt his preparations; 'if there is any danger of war this year I consider it essential that that training should be completed'.[66] One such exercise, conducted in June 1939, involved 250 soldiers of the Darwin Mobile Force, 150 men from the Coastal Defence Force, and the militia company in a week of manoeuvres designed to test the garrison's ability to prevent enemy ships entering the harbour and to repel an attempted landing. The naval survey vessel, HMAS *Moresby*, acted as the enemy. While it may have lacked something in terms of realism, it bore Robertson's energetic stamp and was, as one observer commented, an attempt to 'test the troops under conditions and elements they should meet in a time of war'.[67] As a defended port, control in Darwin in the event of hostilities was to be vested in a Fortress Combined Operational Headquarters with responsibility for area defence as well.[68] Robertson thus worked closely with his naval counterpart, the District Naval Officer, and both dealt with the Administrator of the Northern Territory, Mr C.L. Abbott.

Preparation of the garrison itself was but one, and the lesser, of the tasks facing the commandant. The Northern Territory had featured in Australian defence planning since Federation, but very little development of defence infrastructure had occurred despite much discussion of the need for it. Work now began on a military airfield three miles (between four and five kilometres) from the existing civil airport, an anti-submarine boom was constructed across the mouth of the harbour, the civil hospital was extended and, after the outbreak of war, was supplemented by the 119th Army General Hospital based at Berrimah. Construction began on accommodation for the increasing number of military personnel and civilian construction workers attracted to the town by the defence works programme. Much of this work began under Robertson, although most of it was completed after his departure. The two most important items were the creation of a north-south road to upgrade the standard of communications, and the construction of improved water supply facilities for Darwin, at Manton Dam.[69] Work was undertaken to upgrade the port facilities too, since in August 1939 only two ships could berth at a time in Darwin and the design of the wharves made rapid loading and unloading almost impossible; it could take as much as three weeks to unload 3000 tons of cargo from one of the steamships which regularly plied trade between Darwin and the eastern seaboard.[70]

As war approached further preparations were put in hand to ensure the defence of Darwin should the port and town come under attack. At the beginning of August a militia unit was raised to provide men for the garrison artillery and signals units, and about forty local men enlisted at once. The recruitment level initially was disappointing, given that Darwin now boasted a population of over 5000 people, many of them men of military age. 'Jobs could be found in the militia for men of every profession', Robertson told a recruiting meeting in August. 'All they need do is make application to him and they would be placed'.[71] Numbers did not increase greatly until after the outbreak of war, however, and then there was a considerable drain on eligible manpower as members of the regular and militia forces enlisted in the AIF. Local Aborigines also sought to enlist and, with war's outbreak the following month G.A. Street, the Minister for Defence, gave permission for 'a limited number of selected types of half-caste aborigines' to be enlisted. In the view of the local Protector of Aborigines, 'the militia training to be received will prove of value to them in providing some occupation in hours when they are not otherwise employed'.[72]

From 28 August 1939 the local press representatives agreed to submit their stories for unofficial censorship by the commandant, and on 1 September the intelligence personnel of the garrison began a programme of alien registration of the local Italian and German populations in coordination with the police.[73] As soon as war was declared, all applicants for the militia were called up, buildings were camouflaged, and the Royal Australian Air Force flew in No 12 Squadron, consisting of five Wirraways and one Anson, to operate aerial patrols over the sea approaches to the port. These commenced on 5 September. A temporary military hospital was established, the Darwin Mobile Force was brought into Darwin from its barracks in the Vestey's works, and guards were mounted on strategic points.[74]

Once the initial alert had passed, Robertson ordered a string of exercises for the garrison to give them practice in defence against enemy landings. The Fortress Combined Operational Headquarters was established on 2 September and, in addition, on 5 September the *Defence National Security (General) Regulations* were promulgated, declaring various areas of the port, surrounding shoreline, and buildings occupied by the military to be security areas and prohibited to unauthorised personnel. On 6 September a meeting of the local branch of the returned soldiers' organisation resulted in the enrolment of fifty men in the Class B Reserve after an address by the commandant, and a week later he forwarded a lengthy report on the state of preparedness of Darwin to the Military Board, together with a request for augmentation of his forces since, he felt, they were inadequate to meet all the tasks with which they were charged.[75]

A Defence Coordination Committee was formed, comprising the commandant, the senior officers of the local Royal Australian Navy and Royal Australian Air Force establishments, and their senior staff officers.[76] After the first two weeks of the war, in which it oversaw many of the preparations detailed above, it had very little to do and thenceforth met on a bi-weekly basis. Some initial trouble was experienced in coordinating measures with the local civilian administration since the administrator continued to send reports through the Department of the Interior without reference to the local military authorities, but these were resolved quietly and diplomatically and, at Robertson's insistence, without recourse to higher authority.

Alien registration continued on a more intensive basis, and a census of local manpower was undertaken since it would prove impossible to fill the Territory's quota of recruits for the AIF (initially five officers and 111 other ranks) without the danger of closing down essential defence construction works. In any case, the force in Darwin was being cannibalised already for regulars to help in the training and manning of the new Australian Imperial Force and at the end of September Robertson lost thirty-three NCOs from the DMF and one from the 9th Heavy Battery, all promoted to warrant officer rank and sent south.[77] More applications were received for enlistment in the AIF than the quota would allow, and Robertson sought to divert some of these into the permanent forces to take the places of those already posted, with the promise that they would be trained as 1st and 2nd reinforcements for the 2/3rd Field Regiment, and would thus be sent overseas later.[78]

Despite the slightly unreal atmosphere of the early months of the war, Robertson kept himself and the troops under his command busy. He reconnoitred the beach approaches and inspected the emplacements and defences, presided over the field exercises which became a regular part of the Darwin regimen, inspected guards, chided his officers for the lack of anti-gas preparations among the troops, and in between dealt with labour unrest on the waterfront and elsewhere. In early November there was a strike on the railway which serviced the port area, and Robertson

Robertson and staff, Headquarters, 7 Military District, 1939.

sent in servicemen to keep the line running. Members of the North Australia Workers Union (NAWU), the omnibus union which covered all trades union activities in the Territory, struck on the wharves on 8 November and refused to unload cargo. In concert with the navy, Robertson sent in servicemen to keep the docks operating.

There was to be further industrial unrest on the waterfront in April the following year, when servicemen again were forced to unload ships through strike action by the NAWU, and on this occasion the administrator applied to have essential services legislation proclaimed.[79] This sort of thing had its counterpart elsewhere in Australia at this time and was evidence of the government's 'business as usual' attitude to the war effort. In the first eighteen months of the war government policy aimed at a minimum effort, characterised by the lack of enthusiasm among relevant ministers for recruiting if it should disrupt industry or commerce and the failure to enact serious controls on manpower, industrial disputes, and the allocation of strategic materials.

All the while, Robertson's concern was to get away to the fighting. On 21 September notification had been received that Staff Corps officers might make application to be posted with the 6th Division, destined for service overseas, while the first batch of other rank volunteers for the AIF had left Darwin on 1 December. When the list of command appointments for the 6th Division was issued it contained not a single Staff Corps officer, allegedly on Menzies' instructions.[80] It seemed as if this war would be fought like the last one, with citizen soldiers in the dominant positions. The failure to appoint Staff Corps officers in this way made them 'more firmly resolved than ever to defend [their] interests . . . "All this", said one sage and senior citizen soldier, "bound them up into a close corporation, so that if you touched one of them you hurt them all"'.[81] This understated the degree of personal animosity within the Staff Corps, but there is no question that the prospect of being overlooked again rankled deeply, not least with men like Robertson who were now the senior members of the Staff Corps and had distinguished records from the First World War.

Robertson had been promoted to full colonel in November 1939, and thus was eligible either for a senior staff appointment on a divisional headquarters or, as he much preferred, a brigade command. On 28 February 1940 War Cabinet decided to raise a second division for overseas service, the 7th and, at the same time, to reduce the number of battalions in the infantry brigades from four to three, in line with a decision made in Britain. This meant that three of the battalions of the 6th Division, which was proceeding to Egypt, were now surplus to its establishment. The 18th Brigade, commanded by Brigadier L. J. Morshead, was diverted to England, and the 2/4th, 2/8th, and 2/11th Battalions were brought together to form the 19th Brigade, which would take the 18th's place in the 6th Division. On 4 April Robertson received the command of this brigade, the only Staff Corps officer to hold a command in that division, and four days later he left Darwin by flying boat for Melbourne.[82]

Blamey, a former regular, though not a Duntroon graduate (and Monash's chief of staff in 1918), had been appointed to command of the AIF, and he was not prepared to waste the talent which existed in the Staff Corps. By 1945 nearly half the senior appointments in the Australian army would be held by regulars, although Staff Corps officers would continue to be heavily under-represented at the level of unit command. Robertson's elation may well be imagined. At a meeting in Melbourne soon after he arrived, one senior CMF officer present recorded that '"Red Robbie", as usual, held the stage, and I remember remarking to the cheerful John Moten [commanding 2/27 Battalion], "We'll have to be on our toes to keep up with this fellow". "Don't worry", replied [Moten] with a broad grin, "within a few months he'll be asking us how to train troops"'.[83] The competition between regulars and CMF for positions was already keen, and Lieutenant Colonel George Vasey, now in the Middle East with the advance party of the AIF, wrote to his wife that 'in a letter I had from Syd [Brigadier S. F. Rowell, chief of staff to Blamey] he spoke of the wrangling that is going on for good jobs and I gather from him I may be defeated [for a command], but it will not be for lack of trying'.[84] The suspicions and competitive jealousies which the interwar years had helped foster were evident from the first months of the war.

The years between the world wars were characterised by financial stringency, doctrinal and policy muddle, and organisational and administrative folly which resulted in a state of near-total unpreparedness for war in September 1939. The army trained for the Second World War with the surplus equipment of the First World War, and with many of its operational assumptions. As in 1914, the provisions of the *Defence Act* which precluded overseas service for any but volunteers, and the lack of standing regular troops, meant that the wartime army had to be raised from civilian volunteers, fleshed out in the higher ranks with citizen soldiers who had seen no active service since 1918, to which were added regular officers who had been denied opportunities for professional advancement and who sought now to make up lost ground in the shortest possible space. In time, the Australian army, both Australian Imperial Force and Australian Military Forces, would become highly proficient, but at war's beginning soldiers of virtually all ranks had much to learn still. The existence of 'two armies' did nothing to assist the learning process.

For Robertson, the decades since his return from Palestine had held their share of frustrations but had been marked equally by considerable achievement. He had demonstrated his abilities as an instructor, a commander, and a staff officer. He had engaged in the central strategic debate of the time and had shown himself to be a thinking soldier both in his writings during the 1930s and in his outstanding performance at Camberley in the 1920s. As he rose in rank his egotism and vanity became more marked and made him enemies, but in the tiny and inward-looking army establishment of the day this would have happened regardless. If there were some who did not care for him, there were many at all levels who looked on him as one of the leading military lights of his generation. With his appointment to command an infantry brigade in the first Australian division to be sent overseas, he was now to have his opportunity.

CHAPTER 4

'HIS CROWDED HOUR': 1940-1941

As a consequence of the policies pursued before the war, Australia's capacity to equip the troops it fielded was limited. Following elementary training in Australia the divisions of the 2nd Australian Imperial Force were to move to the Middle East, where more modern equipment would be stockpiled for training and, eventually, for issue to units at full war establishment. This was the theory. In practice, the units of the 6th Division trained with whatever they could get their hands on, and when they went into action against the Italians in January 1941 they scrounged what they could not obtain from British sources and from captured Italian equipment. As one officer of the 2/8th Battalion wrote, 'the tps were later described by an enthusiastic [government] minister as the "best equipped that had ever taken the field"', but when his unit went into action it 'had one and a half mortars — the half was later turned into a whole by the addition of a makeshift mounting from captured Iti material — making two more or less serviceable; and, instead of the prescribed number, only two carriers, one of which might go and might not'.[1] Such shortages were far from unusual.

The first Australian brigade, the 16th, commanded by Brigadier A.S. 'Tubby' Allen, arrived in Egypt in February 1940 and went into training in Palestine. The choice of training area was deliberate, in order to get the Australians away from Cairo and to avoid a repetition of the unseemly behaviour which had characterised the AIF's previous acquaintance with Egypt in 1914 and 1915.[2] The second brigade, the 17th, commanded by Brigadier S.G. Savige, reached the Middle East in mid-May. This served to place greater strain on the available pool of equipment and hampered the training of both formations. The 6th Division's GOC, Major General Iven Mackay, cabled Army Headquarters in Melbourne that 'shortages in essential war equipment deny division any fighting value [in] modern warfare'. The 6th Division possessed a quarter of its light machine guns, one third of its Boyes anti-tank rifles, and only twenty-six old model Bren gun carriers. There were enough crew-served weapons available to equip the infantry battalions with only twenty-two Bren guns and four two-inch mortars each. Web equipment had not arrived, there was no anti-gas clothing, the units had only half their allotment of steel helmets, and there were not enough side arms for the officers. Battalion or equivalent training had begun, but 'shortage of vehicles [is] seriously interfering in all particulars. Division cannot be got ready for war until full scale of weapons and vehicles [is] delivered and period of brigade and higher training [is] completed.'[3]

The third troop convoy left Fremantle on 12 May. On board transport XI — the recently converted Cunard liner *Queen Mary* — was Brigadier H.C.H. Robertson, acting as OC Troops for the voyage. Owing to the submarine threat in the Mediterranean the Admiralty decided to re-route the ships round the Cape to Britain, where they arrived on 16 June. Robertson left the convoy at Simonstown, and by plane and train reached Gaza, in Palestine, on 12 June. News of his appointment had preceded him. George Vasey wrote that 'we have had a complete list [of appointments] from the *Herald* in Melbourne. There are some surprises; but on the whole they are not bad.'[4] Doubtless Robertson was one of the surprises: at forty-six he was not only the youngest brigadier in the division but the only Staff Corps officer to gain a command. As noted, his brigade, the 19th, had been formed from the discarded battalions of the other three brigades when the divisional establishment had been reorganised at the end of February. 'They had been cast out from their original formations and did not like it', wrote one of their number later.[5] Originally intended for the 7th Division, the diversion of the 18th Brigade to Britain had forced them into the 6th. As a result, Robertson was faced with the task of training a new brigade virtually from scratch.

It was the sort of work on which he thrived. 'He believed that physical hardness was one of the first necessities of military efficiency; he took special pains to insist on smartness of dress and deportment.'[6] The brigade was in camp at a site known as Kilo 89, situated in country over which he had operated in the last war, and Robertson had the units out in the hills surrounding Gaza and Beersheba day and night. At battalion and then brigade level they practised 'attacking and retreating, resting only at the point of physical exhaustion, and Robbie was always about'.[7] On one occasion the battalions marched with full equipment from Gaza to Beersheba in a day, 'a hell of a long way as I recall',[8] but the hardening would pay off in the long marches across Libya the following year. Robertson's attitude at this time is epitomised by a remark in a letter to one of his sisters back in Australia that 'this war seems to be going rather badly for us so far and it looks as if we must all pull up our socks soon if we want to win it'.[9]

Training levels intensified as the year drew to a close. In early November the brigades were advised of likely operational roles for the division, and towards the end of that month the 19th Brigade took part in its first divisional exercise, followed by a second over three days at the beginning of December. On both occasions the brigade acted as enemy. The purpose of the exercises was twofold: to accustom the troops to dispersed troop movement and extended patrolling activity, and to exercise the machinery of command and control. Colonel Frank Berryman, GSO 1 (the senior operations staff officer) of the division, noted that by this stage 'as a div[ision] we could manoeuvre without creaking very badly', although the divisional commander, Royal Artillery, Brigadier Ned Herring, thought that the division was not then ready to proceed beyond brigade group exercises.[10] During the second exercise the 19th Brigade completely routed the opposing forces, and the commanding officer of the 2/5th Battalion was captured and released several times by sub-units of the 2/4th and 2/11th Battalions.[11] It was at this stage that the divisional staff began to look at the brigade and battalion commanders from a comparative viewpoint, and to make judgements about their suitability for command in war.

Equipment deficiencies were not the only shortcomings facing the 6th Division as it prepared for battle. With the exception of Robertson himself, the Staff Corps had been confined to staff positions on the headquarters and this clearly grated with some of them. Both Vasey, as Assistant Adjutant and Quartermaster General and then GSO 1, and Berryman, as GSO 1, had regular disagreements with the leading militia officers in the division, Allen, Savige and Herring. The difficulties of supply and administration exacerbated the situation, coupled with the fact that several of the senior regular officers held their divisional commander in low regard initially.[12] Both Vasey and Rowell were frustrated by their situation: 'what Syd feared might happen has. These [militia] generals, who now say they are only colonels, are prepared to step down [a rank] to take a job which will prevent somebody else going up . . . It was really too much to expect our people to let a "young officer" like myself to go on so far.'[13] The clannishness of the interwar army kept coming to the surface: Savige was 'under suspicion as a shooter of the Staff Corps', while Robertson was 'doing very well here. He's really most helpful. He looks after himself in the process but has the interests of the staff corps very much at heart.'[14]

In one sense, none of this mattered very much. Generals are not angels, and few men rise to that rank who lack strength of character and force of personality. Given the tremendous pressures under which commanders operate in modern war it may be wondered that clashes between individuals do not occur more often. And it must be added that when the test of operations came, the headquarters of the 6th Division functioned efficiently and well.[15] The rivalry which developed between the Staff Corps and Savige did have consequences, however, both during the Libyan campaign and later, and these were serious. Savige was a close friend of Blamey's and had stood by him during Blamey's troubled period as Chief Commissioner of the Victoria Police in the 1920s. Savige came to believe that the Staff Corps had it in for him — which was certainly true of some of its members — and the general atmosphere of criticism and derogation came to affect relations between Blamey and some Staff Corps officers as well.[16] It is equally clear that Savige held a restrictive view of the Staff Corps' functions. While commanding the 10th Infantry Brigade in Victoria before the war he had tried to have his brigade major, a regular, removed because he alleged that the latter had 'consistently forgotten his role as a staff officer and had usurped Savige's functions as a commander'.[17] Many of the difficulties were caused by the grinding of the machinery of war, Clausewitz's 'friction', which occurs in all armies in all wars. Some of it was outright careerism, the jockeying for power and position of ambitious men many of whom were conscious of missed opportunities. Taken together, it came to seem like a challenge to the Commander-in-Chief (as he became) on the part of sections of the regular army, and Blamey reacted by dismissing certain of its most prominent members to the outer peripheries later in the war. Lavarack, Rowell and Robertson were all to suffer in this manner.[18]

Robertson had similar problems within his brigade, stemming partly from the clash of personalities and partly from the wider dispute. Unlike many of the brigade commanders in newly-raised divisions, Robertson did not have the opportunity to select his battalion commanders. The first CO of the 2/4th Battalion, Lieutenant Colonel P. A. Parsons, had been posted as Inspector of AIF Canteens in August, and Robertson was assigned Lieutenant Colonel Ivan Dougherty, transferred from the 2/2nd Battalion, to replace him. Robertson had wanted to make the appointment himself, and initially greeted Dougherty rather coolly; 'I did not ask for you and I don't want you. But here you are and I suppose we must make the best of it', he was informed upon arrival.[19] Dougherty replied that they would both have to make the best of it, and within a short time they became close friends. Dougherty impressed Robertson so greatly that when the latter went on leave in October 1940 the CO of the 2/4th Battalion acted as brigade commander, despite being the youngest and most junior of the three unit commanders.[20] He was a brigadier by 1942.

Lieutenant Colonel T. S. Louch commanded the 2/11th Battalion, a Western Australian unit. Louch had joined up as a private soldier in 1914 and had been commissioned from the ranks. He was over-age in 1939, the upper limit for battalion commander being set at forty-five years, but was active and well regarded. Lieutenant Colonel J. W. Mitchell, commanding the 2/8th Battalion, was also over-age. In addition, he had commanded the original 8th Battalion in France in 1918 and had acted

Commanding officers and brigade staff, 19th Infantry Brigade, Burg el Arab, *c.* late 1940.

in command of the 19th Brigade pending Robertson's arrival. The two men did not get on. The 2/8th had come from Savige's 17th Brigade, and Mitchell appears to have shared the anti-Staff Corps ethos of some militia officers in that formation. Robertson believed that a battalion command was a young man's job, and that at forty-nine Mitchell was too old for the physical demands of modern war. Certainly Mitchell thought that there was nothing he needed to learn about leading a battalion in the field. Robertson did not want senior officers with command experience in the First World War because he believed, with reason, that they would not accept the need for different training methods and operational approaches. The result was continuous friction between the two, with Robertson attempting to have him removed on medical grounds and Mitchell making plain his discontent to Savige and anyone else who would listen.[21] Brigadier J.E.S. Stevens, commanding the 21st Brigade, thought Mitchell 'a good soldier in battle, but I was not impressed at our only meeting and was sorry to see my fellows go to him' while Vasey, who took over the 19th Brigade from Robertson after the Libyan campaign, thought him 'a nasty bit of work, as well as pretty useless. My first task is to get rid of him.'[22] The strain of the Greek campaign proved almost too much for him, and soon after Blamey returned him to Australia, along with a number of other over-age officers.[23]

The vast majority of battalion commands in the Second World War went to officers from the militia, or to men promoted from within the AIF as a whole, as had been the case during the previous war. Of the initial battalion commands in the four AIF divisions in 1939 and 1940, only one, the 2/15th Battalion, went to a Staff Corps officer, R.F. Marlan. The overwhelming majority of the commanding officers appointed initially had seen active service between 1914 and 1918, either in the ranks or as junior officers, and nearly half were over the age limit set for the appointment. The average age of battalion COs in 1940 was 42.9 years, ranging from Ivan Dougherty of the 2/4th Battalion, easily the youngest at thirty-three, to Mitchell of the 2/8th and H. Wrigley of the 2/5th, both of whom were forty-nine. By 1945 the average had dropped to 35.6 years of age, ranging from J.R. Broadbent of the 2/17th and P.E. Rhoden of the 2/14th, both thirty-one, to G.E. Colvin of the 2/13th, by far the oldest at forty-two. As in all prolonged conflicts, the average age of unit commanders declined in recognition of the strains placed upon them. Only one thing had not changed in 1945: there was still only one infantry CO drawn from the Staff Corps, T.J. Daly of the 2/10th Battalion.

The end of 1940 found the 19th Brigade in camp at Burg el Arab to the west of Alexandria. Italy had declared war in June, and the large, poorly-equipped and woefully led Italian forces in Libya had launched an offensive into Egypt in September, advancing as far as Sidi Barrani. On 9 December Wavell's forces had attacked the Italian positions there, taking over 38,000 prisoners and numerous guns and supplies in two days of fighting and pushing the enemy back over the frontier towards the fortified border position at Bardia. Wavell then directed that the 4th Indian Division be withdrawn and sent to assist British forces under Major General Sir William Platt in Abyssinia, and that it be replaced by the 6th Australian Division. The 16th and 17th Brigades moved up just before Christmas, and Robertson's brigade was warned to be ready to move on the night of 29-30 December. Shortage of motor transport, which became a recurrent problem during the campaign, forced the brigade to move over a three-day period, but by 2 January it was concentrated west of Fort Capuzzo inside the Italian frontier where it relieved units of the 16th Brigade.

Bardia was the division's first action, one in which the 19th Brigade was not intended, initially, to play any significant role. Still short of equipment and some supporting services, the divisional attack was put back a day in order to get more ammunition forward to the guns and to enable Robertson's leading battalion to arrive. Kept in divisional reserve, they had had to leave their few carriers at the railhead and had no anti-tank

Senior officers of the 6th Australian Division in the Middle East, January 1941. *L to R:* Major Denzil Macarthur-Onslow (divisional cavalry), Squadron-Leader Judge, RAF (air liaison officer), Major Ian Campbell (brigade major, 16 Brigade), Brigadier 'Tubby' Allen (16 Brigade), Major General Iven Mackay (GOC), Robertson (19 Brigade), Colonel George Vasey (AA&QMG), Brigadier Stan Savige (17 Brigade), Lieutenant Colonel L.C. Lucas (CRE), Lieutenant Colonel C.E. Prior (CO, 2/1 Machine Gun Battalion), Brigadier 'Ned' Herring (CRA), Lieutenant Colonel R.M. Jerram (7 Battalion, Royal Tank Regiment), Colonel Frank Berryman (GSO 1). *(AWM 5645)*

guns. The 19th Brigade played no part in the first day's fighting on 3 January but, on the afternoon of the following day, Robertson was instructed to prepare an attack next morning to clear the southern defences of Bardia. The 2/11th Battalion was detailed for the task, to be supported by artillery and six tanks from the 7th Battalion, Royal Tank Regiment, with the 2/4th in reserve and the 2/8th guarding the attack's flank. No serious opposition was encountered at this stage, the tanks penetrated to the enemy gun line and silenced fire from that source, and a short time after the attack commenced a stream of prisoners began to enter the brigade's lines, including two divisional commanders. More than 15,000 Italians were taken, for the loss of three wounded, and by 1.30 p.m. all resistance ceased. A minor role in a larger action, the attack had been a good test of the brigade's training and of the ability of its commander and his brigade staff. Throughout the morning Robertson had been constantly on the move, in touch with his battalions and aware of how the action was unfolding.[24]

The attack on Bardia brought the hostility between Berryman, Robertson and Vasey on the one hand, and Savige on the other, into the open. Robertson was keen to get involved in the action, and early on declared that Mackay was 'not taking the battle seriously',[25] by which he meant presumably that he himself had not yet been involved. Savige appears to have lost control of the action in his sector, or at the very least neglected to keep higher headquarters informed of progress there, which resulted in the commitment of the 19th Brigade and which he claimed later was unnecessary.[26] Berryman suggested the use of the 19th Brigade, and the plan was discussed, and agreed to, by both the divisional and corps commanders.[27] The 17th Brigade had been instructed to mount a demonstration at Post 11 in the Italian defences, but had taken heavier casualties than expected and this had precipitated an argument between Savige and Berryman in the middle of the action. It also led Berryman in future to document carefully all decisions and communications between headquarters and the brigades. Savige was aggrieved at having the 2/5th Battalion placed temporarily under Robertson's command, and over what he felt was lack of confidence in his command; he offered Mackay his resignation, which the latter refused.[28] Antipathy between Robertson and Savige was not lessened by the brusque manner in which Robertson took over responsibility for the attack on the morning of 5 January, and his disdain for Savige is barely concealed in his report of his brigade's activities.[29] The conduct of the attack on Bardia, while it demonstrated the combat readiness of the Australian division, revealed some serious strains among some of its leading officers.

These were not alleviated by the next phase of the campaign, the advance to and capture of Tobruk. Robertson was given a brigade group based on the 19th Brigade and led the advance, setting out from Bardia on the morning of 6 January. Delays were experienced through shortages of motor transport, and the bulk of the brigade did not reach its positions until the evening of the following day. The Italian defences were formidable, with 128 fortified posts along a thirty mile (forty-eight kilometres) front, and the attack could not commence for at least a week until sufficient ammunition was brought up. The 'break' enabled commanders to get their units in hand as well; what Mackay described as 'civilianism' had begun to show itself — soldiers playing with captured Italian equipment, often dangerously — and boots and uniforms needed replacing. Campaigning in the desert was arduous, with men living in

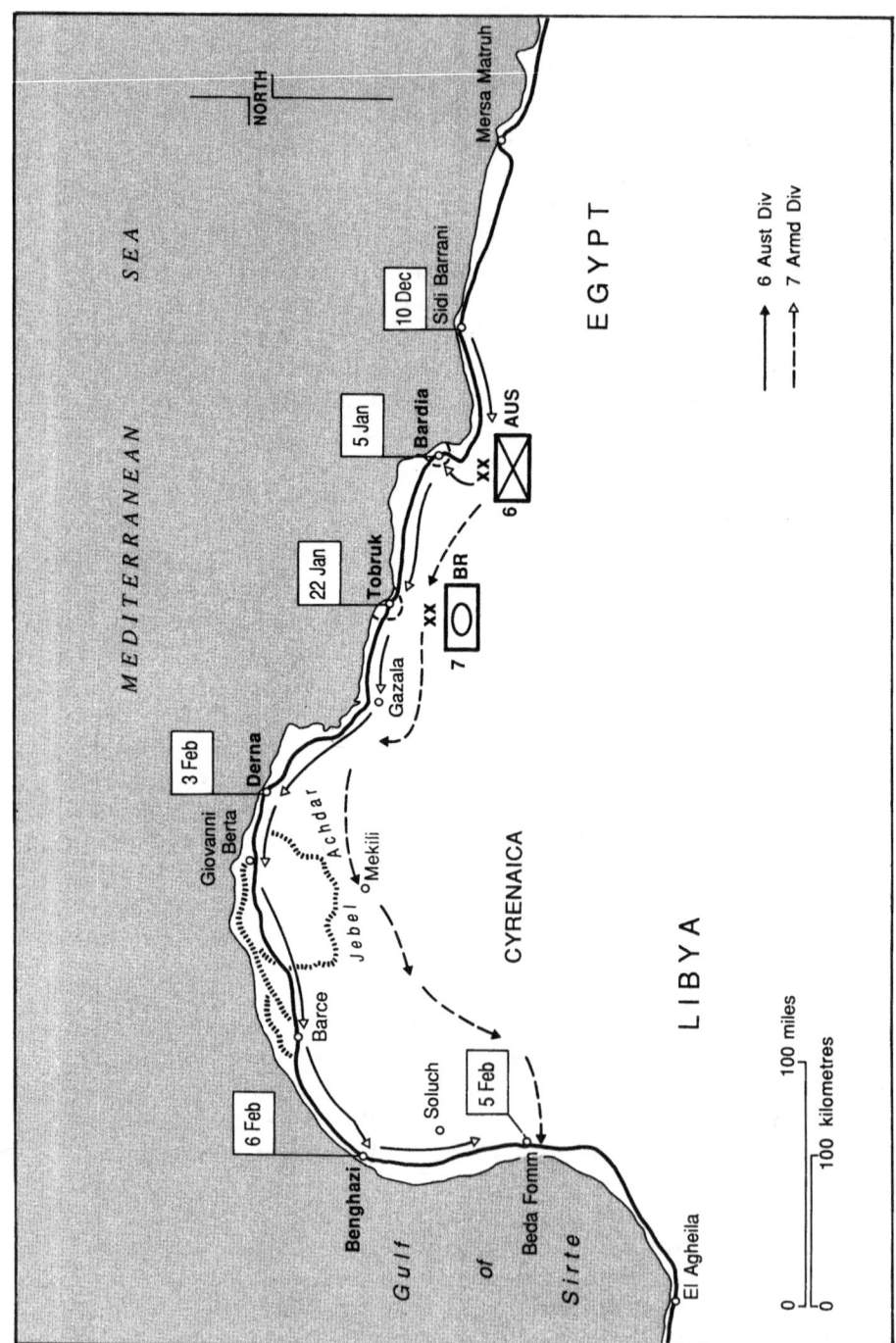

First Libyan campaign, January-February 1941.

holes in the ground and rationed to half a gallon (under two litres) of water per man per day for all purposes. Robertson put all three of his battalions in the line, ostensibly to give them practice in patrolling and to enable a full reconnaissance of the enemy lines, and there they stayed until the night of 16-17 January.

Mackay outlined the plan for the assault to his senior officers on 13 January. The attack would be carried out in two phases, the first conducted by Allen's 16th Brigade to breach the defences, the second by Robertson's brigade to exploit the opening and breach the inner defences of the port. 'Robbie so full of self-confidence I could kick him', Mackay's ADC recorded in his diary after the meeting.[30] Attention focused on the phase one assault initially, 'and other than giving an objective to the 19 Bde, little was done regarding Phase 2 at this stage'.

> However ... I gave considerable attention to a plan for Phase 2, and I spent much time on a detailed examination of the enemy's defences and his battery positions, with the result that I asked the CRA [Herring] for particular attention to be devoted to counter battery work, so that I could contemplate an advance at speed.[31]

Robertson's original plan included the support of several tank sections from 7th Battalion, Royal Tank Regiment, but the shortage of armoured vehicles precluded this and Robertson substituted two companies of the 1st Battalion, Royal Northumberland Fusiliers (a machine gun battalion), and two troops of the divisional cavalry to protect the left flank of his advance. After a twenty-four hour spell out of the line, the 19th Brigade moved into positions south of the Tobruk defences and completed its final preparations for the battle.

Robertson had decided to vary the plan in order to avoid the delays which had held up the Australians at Bardia.

> Eventually I decided to attempt penetrating by the 19th Bde without any pause, and to push my troops through the perimeter while Phase 1 was in progress ... The divisional plan (which many people considered optimistic), legislated for my getting Phase 2 more or less completed at the end of the first day, but my attempt to avoid a pause meant that I might complete Phase 2 by the middle of the morning, in which case I was free to launch an exploitation as Phase 3 in the afternoon, if Arty could get forward in time.

As the objective for exploitation he chose the headquarters of the entire Tobruk garrison, Fort Solaro.

Events justified the risks taken to gain speed. The 16th Brigade completed its phase of the operation on time. The preliminary exploitation was completed by 11.30 a.m. on 21 January after some stiff fighting in places, and artillery batteries were moved forward to provide fire support for the third phase, timed for 2.00 p.m. Dougherty's battalion was given the task of capturing Solaro, which was entrenched and wired and was the scene of some heavy fighting. Robertson trusted Dougherty absolutely and did not issue detailed instructions for the 2/4th Battalion, contenting himself with a general indication of his intentions and a suggestion that if the battalion could push on to its next set of objectives, it was to do so.[32] He kept a much closer control over his remaining battalion commanding officers. The Tobruk headquarters was located about a mile (over a kilometre) to the west of Fort Solaro, and was taken with ease. The fortress commander, General Pitassi Mannella, and a considerable number of senior officers were brought to Robertson, who accepted their surrender with obvious delight. He demanded the surrender of the port and garrison, but the Italian general replied merely that his men 'had orders to fight to the finish'. By dusk, the defences around Fort Pilastrino had been entered, although they were not taken until after dark, and Robertson prepared for the final move into the defended port the next morning.

He was in his element, and the surrender of the senior Italian commander had done nothing to reduce the size of his ego. As he told a group of British and Australian journalists that afternoon,

> *if we capture Solaro and Pilastrino tonight we should have all the Italian generals in the bag. I hope to bring my tally to six. I captured one major general in the last war and I've now got two in this campaign. But I'm going to have a new job tomorrow — accepting the surrender of the Italian cruiser* San Giorgio, *which is aground in the harbour. I'm not very sure of the procedure in capturing admirals, but it should be interesting.*'[33]

Wilmot went on to note that such frankness from a senior officer was greatly appreciated by the press, especially the British who were used to being kept at arm's length by senior officers: 'To our British colleagues therefore Robertson's frankness was something new and in the next few days comments by "a sunburnt, red-headed Australian Brigadier" hit the headlines of the British press — not because he had said something startling, but because he had said anything at all.' Field Marshal Lord Birdwood wrote to Mackay asking the identity of 'the red-haired brigadier we keep hearing and reading so much about over here', but grandstanding in the press did nothing to endear Robertson to his critics.[34]

After a night's rest the advance was resumed, but most of the fight had gone out of the remaining garrison. The 61st Italian Division and its commanding general surrendered to the 2/8th Battalion soon after dawn. At 10 a.m. Robertson went forward into the town with two troops of the divisional cavalry regiment, the brigade staff and a handful of journalists, and established himself in the naval headquarters. While there, he accepted the surrender of Admiral Massimiliano Vietina and 1500 naval

'HIS CROWDED HOUR': 1940-1941

Robertson, Brigadier L. J. Morshead (observer), and Lieutenant Colonel Hogshaw, Royal Northumberland Fusiliers, in the main square of Tobruk after the Italian surrender.

'Surrender of Tobruch [sic]. [L to R] Lt Col Hogshaw, RNF, Robertson, Captain Salventiani, Chief of Staff, Admiral Vietina, General Barberis, Major Key, 2/8 Battalion.'

Robertson and Morshead lunching among surrendered Italian soldiers and sailors, Tobruk.

personnel, having declined to take the surrender of the fortress artillery commander, a colonel, along the way; 'Throw him back', he said, 'nothing but generals and admirals for me today.'[35] The remainder of 22 January was spent in mopping up and organising the huge numbers of prisoners for movement to cages in the rear.

For a total of forty-nine dead and 306 wounded the 6th Division had taken a strongly fortified port city in a day and a half, yielding 27,000 prisoners, over 200 guns, more than 200 vehicles and, most embarrassingly for the Italians, a large number of senior officers. Robertson noted that the success of the operation was owed 'to the speed with which the attack was made, and the fact that the troops pushed on regardless of their flanks, leaving those coming behind to do the mopping up'.[36] The advantages gained by the artillery and tanks had been consolidated and exploited by the infantry with the speed of their attack and their preparedness to go on. 'In the 19th Brigade's attack . . . the diggers kept up with a barrage which lifted 100 yards a minute. They made their own task easier because they could maintain a pace that bewildered the enemy.'[37]

Including the approach march, the battalions of the 16th Brigade covered twenty-one miles (thirty-four kilometres) in two days' fighting, while the 19th Brigade covered twenty-six (forty-two kilometres).[38] The hard training and Robertson's willingness to take a calculated risk in advancing the exploitation phase of the attack had brought results; the 19th Brigade's assault 'which penetrated quickly and deeply into enemy defences, was the cause of the main collapse later'.[39]

Having retained the initiative in spectacular fashion, there was to be little respite for the troops or their commanders.[40] The original plan had called for Savige's brigade to take the lead in the pursuit towards Derna. This now changed, the leading role in the pursuit was assigned to the 19th Brigade, and the resulting disharmony between the brigadiers may well be imagined. Savige's battalions had been used piecemeal during the Tobruk battle, leaving him little role in the action. With an augmented brigade group, dubbed 'B Force', Robertson now pushed ahead towards Derna while the 17th Brigade was held around El Gazala. 'B force' reached the scarp overlooking Derna by nightfall on 25 January, but was held up by the enemy's positions on the western bank of the scarp, rendering it uncrossable. In places it was several hundred yards (metres) wide, nearly 1000 feet (304 metres) deep and with perpendicular sides. By the night of 29-30 January the battalions had worked their way forward and around the Italian positions, capturing a number of forts and gun positions and bringing the enemy position in Derna itself under fire from allied artillery. The capture of Mechili to the south by units of the 7th Armoured Division and the withdrawal of Italian forces there north-west to Giovanni Berta caused the forces remaining in Derna to surrender.

The 19th Brigade led the pursuit once more, with the 2/8th Battalion in the van. The problems between Robertson and Mitchell had not eased, and when on 31 January Mitchell's battalion was held up by Italian defences on the coastal road, Robertson sent an instruction to Dougherty which was calculated to increase the ill-feeling:

> *Once we are on the top the job is easier. If a decent stabbing party could clean up the top during darkness, it would not only let us get on tomorrow but would put such a fear into the Iti [sic] that he would not dare be venturesome again. I have sent a duplicate of this to Mitchell. I don't want either of you to get into serious trouble, but I feel that the Itis don't fear the Australians enough, particularly at night.*[41]

Mitchell faced a difficult position, since the road had been demolished and the Italian positions enjoyed excellent fields of fire which their artillery used to good effect. Nonetheless, spurred no doubt by the above instruction and its implication, Mitchell put three companies up the scarp on the night of 1 February. After hand-to-hand fighting, the enemy

Robertson with General Sir Archibald Wavell the day after the capture of Tobruk.

positions were taken and further demolitions cleared. On 2 February the pursuit continued towards Giovanni Berta.

Savige's brigade was to mount the attack on Giovanni Berta, but the enemy had withdrawn and the brigade occupied the town unopposed. Another dispute between Robertson and Savige developed over Savige's failure to clear the town by one o'clock on the morning of 3 February to allow the troops and vehicles of the 19th Brigade to move through and continue the advance, as set out in divisional orders. Savige argued that the engineers had been unable to clear the minefields and repair the road at which point, he later recorded, 'Brig 19 Bde became somewhat childish', and sent forward his own engineer section 'to put in a special crossing for himself, as he expected to cross at 1000 hours'.[42] Robertson, chafing at the delay, saw Mackay. He convinced him both that the shortage of motor transport necessitated placing all available resources behind one brigade, and that it should be his.

Savige was bitter at the decision. 'Everybody completely fed up as we were one third of the way to Barce and then able to move forthwith with leading elements.'[43] Savige had put forward a plan which called for all resources to be placed behind his own brigade, 'even to the extent of taking some from the 19 Bde', and was furious that Robertson should have been selected instead.

> *It is of course understood that Brig Robertson must be given the honour, particularly in view of his disappointment at being over 10 miles outside Giovanni Berta when this brigade entered it. It is interesting to note also that the 17 Bde will move fwd on foot as best they can and when Barce is taken the 19 Bde will proceed, no doubt in MT [motor transport], by road along the line of the railroad to Benghazi . . . There will not be a repetition of Giovanni Berta. That would not be in the interest of the permanent soldier. Brig [ie, Savige] offered every possible assistance to the 19 Bde which was actively given in order that they should complete their job and obtain the honour and the glory in the capture of Benghazi.*

And elsewhere he noted that the revised plan called for his brigade to be picked up in motor transport 'to proceed through 19 Bde to Benghazi. Perhaps.'[44]

His disappointment was understandable, had he not contrived to bring about exactly the same result at Robertson's expense. It is difficult to see either how the 17th Brigade might have moved immediately towards Barce given his statements to Robertson about the presence of minefields and the state of the road leading from Giovanni Berta. To this extent, his biographer's view that Savige was shocked by this 'cut-throat competition' is not tenable.[45] In any event, the decision was Mackay's, and given Savige's less than outstanding performance to date in the campaign, and Robertson's considerably greater successes, it was a sensible one. The commanding general of XIII Corps was desperate to ensure that the Italians did not get away. 'The thing above everything else is not to let the enemy escape . . . it is essential to the success of the remainder of the campaign.'[46] Mackay's confidence was vindicated; running entirely on captured petrol Robertson's brigade reached Barce on 5 February and the next day, in spite of heavy rains and mined roads, continued on to Benghazi, reaching it in the evening. Pressure from the 7th Armoured Division to the south around Beda Fomm, and with the 19th Brigade at Benghazi and ready to move towards Ghemines, put the final seal on the offensive. On the morning of 7 February the Italian army in Cyrenaica surrendered.

Unable to resist the temptation, Robertson entered Benghazi that morning to take the surrender of the city at the town hall. In a rhetorical flourish he proclaimed 'Give me two stout ships and a bearing on Rome and we'll dine in the hall of the Caesars.' Having taken the surrender, he informed the local authorities that Mackay would be along shortly to take over the city. He wrote to his sister a few days later, 'I am getting quite good at taking surrenders since I have had a lot of practice.' Mackay was not amused at being upstaged in this manner, although Robertson sought to justify it later in his report by stating that, since the divisional GSO1 was present, 'I hoped that the Div Comd would be present at [the appointed] hour [also]'. Mitchell was critical of the surrender ceremony 'while there was still a war on', but commented that Robertson 'wouldn't miss a chance like that'.[47]

An arduous first campaign had been brought to a stunning and successful conclusion. To all intent and purpose the Italian Tenth Army had ceased to exist. The 6th Division had suffered 256 killed, 861 wounded and 21 prisoners; the Italians in total lost 130,000 prisoners, 400 tanks and 1290 guns, amounting to some ten infantry divisions. Robertson's battalions now went under canvas, the 2/11th at Tocra, the 2/8th at Barracca, the 2/4th in garrison in Benghazi. Congratulatory messages flooded in. The Prime Minister, R.G. Menzies, visiting the AIF on his way to London for consultations with Churchill, dropped in to address the troops; 'a picturesque barracks with really lovely camouflague [sic] on the walls, where I address a battalion of infantry. Meet Brig "Red" Robertson, a born salesman and propagandist with great tales of the generals and admirals he has captured. Blamey said later — "Robertson is a competent fellow, but he has won the war about three times already".'[48]

Robertson's ego was to get him into serious trouble at a formal dinner that night, and to open the first public breach between himself and Blamey. The details differ, depending on whose recollections are used, but all agree that Robertson and Blamey argued in front of Menzies over the disposal of some very minor booty taken in Benghazi — depending on the story, either a letter from the Italian army commander, Bergonzoli, or the pennant from his staff car — and that Robertson left the dinner in a huff.[49] It was a stupid and childish incident, doing neither party much credit. Given that Robertson had already 'acquired' several choice pieces, including a bronze of Mussolini on horseback and a relief of the Duce (both later presented to the Australian War Memorial), the incident in retrospect appears even more unnecessary.

It was one of those occasions — and there would be a number of others — where his vanity got the better of him and he proved unable to shut up when prudent counsel might suggest he do so. To be fair to him, his desire for public notice always encompassed the troops under his command and, given his experience in the First World War when British commanders generally begrudged publicity to dominion forces, he may have felt it necessary to counter any such tendency. The pity was, that after his performance in the Libyan campaign, he did not need to indulge in theatrics. O'Connor's chief of staff, later Field Marshal Lord Harding and Chief of the Imperial General Staff, described him as:

> *a somewhat flamboyant character with a liking for public notice, but he was also, in my judgement, a competent brigade commander with drive and initiative, and the confidence of troops under his direct command, and of the units, British and Australian, who operated with him or in support of his brigade. His advance through the Jebel and capture of Benghazi was in my opinion carried out in exemplary fashion and with minimum losses.*[50]

Wilmot, who observed him closely, thought him:

> *second to none as an audacious, brilliant, hard-driving leader ... He possesses undoubted brilliance — a fact of which he is not unaware. His eagerness to exercise his talents in a wider field and his sharp intolerance of the shortcomings of others, have made him a target for criticism, and it is unfortunate that these traits have tended to blind his critics to his real ability.*[51]

And undoubtedly he had friends at court. Long noted that the divisional staff 'did all it could to enhance the prestige of Robertson, who was then the one exception to the rule that Staff Corps offrs would not hold comds', and another officer on the divisional headquarters confirms that 'as most of HQ 6 Div were "non staff", there was much cover for Robertson given by Berryman and Vasey — and when applicable Tom Blamey'.[52] Displays of childish egotism put all that at risk.

By late February the brigade had returned to lines around El Gazala, and Robertson left them to go into hospital for surgery to his left leg. Stories soon spread that the problem was varicose veins and that Robertson was really trying to avoid the Greek expedition, then in preparation, and to get himself returned to Australia. Several versions circulated. One had him stating, 'there's nothing wrong with me. I'm going back to Australia. That's where the promotion is'; a variant had Robertson declaring, 'I am a successful commander, and Greece is going to be a disaster. I am not going to Greece.' Blamey's biographer claimed that 'his ungovernable ambition, not lack of personal courage, was his undoing. He was not unwilling to face an enemy but unwilling to face an enemy whom he knew he could not defeat. He talked himself out of the fighting army while nursing varicose veins in Alexandria.'[53] Both Rowell and Vasey thought that Robertson was trying to 'wangle' something also.[54]

There are several problems with this story. The first is that all accounts rely upon only one witness, Lieutenant Colonel K.A. Wills; others supposedly present when Robertson expressed himself in these terms had no recollection of any such conversation.[55] Given that the war in the Pacific was still nine months away, it would have taken considerable prescience to detect advanced career opportunities in Australia at the beginning of 1941, and being shipped back to Australia as medically unfit would not have done a regular officer's career much good in any case — as Robertson was well aware from his experience during the First World War. Varicose veins suggests a minor ailment of almost cosmetic proportions, but in fact Robertson's leg was giving him considerable trouble. It was the same leg which he had broken in Palestine in 1917, and he had injured it again in April 1939 during a sports meeting in Darwin in which he fell while participating in a race. While the clinical condition was indeed varicose veins, the medical records show that he was treated for 'large varicosities ... causing much discomfort', and in need of 'radical treatment'. He was operated on several times, once for blood clots, and spent a month in hospital.[56]

The notion that he would happily abandon his brigade to the trials of the Greek campaign does not do him justice, nor does it fit with the impressions of some of his key subordinates. Dougherty visited him in hospital before embarking for Greece, and discussed the coming campaign. 'Use mines ... plenty of mines — and cover them by fire, always', was his advice; Dougherty knew him as well as anyone, and does not believe the allegation.[57] Like many good Robertson anecdotes, this one took on a life of its own as his enemies used it against him. There is no doubt that it was a very damaging story. George Vasey finally got his wish and received command of the 19th Brigade, and demonstrated all the technical military flair of his predecessor. The soldiers of the brigade showed that they did not believe the story, if indeed they had even heard about it: when Robbie stood on the station at Gaza to welcome them back from Greece and Crete, he was greeted with an enormous cry of 'Robbie, you old bastard' by a throng of men eager to renew acquaintance.[58]

On one point Hetherington was correct — Robertson was now bereft of an active command. By early 1941 the AIF comprised four divisions. The 8th, under Gordon Bennett, was in Malaya; the Australian Corps in the Middle East had three subordinate formations, Morshead's 9th Division, Lavarack's 7th, and Mackay's 6th, recovering from its ordeal in Greece and destined to see no further action in the Mediterranean. He wanted desperately to get back into the fighting, but there were simply no vacant command slots. As a result, Robertson found himself posted to command the AIF reinforcement depot.

A reinforcement training unit had been created in December 1940 to deal with the problem of reinforcements arriving from Australia who in some cases had never fired a service rifle. The majority of them lacked instruction on modern weapons such as the Bren light machine gun. The original commander, Lieutenant Colonel George Wootten of the 2/2nd Battalion, was posted to command a brigade after only a few weeks, and this set the tone of reinforcement training for some months. An infantry battalion absorbed its first reinforcements within three months as a result of normal wastage — sickness, postings, deaths et cetera — which meant that a division required 1350 men every three months regardless of battle casualties. The 6th Division went into action at Bardia with a full complement of reinforcements behind it, but the Libyan campaign soon consumed this reservoir of trained manpower. There were various problems within the AIF base organisation as a whole, leading Blamey to describe its function as 'to take in one another's washing'.[59] In late January, with the Libyan campaign in full swing, the decision was made to reorganise and expand the training units into the Australian Imperial Force Reinforcement Depot (Middle East), to be based south of Gaza. At this stage, Blamey expected still that the 8th Division would eventually move to the Middle East, and the depot was to be capable of supporting a corps of four divisions, holding and training two months' reinforcements for all units.[60]

The poor training of early reinforcements was not a problem confined to the AIF, by any means. In general, training in the British army was inadequate until nearly halfway through the war. It was mostly a matter for divisional commands, as it had been in the previous war and this, together with the fact that the dominion and empire troops tended to go their own way, meant that there was little standardisation. As late as 1942, one British divisional commander in the desert bemoaned the 'many examples of the limitations of the battle training being given to infantry and armoured formations and even to individuals in the United Kingdom'.[61] AIF headquarters surveyed its technical branches on the subject, and found general dissatisfaction. Reinforcements to medical units 'were notable for the lack of standardisation in their training ... Men of an older age group are common. These men are quite suitable for Base and L of C units but unsuitable for field units. The stretcher bearer in a Field Ambulance has to be young and fit.' Engineer reinforcements were 'insufficient in numbers and inadequately trained ... They are at first a liability rather than an asset to the unit they reinforce.' The standard of artillery officer reinforcement 'on the whole is definitely below requirements on the practical side ... there is much room for improvement in regard both to the type selected and the standard of training achieved'.[62] Things were no better in the infantry. 'Soon after our arrival in the Middle East my Battalion offloaded into the Reinforcement Training Battalion most, if not all, of our "no-hopers"! It didn't take us long to see the error of our ways. That approach to the matter was a very common one and one that most, if not all, frontline units who tried it soon came to regret.'[63]

The training depot comprised the 6th, 7th and 9th Infantry Training Brigades (one per division), made up of three training battalions, one for each brigade. There were in addition training battalions or groups for artillery, engineers, armour, signals, pioneers, machine guns, medical and service corps units, and a reinforcement officers' school.[64] Headquarters was at Julis in Palestine. The staff comprised a brigadier in command, eighteen officers and sixty-nine other rank instructors. On Anzac Day 1941, Robertson took up his appointment as the 'terror of the training battalions'.

He was of course ideally suited to the post, with many years of experience as a trainer of troops behind him, together with very recent experience of active service in the desert under the conditions of the current war, as well as the previous one. There were those who saw the job as a punishment, but Robertson's own feelings were ambivalent. Above all, of course, he wished fervently for an active command.[65] On the other hand, he regarded the training of troops as a matter vital to the success of any army, and prided himself on his reputation as a formidable trainer, a reputation which even his critics conceded. On his first day he was shooting off memoranda to higher headquarters, asking for full distribution of all general staff instructions, not just those confined to training matters, so that 'depot staff and rnfct officers may be kept informed on all subjects ... reports of field formations would be of inestimable value in keeping abreast of training requirements'.[66] As he quickly found, there was much to be done.

The problems were numerous. Some formations failed to appoint training staff to the depot at all. Accommodation was incomplete, and the shortage of equipment in the field units was reflected in the training units. Although the permanent camps south of Gaza were to have been completed in March, construction was still underway in May, further disrupting the programme. Discipline among the reinforcements was poor, but worst of all was the attitude towards reinforcement training manifested by some of the field formations.

> *Generally it is regarded as a punishment and degradation to be sent here from a front line unit, and undoubtedly some of the people sent were in that category. It would help if I could get a clear picture of my powers. As far as I can judge I have none and can merely be a post office. I don't like the place but am always prepared to have a shot at any job while I am in it if I can get the support I need, and I am sure a talk with you [Blamey] would clear up many things and enable me to organise a proper programme. I am very well and itching for work.*[67]

Blamey sent Rowell down to ascertain Robertson's needs, writing in reply that he was 'very much concerned over your difficulties in getting a high standard of discipline into the reinforcements'.[68]

With characteristic vigour, Robertson turned the training organisation upside down and rebuilt it from first principles. He drew attention to 'the necessity of living hard and practising to live hard if we are to have any success against a hard and ruthless enemy'.[69] Drawing on his experience in Palestine with the 19th Brigade, he directed training units to make use of out-of-camp training; 'by stopping out one or two nights in these different areas, variety is introduced, interest is maintained and serious faults in training and administration and command are brought to light'.[70] The training units 'are the servants of the fighting units. Their task is to supply, on demand, drafts of trained officers and other ranks to replace casualties in the fighting units . . . fighting units [must] confidently face the enemy and proceed with their battles undisturbed by problems (which are not properly theirs) of training and equipping their reinforcements'.[71] Full use was to be made of every day, and the length of the training day was increased. Firm measures were taken to improve discipline, backed by an extract from Caesar, the impact of which can only be guessed at.[72]

In July a liaison officer was sent back to Australia to advise on training needs for reinforcements before they left Australia, and Robertson wrote on present inadequacies. Officer reinforcements still contained a proportion of men who were too old, poorly trained, or unsuitable generally, and the shortage of officers in the AIF at large made this a pressing problem. A proportion of the other ranks likewise were over-age; two applicants for transfer to a guard battalion had only been in the theatre six weeks, but were fifty-two years of age. Problems continued with the standard of training received before embarkation, and with a lack of documentation on training standards achieved in each draft. The undesirable element continued to manifest itself, re-enlisting under assumed names after being returned to Australia as unsuitable; the only solution, Robertson felt, was a fingerprint system. Overall, he thought that there was no need for special training missions or even specific instructions to be dispatched back to Australia, if only the authorities in Australia 'will complete individual training, drill, etc, as set out in training manuals and complete SAA courses'. The training units could then add the acclimatisation and general hardening which new arrivals would need before being posted on to units in the front line.[73]

Robertson's view on the state of training in the army was summed up later in a letter to the official historian, Gavin Long. 'I hope you will tell the truth about training', he wrote. 'We really had none until of late and our effort at the last Olympic Games showed that we don't tackle it properly even for sport. If we would only learn from other people it would help us, but I am afraid we will have to get a drubbing in our own country before we really learn.'[74] The equipment and preparation deficiencies which continued to plague the AIF concerned him. As he wrote to one old friend in Australia, 'You can't train without the stuff, and we must have more stuff. I have been brutal and have cleaned up a lot of things here but there remain masses of all kinds of things armies need if my work is going to be worth anything in the near future.'[75] Another element of his philosophy on the subject was reflected by one of his instructors, Gavin Long's younger brother. 'Even that "born soldier" the Aust needs extensive tng. We had a Bn parade thrust upon us today [and] Robertson reviewed the boys and said goodbye before they were sent to the units. They have certainly improved, are tougher to say the least of it, [and] still keen.'[76] Chester Wilmot, whose roving eye missed very little, thought Robertson's period with the reinforcement depot an outstanding success. 'He built up the AIF Reinforcement Depot from little more than a drafting camp to a first-class training centre, which General Auchinleck took as a model for all Middle East forces ... In the task of making soldiers he may be right in thinking there is no place for the gloved hand and the soft tongue. Certainly his methods have produced outstanding results.'[77]

Where previously there had been muddle and lack of a system, he imposed strict standards and orderly procedures, geared always to the needs of the forward units.[78] He ensured a constant rotation of high-calibre instructors from the units to which trainees would be sent, in order that they should receive the best and latest information on the conditions which they would face. As he wrote in the training syllabus:

> *It is a principle of army organisation that a unit in battle should never have to worry about the supply of reinforcements or ammunition. Both are sent forward from the rear and both must be ready for instant use. Everyone on the staff of the AIF Reinforcement Depot should therefore ask himself the following questions: 'Am I fulfilling my task?' 'Will the men I send be ready in every way to take their places in sections of the fighting units and be able to endure all the physical stress of war?'*

The aim of all training must be to 'clothe, arm, equip and toughen these men ... give them a refresher in weapons, and send them forward ready in every way to fight'. One officer commented of his methods that 'he knew soldiering "from the man upwards". He knew what skills were needed to survive and be an effective soldier. . . He "got around" and was not slow to correct mistakes or sloppiness.' Echoing some of Robertson's own judgements on training, this officer thought that 'his standards undoubtedly were high in an Army which, in 1941, was not as skilled and battle experienced as it became'.[79]

All this kept him busy, although he found time to play the odd game of tennis and, as befitted a former light horseman, kept some horses to ride 'so life is not unpleasant'.[80] But above everything else he hankered after an active command; 'considering I am the only man in the AIF with real knowledge and experience of Syria I don't call it falling on my feet to be stuck here when our troops are trying to push into Syria. Added to which I proved in Libya that for speedy movement and seizing chances my show could lick all the others.'[81] The frustrations of being sidelined from the 'real' war had done nothing to curb his vanity, but as 1941 drew to a close his chances of regaining an active command improved.

Back in Australia moves were afoot to create an armoured division for the AIF, and as early as July 1941 Army Headquarters had asked Blamey to indicate the numbers of officers and NCOs he could make available for the nucleus of the formation.[82] Robertson himself had been advocating the creation of just such a division, with himself in command, naturally, but nothing further came of this move for some months. In October Blamey responded to a further request for the return of experienced senior officers to Australia by suggesting him for a posting at Army Headquarters in Melbourne. After declining to send either Vasey or Bridgeford, he wrote of Robertson that 'he is doing first-class work commanding training depots and I do NOT wish to lose him but he broke down through leg trouble after Libyan campaign and I consider absolute physical fitness essential for command of brigade in the field.' Sturdee, now Chief of the General Staff, declined the offer, noting that he did 'not question Robertson's ability but feel he would be a disquieting influence at Army HQ which is now working harmoniously. Have always found him at his best in a semi-independent appointment rather than as one of a team.'[83] The brief exchange is revealing for the light it sheds on the nature of his hospitalisation and Blamey's attitude towards him, together with a shrewd assessment by Sturdee, who had known him since the early 1920s. At about this time Mackay noted also that he was 'at present in an important position to which his training is suited [and is] unlikely to take with zest the training of a new brigade. Has highest ambitions.'[84]

His ambitions now came closer to being realised. The outbreak of war in the Pacific altered radically the assumptions of army planners. Just as the 8th Division was now certain never to join the Australian Corps in the Middle East, so too the requirement in Australia for fit young senior officers with recent war experience became a matter of utmost priority. 'You will appreciate our needs now', wrote Sturdee to Blamey four days after Pearl Harbor, 'and I would be glad if action could be taken earliest date as regards return of personnel already asked for ... by fastest route.'[85] There followed a dozen names, including Robertson's, and the comment that he was marked for appointment 'with probably higher status'. In fact,

War Cabinet quickly approved his promotion to the rank of major general and command of the 1st Cavalry Division, which was to be mechanised and turned into an armoured formation.[86] Blamey's biographer notes that he 'was not eager to spare any of them, with the probable exception of the thrustful and self-seeking Robertson, but Australia's need was beyond question'.[87] This was unfair to Blamey, who appreciated Robertson's abilities however much he may have desired to take him down a peg. If armoured formations were forming for the possible defence of mainland Australia against Japanese attack then Robertson, with both a cavalry and a tank background, was the ideal man to command one.

He relinquished command of the training depot on 17 December and was back in Australia before Christmas. He travelled home by flying boat via Rangoon and Singapore, and spent most of the journey in earnest conversation with Lieutenant General Sir Henry Pownall, a fellow student from Camberley days now heading out to replace Air Chief Marshal Sir Robert Brooke-Popham as Commander-in-Chief, Far East. Ironically, they almost served together again. Within a fortnight of arriving in Singapore, Pownall was superseded by Wavell, who was appointed to head the ill-fated and short-lived ABDA (American, British, Dutch, Australian) Command, thrown together hurriedly at the ARCADIA Conference in Washington in response to the Japanese onslaught. Pownall became chief of staff to Wavell, who asked the Australians for Robertson as AQ, or senior administrative staff officer, on his headquarters. Sturdee declined to release him, and referred the request to Blamey in the Middle East, who sent Colonel C.E.M. 'Gaffer' Lloyd instead. ABDACOM collapsed soon after, and Lloyd was back in Australia by the middle of the following March.[88]

A journalist travelling with the party to Singapore described Robertson as 'a rambunctious and restless spirit [and] argumentative ... an ebullient Australian of the most likable sort [who] would take on anybody, at anything, anywhere'.[89] His high spirits certainly require little imagining. His service in the Middle East had brought with it a setback, but this had proved temporary. 'We are doing our best to be late for everything in this war', he had written earlier to Ernest White. 'We started too late and we still seem to be talking in Australia as if the enemy will wait for us to get ready.'[90] All this had changed, or was rapidly changing, and with the prospect of commanding an armoured division as he had long desired there seemed little he might not accomplish. The next three and a half years, however, were to bring their full measure of doubts and disappointments.

CHAPTER 5

'A TURBULENT SUBORDINATE': 1942-1946

Although Australia had been at war for over two years, the army was poorly prepared for the conflict against Japan when it finally came in December 1941. There were no operational forces available, and shortages of almost every imaginable item of military equipment. Recruitment for the AIF itself had tailed off, and the militia was alternating between periods of 'call up' and 'stand down', while many of its best officers were overseas in any case. The conservative government had fallen in October 1941, and was replaced by a Labor administration under John Curtin which had been in opposition for a decade and which was very short on experience of military affairs in particular. Major General S. F. Rowell had returned to Australia in September to take up the post of Deputy Chief of the General Staff, and found 'the most unwarranted optimism in some political and departmental circles. Indeed, the public at large seemed oblivious to the dangers that lay ahead, and they were given no warning by the political authorities.'[1]

Thus the Japanese onslaught in Southeast Asia was a profound shock to Australian sensibilities, and the reactions among the public and in some government circles were less than edifying. Mackay had been brought back in September, appointed General Officer Commanding-in-Chief, Home Forces, but in three months he could not hope to make good the deficiencies brought about by twenty years of government neglect of Australia's defence. In the days immediately following the outbreak of war and the sinking of the *Prince of Wales* and the *Repulse*, the powers of the Minister for Defence were increased and an additional 100,000 men were called up into the militia. But the first half of 1942 was a time of successive disasters to allied arms, and the very fate of Australia seemed to hang in the balance.

At the war's outbreak, there were 132,000 troops of the Australian Military Forces available immediately for home defence, spread around the country but with concentrations in the major seaboard cities of the southeast. By January 1942 this had increased to 205,431. The state of training and equipment varied widely, but within the first few months of the year equipment improved steadily as production in Australian factories increased. While many of those who commanded CMF units and formations were too old for active service, and drew their ideas from their experience in the Great War, in general this did not affect the normal level of training which units received, although how well it prepared them for combat in the terrain and climate of New Guinea was altogether another matter. But then in the first half of 1942 attention focused as much on the problems of defending Australia itself as it did on the defence of her northern territories.[2]

As part of the urgent preparations against a possible Japanese invasion, the recently-returned senior officers from the AIF were placed in new commands with the task of preparing for the defence of Australia. Many good and able older militia officers found their services dispensed with, often through no fault of their own. On 5 January 1942 Robertson took over as General Officer Commanding 1st Cavalry Division, displacing Major General J. D. Richardson. Like many in his situation, the latter was transferred to the unattached list, but unlike some others he arrived at his headquarters on the morning in question to find his successor already established. This was entirely the fault of Headquarters, Eastern Command, which had failed to inform Richardson of the date of the relief, but the incident served to heighten the unease felt by many older officers. Richardson wrote that he had 'regretfully accepted as sound the policy of placing young men in higher commands, but dismissal at 24 hours' notice in such a manner as this, seems small recompense for thirty years of service and leaves an unpleasant memory'.[3] It should perhaps be noted in passing, however, that Richardson, too, had quarrelled with the Staff Corps before the war, in his case over the details of light horse training during the 1920s.[4]

Earlier, he had written as clear an exposition as could be had of the problems which had faced the militia remaining in Australia. Many militia officers had not been permitted to resign and enlist in the AIF, but had given up business and other commitments to answer the call-up in 1939. There were shortcomings in the training of the militia, but these could be explained by the 'appalling lack of arms, equipment and transport, which the Militia units cheerfully did without in order that the Middle East and Malaya might have plenty'. Serving militia officers had done the best they could with what they had, but existing army orders and the fact that Australia itself was not threatened did not permit the same level of activity as 'could be got away with' in the AIF overseas. 'More and more officers and NCOs with present war experience would be welcome to guide and train the forces in Australia', he concluded, 'but not to displace officers who have done and are doing excellent work ... the officers and men in the home forces in Australia do not differ in quality or fighting spirit from the AIF and should be given their chance.'5

The 1st Cavalry Division was being motorised and became the 1st Australian Motor Division, a light mechanised division, although by mid-1942 it had under command only a single motor brigade, having lost other units to form the new 3rd Australian Army Tank Brigade. After neglecting mechanisation and motorisation in the army between the wars, the authorities now went overboard in the other direction and began to raise no fewer than three armoured or motor divisions and several army tank brigades, despite the fact that Australia possessed few armoured vehicles at the beginning of the Pacific war, and did not at that time have an indigenous motor vehicle industry. The 1st Armoured Division, which had begun to form in July 1941, was intended for overseas service with the AIF in the Middle East in line with British emphasis on the creation of armoured formations in that theatre. The Pacific war put paid to that idea, but in retrospect the formation of so many mechanised divisions with their heavy demands for skilled personnel and equipment does not appear to have been well thought through. As we shall see, none served outside Australia as complete formations.

The return of so many senior officers from the Middle East, and the atmosphere of panic which pervaded Australian affairs in early 1942, led to a renewed bout of intriguing among the senior ranks of the army, culminating in what is sometimes referred to, rather grandiloquently, as the 'revolt of the generals'. As might be expected, Horace Robertson was at the centre of it, although probably not as a conspirator. To the frictions of the preceding decades were added a number of specific events which touched the whole thing off, among them the fall of Singapore and the loss of the 8th Division, followed by the bombing of Darwin. The AIF was still in the Middle East or somewhere on the high seas, as was Blamey. The latter had been recalled to become the Commander-in-Chief of the Australian Military Forces, although the appointment had not been made public. The clash of personalities in the army had been sharpened by events in the Mediterranean theatre, especially during the disastrous Greek campaign, and the return of General Gordon Bennett from Singapore, without his troops, merely added to the tensions.

In mid-March a small group of senior officers approached the Minister for the Army, Frank Forde, and urged that Robertson should be made commander-in-chief and that all officers over the age of fifty should be retired. The chief conspirators were Vasey, Herring and Brigadier Clive Steele, Chief Engineer of I Australian Corps in the Middle East, although they represented a group larger than themselves. They had three principal concerns. The first was the state of morale in Australia and this extended to fears arising from the inexperience of the Labor government;

they also believed that the wrong man was about to be appointed as commander-in-chief. The wrong man was likely either to be Bennett, whose abandonment of his men had outraged regulars and CMF alike but who was the most senior CMF general on the Army List and was well connected politically in New South Wales, or Lavarack, recently knighted and appointed acting C-in-C on 11 March, but who was considered temperamental and unlikely to tell the government unpalatable truths. The plotting was not anti-Blamey, or even necessarily pro-Robertson, as much as an attempt by some desperately worried if rather naive senior officers to impose a solution to the crisis in Australia's defence.

This was not all there was to it, for Robertson's name was being put forward in other quarters. The general manager of the Bank of New South Wales had commended him for the position at a lunch in Sydney, and so had the Murdoch press. Berryman believed that the whole campaign was masterminded by Murdoch.[6] Robertson himself had met the army minister soon after his return to Australia, and 'with a smile on his face as if he had known me for ten years, said: "Well, I am delighted to meet you, Mr Minister, and I am very glad to be back here in Australia, I can assure you, and I would like you to understand that I am ready to take on any job up to that of Commander-in-Chief".[7] This was entirely in keeping with the views on 'over-age' officers which Robertson had been ill-advised enough to express freely in Sydney after his return, and which had found their way back quickly to Sturdee, the Chief of the General Staff.[8]

Blamey's arrival in Melbourne on 26 March saw the complete collapse of the 'plot', which had had little chance of success in any case. Herring later identified Steele as the prime mover, and described the group's concerns succinctly:

> *If you looked at the local scene you wanted somebody who would catch the public eye as well as exercise the commander's powers well. Robbie filled the first part of the bill at least — he had unlimited confidence in himself, plenty of dash. It wanted something to pull the country together — which MacArthur did but we didn't know he was coming at that time. And at that time the invasion was expected within a few days.*[9]

Herring's biographer notes that their part in the 'revolt' did the principal plotters no harm, and Blamey seems not to have been perturbed by their role, expressing surprise merely at their choice. Herring himself declared subsequently that Robertson would have been entirely unsuitable, although he gave no basis for this change of heart.[10] Lavarack wrote later that Steele was uneven in his judgements, 'up in the air at one moment, and down in the dumps the next', a view with which Berryman agreed.[11] More junior officers were divided in their views. Lieutenant Colonel Ragnar Garrett, a Duntroon graduate who served under Robertson on the headquarters of the armoured division and was later Chief of the General

Staff, thought that for all his talents 'he would not have done [as C-in-C]. He could never bear anybody above him — not even a prime minister'.[12] Lieutenant Colonel Denzil Macarthur-Onslow, a CMF officer who had commanded the 6th Division Cavalry Regiment in North Africa and would command an armoured brigade under Robertson, disagreed. In his view only Robertson, Berryman or Herring possessed 'the strength, brains and integrity' for the post of C-in-C, although Gavin Long thought that he too closely echoed Robertson's own views in the matter.[13]

Rowell's role in the whole business was equivocal. When Vasey came to him with details of the plot, he threatened to throw him out, and went straight to Sturdee with the information. His own relations with Blamey had sunk very low indeed after the Greek campaign, and he took to writing disparagingly of 'the lord' in his private correspondence.[14] When Blamey sacked him from command of I Corps in New Guinea in September that year, his loyalty in the 'revolt' was advanced in mitigation to Blamey, who observed nastily that Rowell's behaviour had been prompted by the fact that it was Robertson and not himself who was being put forward.[15] Rowell's own view of Robertson is epitomised in his explanation to John Hetherington:

> *Robbie, although in Sydney, was not unaware of what was going on. The thing that really riled me was Vasey saying that 'perhaps Robbie's vices in peace would be virtues in war', to which I replied that 'if meanmindedness and disloyalty could be counted as virtues at any time I might be prepared to go along with him'.*[16]

Blamey now had the unenviable task of smoothing over the rivalries and jealousies which had come publicly to the fore, and of making appointments to commands in the fight with the army's other enemy, the Japanese.[17]

Lavarack was given command of First Australian Army, Steele became Engineer-in-Chief Land Headquarters, Herring was given command of Northern Territory Force and, after Rowell's removal, command of I Corps in New Guinea, and Vasey got first the 6th and then the 7th Division. Bennett, whose ambitions if anything were magnified by his service in Malaya and who schemed after Blamey's position as desperately as anyone, was sent to Western Australia to command III Corps against a possible Japanese invasion on the west coast. Robertson was given command of the 1st Australian Armoured Division in succession to Northcott, who was promoted to command II Corps. Once again, the niceties of relief as they affected Robertson were not observed, and the first Northcott knew of his supersession was conveyed by the evening newspapers.[18] II Corps at that stage had little more than a training establishment, but within a matter of months he was appointed CGS in succession to Sturdee, a post he held for the rest of the war.

We have discussed already the failure of the Australian army to pay much attention to mechanisation between the wars, and the decision to create an armoured division for the AIF in the middle of 1941. As late as November 1941 it was intended that the 1st Armoured Division should proceed to the Middle East, although difficulties were experienced in raising it to war establishment while keeping up the supply of manpower to the infantry divisions already on active service.[19] The decision to begin motorisation of light horse regiments on the militia establishment had been made late in 1940, but the process was a slow one and by April 1941 the most mobile formations in Australia were still horsed cavalry.[20] Even following mechanisation, it was intended that certain light horse units would remain as horsed cavalry for use in areas not suited to motor vehicles. In any case, the speed of mechanisation was dictated by the availability of suitable equipment, of which there was very little. One year later Headquarters, Eastern Command issued instructions that 'one unit per bde will be selected as a first priority and completely issued to WE [war establishment] with all available equipment, weapons and vehicles required. When the units selected ... are completed, second and third priorities in each Bde will be chosen and completed in that order.'[21] When Robertson took over the 1st Cavalry Division he found that the 6th and 15th Motor Regiments, recently converted from light horse roles, were fulfilling operational tasks at Jervis Bay and Coffs Harbour, but possessed between them only twenty-one motor cycles, sixteen vans, three 30-hundredweight and eleven three-ton lorries, and just twenty carriers each.[22]

Because of their deployment on defensive duties along the coast, the units could not be concentrated for training and Robertson reported that 'the brigades and the Division are incapable of functioning satisfactorily as such'. The divisional signals were largely untrained, while the artillery and anti-tank regiments were deployed on wiring parties and the construction of defences, and also were unable to train for their allotted roles.[23] There was an enormous amount to be done, and Robertson felt the lack of younger officers with recent war experience. He tried to get Dougherty sent to him to command a motor brigade, but Dougherty had already been posted as a brigadier to command the 23rd Infantry Brigade, and operations in New Guinea and northern Australia had priority. 'As you can guess I am up to my eyes in it here', wrote Robertson, 'and would give a lot to have a bunch of the youngsters we had out there [in North Africa]'.[24]

On 1 April the announcement was made of Robertson's transfer to command of the 1st Armoured Division, and he arrived to take up the position four days later. At this stage the division comprised the 1st and 2nd Armoured Brigades, of three armoured regiments each, together with an armoured car regiment as divisional troops. A support group, allotted at the beginning of the year, added a field artillery and anti-tank regiments and three motor regiments to the order of battle. Despite the fact that the division had been in existence for nearly a year, there were many deficiencies. In January Northcott had lost four officers from divisional headquarters, two unit commanders and seven other officers to other appointments, as well as a large proportion of 'the best-trained officers, NCOs and other ranks' of two regiments for service overseas.[25] The divisional establishment had been changed, and then changed back again, and the division operated throughout his time as General Officer Commanding without any tanks, which began to arrive just as he was relieved. A further problem, and one which was never fully resolved during the life of the division, was the psychological effect of being marked for overseas service only to have the deployment cancelled, and then to find themselves allotted a lower priority than some militia formations in matters of equipment and manpower.

Northcott had had a difficult job, but several of the division's officers thought that he had not been fully up to the demands of the position, having little command experience and an infantry background only in the First World War.[26] The new GOC cannot have been unaware of the problems he faced, and from the outset he tackled them with his customary energy and verve. The division's two armoured brigades were spread between New South Wales and Victoria, and Robertson got out among his units to see for himself. In late April he visited the 3rd Armoured Brigade in Victoria, observing exercises, attending practice shoots on the tank gunnery range, and inspecting men, vehicles, accommodation, and training. Discipline was sometimes poor, exercises were being conducted without umpires, gunnery practice was hampered by shortages of tank ammunition, and some of the unit officers did not know their jobs.[27] Sunday was made a working day for all units, with church parades to be held 'at such times as are convenient', and a flood of circulars, training memoranda and instructions followed his inspections. In an order of the day he set forth his requirements and his understanding of the task for which they were preparing:

> *The standard needed for a modern battle lasting days or even weeks means that units must be capable of carrying out under fire a variety of manoeuvres and battle movements without any opportunity for rehearsal. That is why we now train and our efforts must be continued until that standard is automatic to us and so is exhibited in every part of our daily work. [The divisional commander] is confident that the Div will reach that standard.*[28]

But there was still a way to go. In the same month a report on the state of readiness of the 1st Armoured Brigade noted the continuing shortages of spare parts and ammunition for the tank guns, and concluded that while the men were fit and discipline was good, 'the brigade could not be used in either a static or mobile role at present'. The lack of spare parts and the capacity of the workshops were severe handicaps; at that stage it would have taken seventeen weeks to complete the routine 100-hour maintenance on the tanks of that single brigade.[29]

By July, Land Headquarters noted that unit training in the division had been completed, but that much brigade and higher training still lay ahead. There was some confusion about equipment states, with the Chief of the General Staff assuming that the division possessed seventy-nine per cent of its tanks and 100 per cent of its motor transport but only eighty per cent of other equipment, while Robertson reported that in fact he possessed only fifty-six per cent of his tank establishment and only forty-five per cent of motor transport. 'All tanks are deficient of many items of vehicle equipment and tools', and the holdings of spare parts, workshop equipment and machine tools remained 'deplorable'.[30] There were personnel problems also. Armoured units required a high standard of personnel; 'The intelligence and team work required . . . is in no way inferior to that required of an aeroplane crew . . . In addition, their work is more arduous and demands greater endurance and they must be skilled in maintenance of their veh[icles] and weapons.'[31] Robertson was aware of a proposal to reorganise the armoured formations in Australia, resulting in an establishment of one armoured and one motorised brigade in each division. His division would be broken up.

> *It is far quicker and more effective to have fewer units and ample reinforcements than numerous units and no reinforcements. Reinforcements can be trained and absorbed in existing units in months whereas new armd units take years to raise and train. . . A further change which appears necessary is the alteration of the policy which recalls to industry to make tanks surplus to our present needs, the only skilled personnel suitable for training to use the tanks which we at present have.*

His argument was to no avail. Both the government and the munitions ministry were committed to both the manufacture and the importation of tanks, and army headquarters saw an organisational solution in the creation of a third armoured division to the problem of deploying armoured formations to both the eastern and western states.[32]

In the interim, however, Robertson resolved to bring his brigades together for intensive training at the divisional level. The intention was to reach operational readiness by 1 November, and a large area of northwestern New South Wales was given over to army manoeuvres. The exercises were intensely practical, aimed at testing the command and administrative systems of the division, the coordination of all arms and the employment of aircraft in cooperation, and lasted for ten weeks.[33] Gavin Long visited the division at Singleton, and thought that

Publicity photograph of Robertson as GOC, 1 Australian Armoured Division, probably late 1942.

their 'bearing, physique and keenness ... was very impressive'.[34] A report in the *Sydney Morning Herald* commented that:

> It is very doubtful if there has ever been an Australian division fitter than this one, or prouder, or keener for action; or a division in which discipline has been crisper and the bearing of officers and men better.[35]

The troops were denied leave in the surrounding towns during the exercise period but absenteeism remained very low, a sign of good discipline helped no doubt by the example of the GOC, who declined to spend time in towns which he had placed out of bounds to his men. Phases of the exercise lasted from three to seven days, with brigade or divisional training interspersed with regimental drills.

Over all operations hung the prospect of reorganisation, and Robertson spoke long and loudly on the subject to Long and any other journalist who cared to listen. Long recorded one of these declamations in his diary:

> *The equipment of the Div cost £20,000,000. The new base workshop organisation alone cost £2,000,000. He emphasised the vital importance of the rear organisation behind the division, of training in moving the whole division about . . . Contrasted the pay of the man who runs this costly organisation with the pay of any other man running twenty million pounds of equipment, with the pay of a coal miner.*

And on another occasion a few weeks later, Robertson warmed again to the theme of the need for skilled manpower and the inadvisability of the reorganisation.

> *[He] emphasised that you can't have armoured divisions without manning it with men of the tradesman type, and asked where these men were going to come from, when the Govt had ordered that every man in the army not engaged in his own trade must be put to civil work. Where was the division going to be used?*[36]

His disquiet was shared by his senior officers. Brigadier Denzil Macarthur-Onslow, commanding the 1st Armoured Brigade, had used his political connections to see Curtin, the Prime Minister, the Minister for the Army, and the Minister for External Affairs, in an effort to save the armoured division. In his view, 'The one, now trained, armd div is to be dispersed for the sake of creating, on paper, three armd divs. There is neither the personnel nor the equipment for these three divs.' The problem, he felt, lay at Land Headquarters, which was 'empty of officers with recent experience of tank warfare — and pretty empty of officers with any recent experience of warfare.'[37]

The exercises were a considerable success, although they involved hard wear on both men and machines — as would actual operations. At the end of September Robertson felt able to report that provided the necessary equipment, spares and reinforcements were provided, the division 'would be capable of carrying out an operational task'.[38] In the view of one of his unit commanders, they were 'the most realistic [exercises] which I have known'.[39] In the judgement of the official history, 'By the spring of 1942 Robertson had trained the division to as near perfection as a formation is likely to achieve without being in action.'[40] On 18 October, towards the end of the divisional manoeuvres, he told a conference of brigade and regimental commanders that the division as they knew it was to be broken up, and that the reorganised 1st Armoured Division was to be sent to Western Australia as part of Gordon Bennett's III Corps. 'Everyone recognised that their chances of ever seeing active operations as a formation were fading away.'[41]

The division was reorganised on a reduced establishment in November and December, and began its move west in January 1943. As the divisional war diary noted, the delay was occasioned by heavy demands on transport facilities and 'presumably, relatively low priority assigned to despatch of 1 Aust Armd Div to WA'.[42] Morale naturally suffered, the soldiers of the division taking the very reasonable view that they had been shunted off as garrison troops. Robertson issued instructions in March and again in April to try and counter these rumours, but one suspects to little avail.[43] Soldiers of the armoured division feel this frustration to this day.[44] His own feelings may be guessed at. One of his senior commanders thought that he 'did not show resentment at the treatment of himself and his division in 1943. He retained the admiration of the best of his officers and men till the disbandment of the armd div.'[45] Forde, the Minister for the Army, recorded later that on a tour of inspection to Western Australia, he met Robertson again who said to him 'They have sent me to the end of Australia to get me out of the road. This is no good to me.'[46] He put it more bluntly to Rowell: 'the old bastard [ie, Blamey] has sent me to the arse-hole end of the country'.[47] The armoured division was gradually whittled down while based at Geraldton, north of Perth, until it was disbanded finally in September 1943. Robertson did what he could for his officers, many of whom were regulars, trying to ensure that their careers were not blighted by service in a backwater. Virtually his last act as GOC was to arrange the despatch of a party of twenty-five officers, mostly Staff Corps, for attachment to the British 7th Armoured Division then fighting in Italy; 'a good investment' in the future of the postwar army thought Gavin Long, 'in which I see the hand of HCHR'.[48]

The Australian government's policy towards the formation of armoured units in the Second World War provides plenty of evidence for the argument that in that war Australia raised its forces in a haphazard manner, and was then faced with the wholesale disbandment of units which should never have been created in the first place. The formation of the 1st Armoured Division in 1941 and 1942 was a sensible measure given the needs of the allies in the Mediterranean, the parlous state of Australia's defences against Japanese invasion and the opportunities which operations in Australia itself would provide for armoured, mobile warfare. By late 1942 it should have been clear that the Japanese neither intended, nor were capable of mounting an invasion of Australia, and the moves made to create additional armoured formations and basing them in Australia were a waste of resources which were needed elsewhere. It was a waste of existing assets also, since the 1st Armoured Division had been built up at tremendous cost and was then squandered. It is difficult to disagree with the judgement of the official historian, who wrote that:

> *in retrospect it seems unfortunate, for a variety of reasons, that a more sanguine view of the possibility of the invasion of Australia was not taken in the summer of 1942-43 and that this fine division was not transferred to Africa, perhaps in the transports which brought the 9th Division home, to play a part in the coming campaigns there and in Europe'.*[49]

A more recent commentator agrees that 'in retrospect it would appear that the Australian armoured forces were greatly over-expanded'.[50] The 1st Armoured Brigade remained in Western Australia for the time being, under command of the 2nd Australian Infantry Division.

His station in Western Australia brought Robertson under the command of Gordon Bennett's III Corps, which by early 1943 comprised the armoured division, the 2nd Division, commanded by Major General H.W. Lloyd, and the Western Australia Lines of Communication Area, the supporting base headquarters under the command of Brigadier O.V. Hoad. Lloyd and Hoad were both regulars, although not graduates of Duntroon, and, given Bennett's detestation of the Staff Corps, relations within this command must have been less than harmonious. In early 1942 the threat of invasion had made the Western Australian command an important one, but as the threat receded it became obvious that Blamey, and indeed many other senior officers, would not tolerate Bennett's appointment to a senior active command against the Japanese after his flight from Singapore, and so the latter languished. Negative views of Bennett crossed the divide between Staff Corps and militia, and Major General Jack Stevens, a CMF officer, recorded that when he was sent to command the 4th Division in Western Australia Rowell had informed him, 'You're the only one we could find who would serve under Bennett without kicking up a fuss.'[51]

The period in Western Australia was not an easy one for Robertson. On top of personal disappointment at his relegation to the periphery of military activity, his relations with Bennett were never more than correct, and more often were poisonous. Hetherington noted the emotional tension between them,[52] and Garrett wrote later that 'with Bennett intriguing against Blamey and Robbie intriguing against both of them, the situation in WA was not altogether happy'.[53] Blamey was well aware of the tensions and jealousies in III Corps, and once remarked to Brigadier C.M.L. Elliott that he had thought that 'those two red-headed bastards would cut one another's throats'.[54] Bennett did everything in his power to get rid of Robertson; when the armoured division was broken up he made remonstrations to Blamey that Robertson should be posted out of his command. Blamey's response was to appoint him to the command of the 2nd Division, which now became the only field formation in the west.[55] Bennett then returned to the attack, arguing that Major General Lloyd had been treated unjustly. Blamey replied that since the 2nd Division would retain a motor brigade from the armoured division under command, 'it [seemed] advisable to retain in Western Australia for the present at least the commander who has had the greatest experience with Armd training'.[56] Getting nowhere with this, Bennett then tried to abolish the motor brigade and have it converted to infantry and, when that failed, began to make complaints about the competence and efficiency of its commander, Brigadier F.E. Wells, a Robertson appointment and a Staff Corps officer.[57]

There can be little doubt that Blamey was keeping two of his most troublesome rivals well out of the way, nor that when it came to a choice, he would back the more able Robertson against the discredited Bennett. Colonel Eugene Gorman, Chief Inspector of Administration at Land Headquarters and an old friend, advised Blamey to either 'conciliate or exterminate' the dissidents within the senior officer corps, but Blamey preferred simply to play them off against each other.[58] Bennett finally gave Blamey the excuse for which he had been waiting by demanding an active command and threatening to resign if it was not granted. His resignation was accepted.[59]

Robertson, who had been given command of the 3rd Division in February because the 2nd Division 'had practically ceased to exist, the units comprising it being absorbed in other formations', had not yet taken it up,[60] and was now given temporary command of III Corps. This was bad luck, since although Western Australia was a corps command, at least nominally, the 3rd Division was a frontline formation based on the Atherton Tableland in Queensland, where it was to undergo retraining before again seeing action on Bougainville.[61] There was irony for Robertson in the fact that Savige had commanded the 3rd Division in the bitter fighting in New Guinea, and had now been appointed to the command of II Corps. Major General William Bridgeford got the 3rd Division instead.

Relative idleness and the disappointments of his circumstances did not translate into a diminution of his usual exacting standards or fearsome drive. One medical officer in charge of a convalescent depot recorded a tour of inspection by the General Officer Commanding in mid-1944 which captured perfectly all the elements of Robertson's style of command. Having been tipped off that the general was in the area,

> *true to form* ... *'Red Robbie' duly swooped upon us like a tornado but the gate sentries were ready, saluted smartly and paid all the required compliments. Later, in the mess, in conversation with me I noticed that he was, theoretically at least, very much 'au fait' with the running of an army convalescent depot. He had apparently done his homework* ... *Among other things he said that last year my convalescent depot had made him 'sick'. He looked pretty hale and hearty today with no apparent signs of nausea, so I assumed that we had passed muster* ... *Finally, having reduced us all to impotent, quivering jellies he and his entourage took their departure as quickly as they had arrived.*

And he noted, only half in jest, that 'later that day . . . but almost as an anti-climax, we heard the news of the Normandy landings'.[62]

But a high level of activity was no compensation for the feeling that the war was passing him by. In a letter to Berryman after the latter had been appointed to command of I Australian Corps, he complained that he was

> not very pleased at being left in the cold myself, and I have been so very long away from a fight that I am almost despairing of getting one again. Some influence which I don't understand always seems to be working against me and the more I try to counteract it the worse it becomes . . . As a result I am well and truly in the discard and have not even the compensation of being able to save a little money by avoiding income tax as I have been paying over £500 a year since I came back. I also seem to miss all the ribbons.

And in a characteristic note of Staff Corps solidarity, he concluded with the comment that 'even if I have to bury all my hopes I am glad you have got a chance (I have no fears that you will fail us) and get Duntroon at last on top'.[63]

An additional factor in his continued relegation to the sidelines has generally been overlooked, however, and that was the state of his health. In February 1943 Blamey had issued a detailed instruction that 'all officers holding high rank in the Army should be medically fit and under existing conditions this fitness should include a) fitness for active service b) fitness for service in the tropics'.[64] This reflected his longstanding belief, formulated in North Africa, that all senior officers must be in peak physical condition, and reinforced his view that a fit general of fifty-eight was the equal of a fit general of forty-eight (a position with which Robertson publicly disagreed, as we have seen). The simple fact is that in the middle of 1944 Robertson was not only not fit for active service, he was in fact seriously ill. On 26 July he was admitted to No 110 Military Hospital with internal haemorrhaging, probably of the duodenum, and was in hospital for a month. He required several blood transfusions and was on the seriously ill list for nearly a fortnight.[65] After release from hospital, he travelled to the eastern states to convalesce.

Major General George Vasey, back in Australia from commanding the 7th Division in New Guinea, was also recuperating after acute polyneuritis. In October that year, together with the Commandant of the Royal Military College, Brigadier Bertrand Combes, they were approached by the Chief of the General Staff, Northcott, to conduct an inquiry into the future organisation and training of Duntroon. The idea seems to have originated with Blamey, who was thinking ahead to the postwar organisation of the forces and who may have felt that certain of the practices at RMC were in need of overhaul.[66] The committee finalised its report on 30 November, although it was not presented to Blamey until the following January.[67]

It was scarcely a hostile committee, since all three members were Duntroon graduates, and its findings were sensible, forward-looking and, no doubt in the view of some CMF officers, geared to protecting the place of the regulars in the postwar army. Among the recommendations were that Duntroon's curriculum should be upgraded to university degree status — which was not to happen for more than two decades — and that higher calibre staff be posted to the college, rather than personnel chosen on a basis of availability and convenience as had often been the case. Perhaps the most important aspects of the committee's findings were that graduates entering the army should be appointed to regimental postings in permanent units, and that officers below the rank of lieutenant colonel should be alternated between staff and regimental duties. This predicated a standing regular army along the lines recommended by Squires just before the war.

A regular army run by the professional military was dear to the hearts of all those Staff Corps officers who had suffered the cutbacks and frustrations of the interwar decades. As the war seemed to be nearing its end, the senior members of the regular establishment made it clear that they would not accept again the slighting treatment accorded them in the aftermath of the last war, nor see their juniors so treated, and in 1944 established a section in the Adjutant General's department to oversee command postings in the postwar army.[68] Gavin Long turned his mind to the problem in late 1943, noting that 'the time has come to take a long view of the staff corps, and send these [younger] officers who have little or no active regimental service into regiments before it is too late. Otherwise, after the war, for years the army will be run by officers who have not a fraction of the active service in bns and regts that the last war generation of Duntrooners had.'[69] On another occasion, while discussing Allen's strengths and weaknesses as a commander, he wrote that:

> *the regular officer is inclined to say that a militia officer can rise to command of a unit, and succeed in such a command, but that commands of formations should as a rule be reserved for professional officers. The coordination of all arms and the staff work is [a] task beyond all but the most exceptional amateur officers . . . Allen is probably a case in point — a fine colonel, a better brig than div comd, and not a suitable corps comd.*[70]

In Long's view the outstanding divisional commanders of the war were Vasey, Wootten and Robertson, all Duntroon graduates. Savige was another case in point. Berryman thought his two major attacks as a divisional commander in New Guinea were 'NBG [no bloody good]', while Rowell held that he 'lacks the rudiments of manoeuvre above a company', and even officers better disposed towards him thought him very reliant upon his gifted GSO 1, Colonel J.G.N. Wilton, a Duntroon graduate of 1930.[71]

Robertson returned to Western Australia and supervised the gradual rundown of his command, which by the end of 1944 had been reduced almost to nothing. At this late stage of the war Blamey had six formations under command: First Army, based at Lae, Second Army, in reserve in Australia, I Corps, retraining on the Atherton Tableland, the 11th Division, a reserve formation in Queensland with no units under command, Northern Territory Force, with one brigade, and Western Command. The pressures to redeploy available manpower to agriculture and industry, together with the allied advances to the north and the end of any invasion threat to Australian territory, saw the rapid rundown of those remaining reserve and defensive units based in Australia.[72] At a stage when it must have seemed that further active command in this war would pass him by, Robertson was posted as GOC of the 5th Division in New Guinea on 4 April.

The circumstances of the reshuffle in divisional commands was tinged with sadness, for it arose through Vasey's death in an aircraft crash off the Queensland coast as he was returning to the 6th Division. They had been good, rather than close, friends of long standing, and had each admired the strengths of the other. Vasey had been a defender of Robertson's in the previous eighteen months, going so far as to tell Prime Minister Curtin on one occasion that he would happily serve under Robertson as a corps commander, so highly did he think of his abilities, and that together the two of them would 'remake the army' after the war.[73] After the accident, Major General Jack Stevens remained with the 6th Division for a time, and Robertson took over from Major General A.H. Ramsay, who was given the 11th Division on Bougainville.

Robertson's appointment may have owed something to the pressure under which Blamey had found himself at the beginning of the year, when Senator Foll of Queensland had raised the issue of the dispositions of the army. The fates of Rowell, Lavarack and Bennett were raised in the parliament, as was Robertson's: 'well known as a dashing commander in the Middle East . . . He was sent home and put on the shelf, never to lead his men again. What is the use pretending that all is well with our army in the light of these things?'[74] Blamey defended himself stoutly, pointing out that in the crisis of 1942 all those named had held important posts for the defence of the country should the Japanese attempt an invasion.[75] This was true, but it rather avoided the issue of their subsequent employment; Lavarack heading the Australian Military Mission in Washington, Rowell banished to a make-work job in the Middle East and then in the War Office, Robertson, as we have seen, nursing his ego and on occasions his health in Western Australia. Berryman, who managed to juggle loyalty to Blamey as his chief of staff with tribal loyalties in the army, thought later that:

> *at this time [1943] Morshead, Lavarack and Northcott had had no experience in operations in New Guinea nor had their staffs and at this stage I think General Blamey was wise in sticking to Herring and Mackay. At a later date when I took over II Corps from General Morshead I was surprised that so many senior members of the corps staff were still thinking in terms of Alamein and not New Guinea where the problems were totally different.*[76]

Returning Robertson to active service was nonetheless a useful way of mollifying the critics within and without the army.

The 5th Division was a militia formation, although this designation increasingly meant less as the war went on because militia units which volunteered to serve outside the tightly circumscribed geographical limits laid down by the *Defence Act* were known as AIF. The original units of the division were militia ones, and had seen hard fighting at Salamaua, Alexishafen, Hansa Bay and in the Sepik River valley. In October the previous year they had been moved to New Britain, and Robertson joined the headquarters at Jacquinot Bay on 21 April 1945.[77] As a result of MacArthur's decision that only American units would take part in the reconquest of the Philippines, the Australian army found itself in the last months of the Pacific war engaged in secondary operations against Japanese forces which had been cut off from the rest of their positions in south-east Asia. These campaigns were, and remain highly contentious, since it has been argued that there was little strategic justification for fighting enemy forces which were now incapable of any sustained offensive activity and which should merely have been 'held' and allowed to 'wither on the vine'.[78]

Ramsay had employed one brigade at a time to secure the central part of the island and maintain ascendancy over the estimated 50,000 Japanese troops isolated there. He had wanted to step up operations in order to maintain morale and fighting efficiency, but Blamey ordered that such operations were to be cleared with him through Sturdee before being undertaken, since they might 'involve demand for further resources which cannot be met'.[79] By the time Robertson took over command, the division was involved in semi-static operations designed to keep the enemy confined to the area of the Gazelle Peninsula. The emphasis was placed on the maintenance of physical fitness, morale and thoroughness in training, and Robertson visited his brigades each day, usually the one(s) in action on that occasion. From time to time he would visit the battalions in similar circumstances.[80] This was the most successful and least costly of the 'final campaigns', the 5th Division suffering a total of fifty-three killed, twenty-one dead from other causes, and 140 wounded. But as the divisional war diarist noted, 'official wording such as patrol activity continued gives no indication of the rigours of service.

Terrain, weather and virgin jungle country play havoc with equipment and personnel.'[81]

As a result of strong pressure from the government to accept the position of Assistant Public Service Commissioner, Major General J.E.S. Stevens relinquished command of the 6th Division in July and returned to Australia, his post as GOC being taken by Robertson, who was transferred from the 5th Division on 26 July.[82] The 6th Division was in positions around Wewak facing the remnants of the XVIII Japanese Army under General Hatazo Adachi, estimated to number 8850 troops, 3000 of whom were classified as 'base troops'. The 6th Division was badly understrength at this stage of the war, 132 officers and 1966 other ranks below establishment and with 176 officers and 2566 other ranks detached from their units for various reasons.[83] Operations had proved more extensive than originally sanctioned, and had prompted a highly critical report from the acting Minister for the Army, J.M. Fraser, after his visit there in April.[84] Robertson arrived on 1 August and offensive operations by units of the division ceased on 9 August, although defensive positions were maintained for a further four days.

Arriving at his new command, Robertson nearly shared the fate of his friend George Vasey. His own wife was seriously ill in Melbourne, and he arranged to take the flight back to Lae and thence to Australia with Stevens. The aircraft designated for the trip failed to arrive, so the pair hopped an ancient Anson to Madang. On arriving there they found that the Beaufort scheduled to meet them was not available, and Robertson insisted that they continue on to Lae, despite the fact that one of the Anson's engines had been causing trouble. They took off again late in the afternoon and ran into thick cloud over the Ramu valley, finally arriving over Lae in darkness at about 7p.m. Ten minutes later the plane went straight into the sea, between one and two miles (one to three kilometres) offshore. There were no serious injuries and a landing craft arrived about an hour and a half later to pick them out of the water. They spent the night at the 2/7th Australian General Hospital, and Robertson took the Qantas flight to Australia at 5 o'clock the next morning. When he reached Melbourne, however, he was put into Heidelberg Military Hospital for ten days, and did not return to the division until late in the month.[85]

By then the Japanese had surrendered, following the atomic bombings of Hiroshima and Nagasaki. But the surrender of Japanese forces throughout south-east Asia had to await the main surrender in Tokyo Bay, and as a result the troops in operational areas maintained a wary, if more relaxed, eye on the Japanese positions facing them. On 7 September news was received from Sturdee at Headquarters, First Army that the surrender of Adachi's army was to take place no earlier than the following day. Although contacts had been established with the enemy as early as 17 August in an attempt to hasten the formal cessation of hostilities in the area, Adachi refused to surrender without express orders from his superior, General Hitoshi Imamura commanding Eighth Area Army, and this took time. On 10 September Robertson demanded the surrender of the islands which covered Wewak from the sea and the local commander, Rear-Admiral Sato, proffered his sword the same day. On the 13th it was Adachi's turn, and he was flown to Wom airstrip where, at 10 a.m., he signed the instrument of surrender and handed over his sword before 3000 Australian soldiers drawn up on parade. 'I was right-hand subaltern for our battalion and was opposite the surrender table. "Red Robbie" had the Japanese general debus from the jeep at the far end of the airstrip and march through the ranks of 6 Div while the parade was "at ease". [He] was rubbing his hands in glee and positively gloating as Adachi approached.'[86] The proceedings were broadcast on the divisional signals net so that all might hear it, and the GOC ordered the issue of a bottle of beer per man to mark the occasion. Berryman noted to Mackay that the surrenders in the Australian areas had all gone smoothly, 'except that as usual Red Robby seemed to have all the difficulties, in consequence of which he evidently enjoyed the attendant publicity. It would, indeed, be a hard war if we all had such great difficulties as seem to rise up and confront our well-known friend.'[87]

Neither the work nor the problems had lessened, however, merely because the war had ended. The Japanese had to be disarmed and concentrated in POW collection areas on Muschu Island off Wewak. Contrary to intelligence estimates, the XVIII Army was found to be still a relatively cohesive fighting force numbering over 13,000 men.[88] There was also the question of demobilisation and repatriation of the Australian army scattered through the islands. The 6th Division was ordered to scour its area for remaining groups of Japanese troops, and as a result its repatriation was delayed. This led to a drop in morale and what was described by Sturdee at First Army as 'organised criticism of labour troubles and strikes in Australia', which many of the troops blamed for the delay.[89] It had been decided that neither the 6th Division nor any other formation would be repatriated as a formation, but rather that men would be sent home in groups under the long service release system and a scheme of demobilisation 'points' amassed on the basis of length of service, civilian job, marital status, etc.[90] Robertson had done all this before, of course, and understood the feelings of his men. He told Sturdee that the dissatisfaction expressed was 'over time waiting return Australia and impression that shipping disputes responsible that delay. Whole matter mixed up with feeling prevalent formerly that this was forgotten div and tendency to fall back into that frame of mind.'[91]

Once the troops began to move all such problems rapidly disappeared. On 1 October there were some 19,350 personnel still serving in the Pacific, but by 31 December this had been reduced to 10,400, and further

Robertson with Lieutenant General Adachi, Japanese XVIII Army commander, and staff, Wom airstrip, 12 September 1945.

demobilisations were planned at a rate of 1850 a month.[92] On 16 November Robertson was advised that he was to administer command of the First Army; Sturdee had returned to Australia to assume the position of Commander-in-Chief. There were three infantry divisions (3rd, 6th, 11th) in the process of disbandment, plus Nauru Force, the 2/6th Cavalry Commando Regiment, and the 2/4th Armoured Regiment.[93] The concentration and disarming of the Japanese in the First Army area was completed by 31 December, and all former enemy soldiers had been repatriated by 17 January, except for 144 accused of war crimes who were held awaiting trial.[94] By the time Robertson was ready to vacate the command at the beginning of March 1946, First Army had been disbanded.

Ahead lay the organisation of the postwar army and Robertson's appointment as GOC Southern Command in the rank of lieutenant general. Every appointment to the newly-reconstituted Military Board at the beginning of 1946, other than the Chief of the General Staff, as well as the three senior area commands, went to a Duntroon graduate.[95] For the first time in Australia's history, the military professionals were to be the chief source of military advice to the government of the day. The Second World War ensured for the Staff Corps the domination of the postwar army. For the individuals concerned there was to be no repetition of the slights and frustrations experienced after 1921, and instead they could look forward to high rank and appointments.

For Robertson himself the war had been a mixed experience, although he had come out well in the end. He squandered his considerable early advantages through an inability to curb his ego and his tongue. Once out of active command, it proved very difficult to return and his uncertain health was a factor in this, although it is doubtful that he would have returned to active command any earlier had his health been better in 1944. Including the period with the 6th Division at the end of the war, he had commanded at all levels in action for only six months. This did not disadvantage him greatly against his contemporaries who were now running the army, half of whom had spent the majority of their war service in staff and headquarters positions. (Rowell commanded I Corps for just over five months; Berryman had I Corps for only three months, plus a short period as an independent commander in Syria in 1941; Bridgeford was GOC of the 3rd Division for a year. Clowes had led Milne Force and the 11th Division in 1942 and 1943, but spent the rest of the war commanding the Victoria Lines of Communication Area. Only Milford and Boase had commanded in the field for prolonged periods — Milford with the 5th and 7th Divisions, 1942-45, and Boase with the 11th Division for eighteen months, 1943-45. Beavis had occupied senior staff positions for the entire war.)

The adjustment to peacetime conditions was not easy for many, and was not helped by those on both sides of the Staff Corps versus militia divide who could not restrain their antagonism. Many officers who had done well in the war and who, for whatever reason, wished to stay on in the peacetime army, were made to feel that there was 'no room for amateurs'. Robertson at his arrogant worst told one young lieutenant colonel with a good war record and a Military Cross, 'You don't imagine you're a soldier do you? You've never been to a staff school. You've had no military education.' Another, who had also commanded a battalion, was told (not by Robertson) that he might manage a commission as a lieutenant.[96] Blamey spoke out against the domination of the army by Royal Military College graduates and argued that this was inappropriate in what remained a citizen army. He was joined by Savige, who vented his spleen against the Staff Corps by charging that during the war 'a very high percentage of Duntroon graduates . . . not only failed as commanders but also proved inefficient staff officers.'[97] There was an exchange of letters in the papers, which resolved nothing, but the fact was that the tide had shifted in favour of the regulars. The creation of a peacetime regular army in the years immediately after the war was the next step in the eventual reversal of army policy as it had existed since Federation. Now the Citizen Military Forces would exist to augment the regulars, and not the other way around.

PART TWO

The value of 'tact' can be over-emphasised in selecting officers for command: positive personality will evoke a greater response than negative pleasantness.

B. H. Liddell Hart

CHAPTER 6

THE OCCUPATION OF JAPAN: 1945-1946

The Australian army demobilised rapidly with the end of hostilities in the Pacific, and was replaced by the 'interim' army. As is always the case in the aftermath of a great war, the adjustments to the size and scale of the army necessitated reductions in the officer corps, and this presented the military authorities with some problems, since more men wished to stay on in the service than could be accommodated under peacetime establishments. 'The officer position in the AMF ... is at present a very difficult one', noted the Adjutant General's office. 'Maximum economy and efficiency is [to be] effected in the posting of officers, whilst at the same time every possible consideration is given to the officers themselves.'[1] Officers of the Permanent Military Forces who had held commissions prior to 3 September 1939 were to be given preference, followed by those who had been members (ie, other ranks) of the PMF prior to that date but who had obtained commissions during the wartime expansion of the army.

The second problem facing the military authorities was what to do about the large number of senior officers left over by the war. Blamey was retired in November 1945, and many of the senior CMF generals likewise returned to civilian callings at the end of the war, or in some cases even earlier. The Staff Corps generals who remained all held temporary general officer rank; Rowell, Robertson, Berryman, Milford and the others were all still substantive colonels. While the shape of the postwar forces was yet to be decided, the government resolved originally to maintain these senior officers in their temporary generals' ranks. On the other hand Sturdee, the Chief of the General Staff, recommended that all officers who had been promoted to general officer's rank during the war, and who still held that rank at retirement, should transfer to the Reserve of Officers as generals or, in the case of the regulars who were still serving in that rank, should be promoted substantively to it.[2] Approval was forthcoming, since the number involved was small and the conversion of temporary ranks to substantive ones had already been conceded for officers below the rank of major general. Importantly for a government concerned to divest itself of high levels of military expenditure, the move did not involve any increased financial disbursements, since temporary and substantive ranks attracted the same rates of pay and allowances.[3] Thus there was no repetition of the situation after the First World War when reductions in the military establishment had brought savage cutbacks in rank, two moves which ensured the direction of military policy for the next thirty years.

Robertson was promoted substantively to major general, and went off to Southern Command in Victoria as GOC in March. After years of the peripatetic life which servicemen know well, he was to return to his home state and wider family and could expect a more settled existence for the first time in many years. The moment did not last long. Within a month of taking up duty in Melbourne he was nominated to the post of Commander-in-Chief of the British Commonwealth Occupation Force based in southern Japan, in succession to John Northcott, the last of the wartime Australian Chiefs of the General Staff, who had accepted the post of Governor of New South Wales.[4] The Prime Minister, Ben Chifley, decided to delay the changeover in command until June because of his own scheduled visit to Japan in May, and so Robertson was given a few weeks in which to prepare himself for his new duties. Additionally, because the C-in-C was answerable for a multinational force to the various Commonwealth governments which deployed units to Japan, the nomination required the approval of those other governments concerned.

Robertson had been Sturdee's choice for the job, and in the circumstances one is reminded of his observation in 1941 about Robertson's suitability for semi-independent commands. Sturdee had nominated Northcott to Japan also, on that occasion as the price for again taking up the post of CGS. He felt that Northcott had missed the opportunities for overseas service through being tied to Melbourne and saw the post of C-in-C in Japan as a reward for services well and faithfully rendered.[5] When Northcott accepted the governorship of New South Wales, Sturdee informed the government that Robertson was 'the best practical field commander of troops that I can make available'.[6] The appointment may have come as something of a surprise to Robertson. As he wrote to Sir John Latham, former ambassador to Japan, after the posting was announced, 'I did not seek the appointment as I felt that I had wandered enough and it was time for me to try and settle down, but I cannot but feel very proud of having been given it ... I will be very sorry to leave this interesting and very active command but at least I have completed the first phase.'[7] On 5 June 1946 he boarded a Liberator at Laverton air base and departed for Tokyo. Apart from a couple of short periods for leave and government briefings, he was not to return to Australia and the central concerns of the army for over five years.

THE OCCUPATION OF JAPAN: 1945-1946

The role played by Australia in the postwar occupation of Japan illustrates the changes in Commonwealth and international affairs brought about by the Second World War. The collapse of British power in the Far East in 1942 not only heralded the beginning of the end of Britain's role as a great colonial power, but affected fundamentally the ties between the metropolitan centre and its self-governing Pacific territories. Given also the fundamental importance of postwar relations with Japan to modern Australia it seems strange that the first phase of this relationship should have been so completely overlooked by later generations of Australians. The foundation of the modern economic partnership was formed by the 1957 trade agreement, it is true, and to that extent the occupation period may be said to have led nowhere. It may even be the case that the occupation was thought best forgotten since it served only to remind both parties of a war which had ended in a resounding defeat of the Japanese and during which Australian passions had been inflamed by Japanese atrocities committed on Australian POWs. The only significant study of Commonwealth involvement in occupied Japan has noted, however, that 'by its commitment [Australia] demonstrated a new maturity in its Pacific foreign policy. The presence of Australian troops supported Australia's claims to be taken seriously as a regional power.'[8] On another level again it marked a departure for the Australian services, especially the army, which was required to maintain substantial forces overseas in peacetime for the first time in its history, and to take responsibility for policy, command and administration of a combined Commonwealth force. So Australia's involvement in the occupation is not without interest on a number of fronts.

The planning for a Commonwealth role in the occupation of Japan had begun before the Pacific war had ended. Indeed, the first call for volunteers for an Australian brigade had gone out while Robertson had been commanding the 6th Division in New Guinea.[9] Participation in the occupation of Japan was complicated by the fact that while all the major allies sought a role for their forces, the Americans, and MacArthur in particular, were concerned to assert a dominant role for themselves in a theatre in which, as they saw it, they had done all the fighting and borne all the costs. As the Joint Staff Planners of the American Joint Chiefs of Staff succinctly expressed it, 'participation by the Allies should ... be limited to that minimum size necessary to obtain the political objectives of the United States'.[10] MacArthur in particular was concerned to exclude the Soviets from any useful role in postwar Japan but, as during the war itself, his exclusivist views extended to other allies as well, without much distinction being made.

The Americans were not the only ones with political objectives in Japan, and the decisions surrounding the Commonwealth contribution to the occupation force provide some of the earliest evidence for the growing divergence in attitudes between Australia and Britain in the Far East. The original proposal called for an empire force of five brigades, fielded by Britain, India, Canada, Australia and New Zealand, together with air and naval elements, and built on the proposals for participation in Operations OLYMPIC and CORONET, the intended invasions of the Japanese home islands. The sudden surrender of the Japanese and their passive acceptance of the American occupation caught the Commonwealth governments unprepared, and by the time their contingents actually reached Japan some of the initial justification for their presence had disappeared. Successive British governments in 1945 were determined to acquire a military stake in postwar Japanese affairs.[11] The government in Canberra was equally firm in its insistence that Australia would play the leading role in Commonwealth affairs in the Pacific which its role in the war against Japan had earned, and which it was felt had not been sufficiently appreciated by the major belligerents — as indeed it had not.

Canada had no interest in Asia and declined to participate, citing its commitments in Europe as justification. The real barrier to British desires to present a united Commonwealth effort to the Americans came from the Australians who, on 17 August 1945, informed London that any Australian troops sent to Japan would operate separately from the rest of the Commonwealth in an independent role directly under the Supreme Commander for the Allied Powers (SCAP), MacArthur. Chifley told MacArthur that this action was being taken by Australia 'as a separate belligerent of Japan'. There was a range of complex motivations behind the Australian decision, tied up with views about the future roles of smaller states and of Australia in the Pacific,[12] and later observers may be struck by the lack of unanimity in viewpoint between two Labor administrations. Australia's decision to 'go it alone' had serious implications for postwar Commonwealth defence cooperation, and on these grounds alone, the British Chiefs of Staff Committee recommended to Attlee that a renewed approach should be made to Canberra advocating a unified Commonwealth force and offering command of such a force to an Australian senior officer, who would then be responsible to both the Australian and British governments. Sir John Stephenson at the Dominions Office thought the Australians in a 'somewhat truculent mood', and recommended that the matter be discussed personally with the Australian external affairs minister, Dr H.V. Evatt, when he arrived in London in September, but the recommendations of the British Chiefs of Staff prevailed, and Attlee cabled Chifley with the new offer.[13] Initially, this produced no change in the Australian government's attitude, and as late as 12 September Chifley replied to Attlee that his government's intentions remained unchanged.[14] The matter was discussed with Evatt in London, however, and on 21 September Chifley advised acceptance of the British offer, with certain conditions relating to command of the air contingent, the joint control machinery and British representation in Australia.[15]

The Australian suggestion that the command of the Commonwealth air component go to an officer of the Royal Australian Air Force was not accepted by the British, who argued that as the Royal Air Force fielded most of the air force component, and since the Australian proposal would leave them without any senior representation in the British Commonwealth Occupation Force as a whole, the post should go to the RAF. This was agreed, especially when the British Chiefs of Staff conceded the Australian alternative, which was that the chief of staff to the commander-in-chief should come from the RAAF, on the grounds that a commander should always have the major say in the selection of his principal headquarters staff.[16]

As we have noted, initially Northcott was selected as Commander-in-Chief BCOF. The controlling mechanism for the force was a joint Commonwealth body, the Joint Chiefs of Staff in Australia (JCOSA), essentially the Australian Chiefs of Staff augmented by representatives from the British, Indian and New Zealand chiefs of staff, which met in Melbourne. The Australian government conducted all negotiations with the Americans on behalf of the whole, and the discussions leading to American acceptance of the British Commonwealth force in the occupation were conducted in November 1945 by Evatt, the Minister for External Affairs, Sir Frederic Eggleston, the Australian Minister to the United States of America, and the head of the Australian Military Mission in Washington, Lieutenant General Sir John Lavarack.

These discussions led to the declaration of a Statement of General Principles, which laid down the size of the force and its operational control, which would be exercised by MacArthur, and ensured that internal policy remained a Commonwealth responsibility which Australia would exercise in the first instance on behalf of the others.[17] This was followed by more detailed negotiations on the areas which BCOF would be allotted and the administrative and other arrangements which would have to be made, and were conducted by Northcott with MacArthur's chief of staff, General Richard Sutherland. The result was the Northcott/MacArthur Agreement, formally ratified on 30 January 1946.

Even as the agreement was negotiated in December, problems arose over the forces to be contributed. Northcott advised his government that MacArthur had agreed to an Anzac and a British Indian Division and a combined air force presence of 9000 personnel, to be based in Hiroshima prefecture and including the cities of Kure and Fukuyama in its jurisdiction.[18] The role of the force at this stage was confined to the demilitarisation and destruction of arms and defences in the area, and to the military control of the prefecture. Control of BCOF would be exercised through Lieutenant General Robert L. Eichelberger, the

Commanding General, Eighth United States Army, for operational matters, through BCOF headquarters itself for matters of administration and maintenance, and by direct negotiation between MacArthur and the Commander-in-Chief, BCOF on all matters of occupation policy which might require government agreement. The final form of the agreement, recorded in a 'memorandum of record' on 18 December, allocated control of Commonwealth air components to the Commanding General, Fifth Air Force and of the Royal Naval Port Party which operated out of Kure to the US naval commander exercising jurisdiction over Japanese ports.

The BCOF area of responsibility would be increased over time, but the basic arrangements under which the force operated in Japan would remain unaltered in essentials till the end of the occupation.[19] It became clear very quickly, however, that with Australia and New Zealand demobilising rapidly and with various urgent imperial tasks in hand the British and other Commonwealth governments concerned could not meet the force contributions they had undertaken. Such difficulties had been foreshadowed back in September, when the New Zealand government had been forced to justify its involvement in BCOF in the face of considerable domestic opposition to the inclusion of conscripts in the New Zealand brigade.[20] On 24 December Sturdee, the Australian CGS, reported to a meeting of JCOSA that the Australian and New Zealand services were unable to raise the personnel for the Anzac Division headquarters, and that neither would be able to meet their quota of force and base troops. This placed pressure on the British and Indians to provide engineer, signal, provost and other base area troops, an imposition unlikely to be welcomed given the manpower pressures facing all three British services at this time, and in particular the RAF. Although committed initially to a force of 6000 men in five squadrons, the air staff decided to withhold two squadrons from the force for Japan for duties in South East Asia Command, where the British were policing the violent confrontations developing between Indonesian nationalists and the returning Dutch in Java in the aftermath of the Japanese surrender, and through more generalised fears for the future stability of India. The British Assistant Chief of Air Staff for Personnel expressed some concern at 'the risk that the Australian Government may feel that we have obtained their agreement to the appointment of an RAF officer as the commander of the air contingent on false pretences', but commitments in Java and potential commitments in India warranted the decision.[21] This was to become a persistent theme in 1946 and 1947 in the debate over the withdrawal of British and Indian forces.

Northcott returned to Melbourne in late December 1945 to explain the terms of the agreement to JCOSA and gain their concurrence. He had selected Hiroshima prefecture from three zones offered him by MacArthur on grounds of climate and general suitability, and with the understanding that the area could be expanded if necessary.[22] There was only one airfield, at Iwakuni and in fact outside the boundary of the original zone, but this could handle six or seven squadrons once necessary repairs had been completed. There were few good roads, water supply was a serious problem, and there was a considerable shortage of accommodation of European standard despite the presence for some months of US troops, from whom BCOF units would take over. Food supplies were precarious in Japan itself, there was a growing black market problem, the Japanese currency was nearly worthless, and training facilities for the force were limited. And there were to be other problems, both within the force and in attempting to reconcile policy differences between the contributing governments.

The 34th Australian Infantry Brigade, under Brigadier R.N.L. Hopkins, began to arrive in late February and was established first at Kure and then at Hiro. Major General D.T. 'Punch' Cowan's British Indian Division, or Brindiv, comprising the 5th British Infantry Brigade, the 268th Indian Infantry Brigade and the 7th Indian Light Cavalry Regiment, had its headquarters at Okayama, while when it arrived the 9th New Zealand Brigade under Brigadier K.L. Stewart, shipped from Bari in Italy, took over Yamaguchi prefecture in a newly-expanded BCOF area with its headquarters at Shimonoseki. All three formation commanders were under Northcott's direct command, and the senior officer in each national component was also the national representative of his government and was responsible for all forces of that nationality, whether serving under his direct command or not, and with rights of direct communication to his home government.

This was an involved system of competing jurisdictions and, as we shall see, was complicated still further by the existence of one or more national representatives outside the military chain of command who attempted to exercise some jurisdiction in both military and civil aspects of the occupation. British and Indian units continued to be carried on the Brindiv order of battle, whether located in the Brindiv area or not. This made administrative arrangements for units supposedly carried on integrated Commonwealth establishments in the base areas particularly difficult, as did the directive issued to the 9th New Zealand Brigade which meant its commander was virtually independent in all matters other than operational control.

Command of the force was made more complex still by the failure to agree on the sharing of staffs at BCOF headquarters. Reports appeared in the Australian press of 'officers of other units complaining that Australians predominate in the executive posts'.[23] A large force of all services drawn from four nationalities is a complicated proposition even in peacetime — perhaps especially in peacetime. It really required a fully integrated headquarters with appointments shared between all components, but

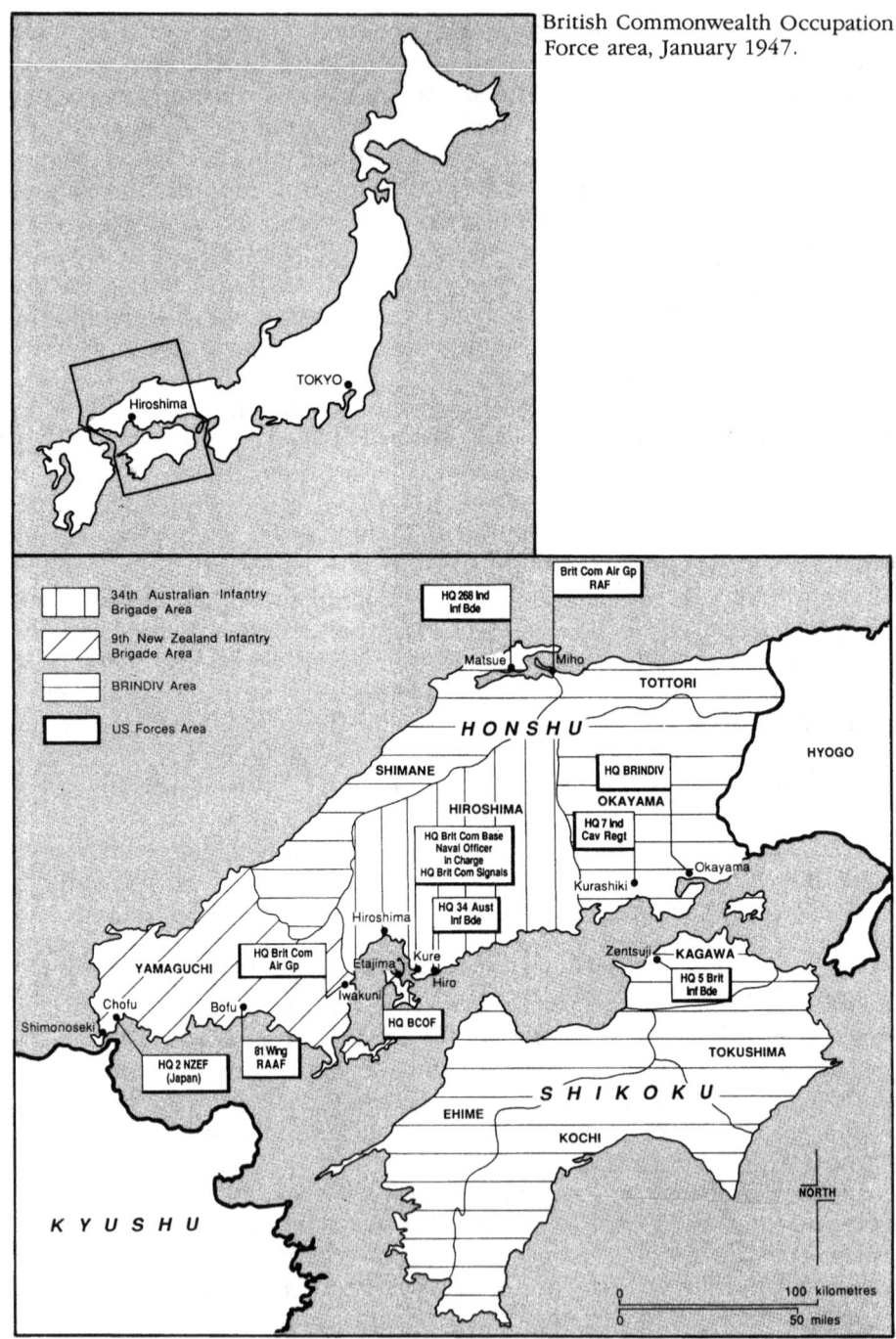

Japan, showing British Commonwealth Occupation Force area.

this never happened and the majority of positions were filled by the Australians and the British. Much of this might have been avoided had Northcott's own directive as Commander-in-Chief been issued, but it was still in draft form and under discussion when he was superseded by Robertson, as was the detailed plan governing the deployment of BCOF, which was not issued until May 1946. Robertson was able to take a draft of this last with him when he departed for Tokyo, but the situation emphasises the *ad hoc* manner in which BCOF was put together and deployed, at least in the crucial initial months of the occupation.

Northcott noted later the problems of integration, especially on the force headquarters. Officers and other ranks arrived 'in small numbers from all possible directions over the whole period', and before the headquarters was fully staffed some at least of these found themselves due for release and repatriation.[24] Robertson inherited the problem. He favoured integration on the headquarters so that 'everyone, Army, Navy and Air Force from each country . . . could watch the interests of his own particular section as well as cooperating in the general control of the force'.[25] Failures at this level led to difficulties with units of Brindiv, which complained about the level of rationing and general resupply received from Australian sources. These were symptomatic of difficult personal relations between Robertson and the division's commander, Major General D.T. Cowan, who had commanded the 17th Gurkha Division in Burma for several years against the Japanese. Together with many of his officers and men he had a long and distinguished war record. Suspicious of outsiders, he was not therefore perhaps the best choice for the position he occupied in Japan, and he made it clear in various ways that he resented being placed under the command of an Australian senior officer. Gradually the points of administrative difference were rectified, but relations between Cowan and Robertson were never warm, and Robertson wrote later that 'it did not occur to me that officers of the British and Indian army looked upon us from Australia and New Zealand as they looked upon the Indians, and were prepared to do anything to avoid being publicly commanded by us'.[26] There is some suggestion that relations between British and Australian troops were not particularly good either, and on one occasion Australian and Indian soldiers actually opened fire on each other, although this was an extreme case. Ill-feeling between Brindiv and the Australians was a function in part of the confusion over rationing and logistic arrangements. Robertson was able to show that the distribution problem lay not with the Australians, who had supplied the necessary items promptly, but at Brindiv headquarters at Okayama where the 'missing' items were found in storage. But the other ranks cannot have been expected to know this, with resulting difficulties between the troops on all sides.[27]

Policy differences and competing national interests also had to be reconciled. To competition for the senior command posts in the force must be added much more serious differences concerning the purpose of the occupation. There were a number of officials in the Foreign Office who saw the whole aim of participation in BCOF as a means to renew British economic penetration of Japan based on prewar associations.[28] An area of operations confined to the devastated rural margins of the country did not serve this purpose at all and, as early as December 1945, with the Northcott/MacArthur Agreement under discussion in London, Attlee's personal representative on MacArthur's headquarters, Lieutenant General Sir Charles Gairdner, was advising the British Chiefs of Staff that as 'the port and hinterland agreed upon for the use of the British Commonwealth Occupation Force had little to offer British commercial interests, it might be to our advantage to secure provisional agreement with the US Government for an extension of the area'.[29] The British were particularly interested in Kobe, which the Americans had secured for themselves. The Chiefs of Staff resolved not to press the matter at that time for fear of upsetting the agreement with MacArthur, but the issue of the lack of opportunities for British economic activity in Japan was to be raised several times in 1946 and 1947. It is worth noting also that Gairdner's suggestion was couched entirely in terms of a direct approach from the British to the American government, with no thought given to the role of the Australians as principal Commonwealth authority in occupation matters. This too was to become a regular theme over the ensuing two years.

The area originally designated for BCOF was too small for the growing force which occupied it, and in March Northcott gained agreement for expansion into neighbouring Shimane and Yamaguchi prefectures, gaining additional airfields at Bofu and Ozuki for the air component. In May his area expanded once again, not into Kobe or Osaka as London had hoped but into Tottori, Okayama and Shikoku Island, thus replacing US forces entirely throughout the Shikoku and Chugoku regions. It seems virtually certain that the Americans blocked any attempt by the British to resume commercial activities in important economic centres; the British-Indian representatives on JCOSA reported that the incoming commander-in-chief would be informed 'of the political and commercial importance of BCOF assuming control of these industrial areas as soon as this is feasible', but in the meantime Brindiv units continued to garrison seven of the nine prefectures in the BCOF area.[30]

The tasks allotted to BCOF were varied. The major one initially was the cataloguing and disposal of Japanese war equipment; large quantities of this were scattered across the BCOF area, which had contained a number of military installations, especially around Kure and Hiroshima. The Japanese had stockpiled munitions and chemical agents in preparation for the defence of the home islands, and this material had to be located and destroyed. Over 70,000 tons of explosive and 30,000 tons of poison gas were disposed of in this manner.

The second major duty involved supervising the Japanese repatriation centres. More than 700,000 returning Japanese personnel were processed through the three centres in the BCOF area, and 65,000 non-Japanese were repatriated from Japan, including 17,000 Koreans. One Brindiv intelligence report in October 1946 estimated that there were nearly 600,000 demobilised Japanese servicemen in the divisional area, with 210,000 in the prefecture of Kochi.[31] This huge pool of potentially disaffected manpower was a cause of concern to allied authorities, and much effort was expended in monitoring the activities of ex-soldiers and sailors of the Imperial Japanese Army and Navy in case they should attempt some form of violent opposition to the occupation. Over and above these activities, BCOF units were involved in extensive 'flag waving' exercises, patrolling their localities and mounting guard regularly on the Imperial Plaza in Tokyo, where the Commonwealth had jurisdiction over a 'sub-area' within the city.[32]

For most Commonweath personnel the real challenges of occupation duty lay in making the best of conditions in a devastated country in which relations with the locals were made more difficult both by the barriers of language and official prohibitions on such contact. Areas taken over for accommodation were not suited to European occupation even when still in a reasonable state of repair, and the early months of duty in Japan were spent by many soldiers on labour detachments, building and renovating barracks and other facilities against the advent of the coming Japanese winter. The battalion medical officer with the Australian 65th Battalion noted in one monthly report that 'the hygiene of the camp at Hachihommatsu was very unsatasfactory [sic] when first occupied by this unit, but measures to correct this have improved the standard greatly.'[33] Gradually some of these tasks would be performed by locally-engaged labour, but initially it was performed by the soldiers themselves.

If the troops found conditions difficult, the civilian population was faced with greater hardship still. In addition to the dislocation of defeat and the damage wrought by heavy allied aerial attack in the last months of the war, food shortages and epidemic disease were more or less serious problems at different times. Soon after arrival one Australian battalion noted an uncontrolled cholera epidemic in Fukuyama city which led to a ban on all Japanese personnel within the unit area. By the end of the year the situation had eased, although the war diarist noted again a 'slight increase in the endemic typhoid rate in Onomichi . . . but the situation appeared to be under control, and the town was not placed out of bounds'.[34]

Once the pressing matters of accommodation and supply had been sorted out, the biggest problem for unit commanders was to keep their men busy. Some of the Commonwealth areas were former training sites of the Imperial Japanese Army, and these were pressed into service. A constant round of training was leavened with unit and formation sporting competitions and, once the force was established and leave facilities acquired from the Americans, the opportunity to relax and see something of the country. From time to time Commonwealth units would be called on to perform security duties. In July 1946 and again in March 1947 D Company of the Australian 65th Battalion provided troops to accompany intelligence officers raiding Japanese shipping in Onomichi harbour, looking for weapons, foreign currency, medicines and other evidence of black market activity.[35]

Both American and Commonwealth authorities took the black market problem seriously, and in January 1948 Commonwealth units again were called on to supply men for use in a crackdown on such activities. But as with the monitoring of the Japanese elections the previous year, only small numbers of officers and specialists — mostly intelligence personnel and interpreters — were called on to form surveillance squads and assist the American Military Government Teams in the Commonwealth areas of Shikoku and Chugoku. BCOF provided eleven teams of three men each in the drive against black marketeers, and these men were detached from their units for some three months. But as with the supervision of the elections, when BCOF had supplied 115 personnel drawn from the Australian, New Zealand and Brindiv components, these duties fell to very few members of the force, and the vast majority took little or no part in even this indirect administration of the occupation.[36]

The failure of attempts to expand BCOF into centres of greater immediate interest to the British may have been behind moves to replace Northcott, although there is no evidence at all that he was dismissed as has been surmised.[37] His appointment as the first Australian-born Governor of New South Wales was a considerable honour, but should not blind us to the fact that his tenure of command in Japan was a less than unqualified success. He probably extracted the best bargain possible under the circumstances from MacArthur, but the limitations of the agreement were such as to reduce BCOF's role in Japan and to frustrate British ambitions, in particular, which would in turn lead to an early withdrawal of British components of the force. He faced formidable difficulties in the early months, but never really imposed organisational order, although to be fair he was not really in Japan long enough to leave a personal stamp on the units he commanded. But as a judgement on his tenure of command, and in presaging the work of his successor, it is probably fair to note the observation of the Australian Vice Chief of the General Staff at this time, S.F. Rowell, who wrote later,

THE OCCUPATION OF JAPAN: 1945-1946

> *Without being critical of Lieutenant General John Northcott . . . who faced a dreadfully difficult task in a devastated area [of Japan] with a staff and multi-national force hastily put together and in no way 'run-in', it is true to say that his successor, Horace Robertson, was able to correct the situation and establish this force firmly. This was his finest piece of work in a not undistinguished career.*[38]

Neither Robertson's qualities nor his achievements would commend themselves to everyone.

Robertson arrived in Japan on 9 June 1946. W. Macmahon Ball, the Australian nominated by Evatt as Commonwealth representative to the Allied Council for Japan, met him that night and described him as 'saturated with influenza . . . and generally looked a wreck'. They dined the following night in company with Northcott and the French and Soviet representatives on the ACJ. While Macmahon Ball's judgements in Japan were erratic — he managed to antagonise both the British and the Americans, and in the end resigned in July 1947 after it became clear that Evatt had lost confidence in him — his portrait of the two commanders is interesting:

> *After the guests left, I talked a long while to Northcott and Robertson. Although Robertson is the more energetic, more incisive in his views, and I should think a more efficient administrator, I get the impression that he may easily be a blunderer. He seems overconfident about his views. Northcott, while lacking Robertson's fire, is more moderate and far-seeing in what he says and does.*[39]

But within a fortnight he was able to write that 'I was greatly impressed with his general attitude towards the job in Japan and found him most friendly and understanding', and a few days earlier, 'I was altogether very impressed with him . . . he [is] a man with some element of greatness [in] that he can accept this [a reference to an earlier heated argument over BCOF's responsibility for provisioning the civilian missions] all in such good part and be so friendly.'[40] Japan was to be a frustrating post for both of them.

With characteristic energy, Robertson began work from the first day he arrived. Northcott arranged for him to meet MacArthur, Eichelberger, and his own senior officers at Hiro, and had arranged a 'grand tour' of the BCOF area by rail, to be undertaken jointly by them both. The 'flu which had struck Robertson on the flight to Japan now came to his rescue since, as he recorded, 'I have never been in favour of such things once command has been transferred, and I consider that from the moment a new commander takes over, the sooner the old one leaves the better.'[41] Northcott made the tour on his own, although he no longer exercised any command function over BCOF units, and after he had departed at the end of June 'I arranged my own tour and went round to see all the places for myself.'

There was much to see, and much to be done. Before he left Australia he had had an interview with Chifley, who had expressed concern on a number of subjects to do with amenities and conditions for the Australian component of the force, a subject which received periodic airings in the Australian press in the course of 1946. This was not merely journalistic mischief-making. Most of those who served in Japan in the early days draw attention to the harsh conditions and primitive amenities which the troops endured.[42] Hopkins recorded that to begin with his units in Kaitaichi lived in large store sheds along the rail sidings of the port; 'space was their only attribute; otherwise they were cold, draughty and comfortless. Some only were floored . . . Kure was twenty miles away, for what it was worth; Hiroshima was quite close, and the only outlet for troops seeking relaxation. It can well be imagined that it had little to offer.' Other units lived four or five men to a room in workmen's quarters on the site of the Nippon Steel Company, or in ruined Japanese barracks in Kure amid the bombed-out wreckage of the docks and city itself.[43] Only as the force settled into permanent locations did it prove possible to provide amenities 'on a scale more suitable for the conditions', bearing in mind of course that at this stage there was a strict 'no fraternisation' policy which prevented troops from any informal dealings with Japanese civilians.

On the matters which Chifley had raised with him, Robertson was able to reply that mail was getting through as regularly as could be expected in the circumstances, and that JCOSA was working on a policy to cover entertainment for the troops since two cinema shows a week were scarcely adequate to the recreational needs of a force of 40,000 men. On the question of provisions, especially fresh vegetables, he reported that frozen cargoes had been received of late and that these should be continued and, wherever possible, expanded since 'the Americans are lavish with their freezer cargoes and . . . so they are better off . . . That however applies to many things other than vegetables.'[44] The most serious problem Robertson foresaw with the Australians, however, was 'the feminine one'. The only women with the Australian formations were nurses and members of the Australian Army Medical Women's Service at the hospital,

> so Australians live a kind of monastic life and never even speak to a woman except when they fall for a Jap girl in the street with subsequent trouble . . . The great bulk of Australians never go near the hospital and on account of their location cannot do so. They live lonely lives and the fraternisation and consequent evils are more or less forced on them.

The provision within BCOF of a couple of hundred members of the Australian Women's Army Service would 'be a profitable investment for Australia as not only would these girls 'do our essential typing, clerking, telephoning etc', but would help to alleviate the 'monastic ritual' to which he referred through providing the Australian soldiers with female company. 'The saving in hospital costs alone judging on the British figures would be very large, and that does not take into account the saving in after effects in Australia.'[45] Over and above this again was the question of whether wives would be allowed to join their husbands in Japan, as seemed likely to happen for the British troops stationed there.

The issue here, of course, was the high incidence of venereal disease among Australian troops in Japan and the related issue of fraternisation with the Japanese. The matter was viewed sufficiently seriously for JCOSA to commission a report into the subject in August 1946. Far and away the highest proportion of VD cases within the force came from the Australians, consistently over 64 per cent of the total in the period surveyed in June and July that year.

Fortnight	Total	Australian cases	Percentage
14 June	2245	1655	73.2%
28 June	2659	1713	64.4%
12 July	3080	1942	64.02%

Several reasons were advanced for the situation: the Australians occupied areas more heavily devastated by the wartime bombing than the other components and here Japanese women were forced to turn to prostitution for economic survival; recreational amenities were inadequate; MacArthur had placed all brothels out of bounds to occupation forces, forcing the women workers to ply their trade on the streets and away from the normal system of inspection, control and treatment; and finally, that the Australian soldiers were generally younger than their British counterparts 'and are more irresponsible'. The New Zealanders had suffered even higher incidences of infection in Italy before arrival in Japan, it was alleged, but the prospect of their imminent return to New Zealand and demobilisation now made them more cautious.[46]

Like reports of violent crime among the occupation forces, the incidence of venereal disease provided the newspapers in Australia with good copy, even after the problem was checked by educative and prophylactic measures. Hopkins instituted various measures to control and limit the incidence of the disease 'with reasonable success', but as he went on to note, 'infection was widespread among Japanese civilians'.[47] The incidence of venereal infection among Australian soldiers in Egypt in 1914 and 1915 had scandalised C. E. W. Bean, and in 1917 and 1918 hospitals treating the British Expeditionary Force in France recorded 18.79 per cent of total admissions as venereal in origin, while in the AIF between 1916 and 1919 over 13,000 cases of venereal disease were admitted to the field ambulances in France, accounting for 6.19 per cent of total non-battle casualties.[48] The Australian media has always taken a prurient interest in such matters, and the coincidence of soldiering and sexually transmitted diseases is an old one, never more so than in armies of occupation. But the dimension of the problem in Japan may be gathered from the fact that when No 130 Australian General Hospital was established in 1946 a 200-bed ward was set up specifically to cater for venereal patients, and Northcott ordered that any officer in the force who contracted the disease was to be sent home.[49]

The broader issue of fraternisation was dealt with less easily. Northcott had made it clear that members of BCOF were to eschew social contacts with the Japanese, 'a conquered enemy', with whom relations must be 'formal and correct', a position endorsed by JCOSA. Robertson reinforced the edict, although with increasing difficulty since once it became clear that the Japanese in the main had accepted the fact of their defeat the Americans, with MacArthur's encouragement, relaxed their own orders concerning fraternisation with the civilian population.[50] Increasingly the strict insistence on maintaining a distance between the Japanese and BCOF troops seemed out of step with the general tenor of the occupation and eventually it was broken down, providing Australian immigration authorities with the problem of dealing with Japanese war brides returning to Australia. Robertson himself, however, maintained a hard-line attitude towards the Japanese throughout his time there.

A perfect instance of this was provided in 1948 at the ceremonies marking the third anniversary of the atomic bombing of Hiroshima. Speaking at the ceremony Robertson told the assembled Japanese that the bombing 'was your own fault, and we hope you won't forget it'. 'The punishment given to Hiroshima was only part of the retribution of the Japanese people as a whole', he told them, and he reinforced his point by detailing a squadron of Mustang fighters to fly low over the ceremony. 'I never fail to remind them it was their own fault', he told a journalist afterwards, 'they will forget it soon enough.'[51] Behind this display was a great deal of British and Commonwealth misgiving at the 'lenient' treatment of the Japanese which characterised MacArthur's rule, and the feeling that the rebuilding and restitution of Japan was outstripping the more punitive measures of occupation. Robertson was not unsympathetic to the plight of the Japanese or to the task which they faced in rebuilding the country, as his efforts to have Australian civil engineers and town planners brought in to assist in Hiroshima itself demonstrated,[52] but his words and his attitude found a sympathetic echo nonetheless among many of his fellow countrymen.

The early months of his tenure as Commander-in-Chief BCOF were hectic as Robertson sought to put the force on a sound administrative and organisational footing.

> *The first task for all the troops was ... a proper programme of rehabilitation of the barracks and, in some cases, the demolition of existing ones and replacement by new barracks ... the period from 1946 and well into 1947 was an extremely strenuous time for all the engineers in the force, planning, designing and drawing up detailed specifications for all the requirements as well as supervising the work being carried out by the Japanese contractors once contracts were let.'*[53]

The construction of barracks, proper establishment of base areas and hospitals and provision of sufficient and suitable recreational facilities had begun under Northcott, but it was pursued with renewed vigour under his successor. Accommodation was at a premium in war-devastated Japan, and because of the late arrival of the Commonwealth force most of the desirable areas had been sequestrated by the Americans for their own use. No provision had been made for leave centres for BCOF troops, and the use of American leave centres, of which there were any number, was impractical because this necessitated the expenditure of dollars with which the sterling area was not well endowed. After he had selected a number of likely sites in Kyushu, the Kobe-Kyoto area and outside Tokyo, Robertson pushed the issue hard with his American superior, Eichelberger, who agreed to hand over various assets since, as he noted in his diary, the Commander-in-Chief, BCOF 'has quite a large nuisance value'.[54] A number of the sites given to the Commonwealth force were in need of substantial renovation, 'requiring much engineering work before they could be occupied'.[55] On one occasion, when he felt he was being thwarted by Headquarters, Eighth Army in his drive to establish a leave hotel outside Tokyo, Robertson took the issue straight to MacArthur, who intervened in his favour in procuring what later became Robertson's own favourite recreation spot, the Kawana hotel, with its excellent golf course. That the issue was not a trivial one is exemplified by his observation after his first full tour of his units in mid-1946: 'I was struck more and more by the feeling that had I been a private soldier in one of these units at the time, I should have felt rebellious against the whole thing. That the troops continued to loyally do their work throughout that period is deserving of the greatest praise'.[56] By a mixture of cajolery and force of personality he extracted what he needed from an American system which was not always as cooperative as it might pretend; Eichelberger again recorded in his diary in December 1946 after another round of representation from Robertson on the subject of leave facilities that 'there are two schools of thought among my men. One — to make the British [*sic*] fix themselves up as we did; I take a middle course and want to share some of our nice hotels with them.' And on this occasion at least 'the conversation ended on a high note', assisted no doubt by the case of champagne sent as a Christmas gift from the Australian general to his American superior.[57]

Comment continued on the alleged indiscipline of the Australians in Japan, and following the federal election in October 1946 the new

Minister for the Army, Cyril Chambers, made an official visit to Japan to inspect BCOF and Robertson. A report in the *Chicago Tribune* in November had charged that 'the Australians are out of control and should be sent home'. It spoke of gang rapes and violent robberies, and described Robertson as a 'self-indulgent general' who demanded much for his own comfort in a bombed-out country. (This was probably a reference to the former Thai embassy in Tokyo, which Robertson had taken over as his own quarters. Accommodation of any sort was at a premium, and for the first year of his stint as C-in-C he shared the house with some of his senior staff.) The Australians 'are distinguished for a lack of discipline', and this began at the top.[58] There had been similar reports earlier in the Australian press, although it is unclear what had given rise to them. There was some suggestion at the time that the previous, long-serving army minister, F. M. Forde, had lost his seat at the 1946 federal election in part because of allegations about conditions in Japan. While this may be open to question, it cannot be doubted that the image of the Australian component was in need of some rehabilitation, at least within sections of the Australian government. Robertson noted of Chambers, a dentist by profession who had seen some service in New Guinea in 1942, that he was 'a conscientious man but rather imbued with Labour ideas, convinced that all generals were useless and with a mission in life to reform the Army.'[59] In many respects, therefore, he was an excellent choice to review the conditions under which the Australians in Japan operated.

While problems still remained, the minister was gratified by what he saw and the BCOF organisation was judged generally sound. There were disciplinary problems, but on a scale far removed from press reports. Robertson advised that some of the officers in the component were unsuitable, and that men who transgressed were discharged and sent home, but that this would prove effective only if the authorities in Australia took care in the selection of replacements. The incidence of venereal disease was greatly reduced, but Chambers advocated the despatch of religious and philanthropic organisations to work among the troops 'to provide some distraction from the monotony of barrack life and the attractions of the Japanese cities and towns, which have had such an unfortunate effect on the troops to date'. Leave centres, problems with rations, currency issues and a host of other matters occupied the minister's attention.[60] He had an interview with MacArthur and was given the opportunity to talk to the troops. Robertson thought him still 'a critic of the army . . . still seized with the fact that all generals were stupid and useless and that the private soldier knew best', but used the opportunity to point out to him 'that if he did not look after his generals and senior officers he could not expect to have an efficient army . . . and that the troops knew that only too well'. But he pronounced himself pleased with the conditions under which the Australians were operating, especially in light of earlier press comment, and before his return to Australia told journalists that,

> *These soldiers, who were the pioneers in their sphere, deserve the highest commendation for the results they have achieved ... I am convinced that the troops as a whole are doing a grand job under most difficult conditions and whatever action can justifiably be taken to improve their conditions, I shall endeavour to provide.*

Of greater moment than the administrative minutiae with which he concerned himself largely in his reports was the broader issue of the aims and purpose of the occupation as a whole, and of Australia's part in it. 'I doubt whether many of the men now in Japan have any great knowledge of the purpose and object underlying their presence there ... This would also apply to a considerable number of officers.'[61] He was concerned too by the failure of the Commonwealth force to carry out the military government function within its area, an issue he had taken up with MacArthur without success. As Robertson told the civilian head of the United Kingdom Liaison Mission, Sir Alvary Gascoigne, '[Chambers] could not appreciate the purpose which was being served by the continued maintenance of a Commonwealth force which was not having official contact with the Japanese, and was merely fulfilling functions which saved the Americans expense and manpower'.[62] While not disputing the truth of these observations, the chief of staff of the United Kingdom/India Element on JCOSA, Major General J.C. Haydon, thought that nonetheless 'for what it is worth ... BCOF, despite all its difficulties, despite its rather inferior position *vis à vis* the Americans, and despite its cost, pays a dividend'.[63] This was a purely personal view and, as we shall see, not one shared in London either in the Foreign Office or on the Chiefs of Staff Committee. The purpose and continuing viability of BCOF was to occupy JCOSA, Robertson himself and Australian policy makers throughout 1947 and 1948.

Numerous difficulties beset BCOF in its first year of occupation in Japan. Insufficient thought had been given to the demands which the occupation would make on the forces committed to it, and the physical conditions under which British, Indian, Australian and New Zealand units laboured in 1946 were difficult in the extreme. After securing command of the force and of the Commonwealth position on the Allied Council for Japan, the Australian government appears to have paid little attention to its forces in Japan except when sensational press stories made for short-term domestic political embarrassment. Macmahon Ball recorded in his diary after one conversation that Robertson felt that he received 'very poor support from Australia and that the Americans here are officially half-hearted and obstructive about giving him the things he asks for', a plaint with which Macmahon Ball could duly sympathise.[64]

Thanks to the Northcott/MacArthur Agreement, the essential link between the occupation forces and the Japanese — military government — was staffed and run entirely by the Americans. Given the attitudes of Robertson, Northcott and many other Australians towards the former enemy this was no bad thing from the Japanese point of view, but it undermined further the rationale for a Commonwealth presence in the occupation, especially one of some 40,000 men which, in 1946, represented twenty-five per cent of the forces deployed in Japan. The best justification Northcott could provide for their continuing presence was that 'our main influence upon the Japanese depends upon the military bearing and conduct of our troops'.[65] With the principal positions taken by the Australians, with attempts to regain an economic advantage in Japan stymied by American policy, and with BCOF's role increasingly peripheral for all the increase in territory occupied, it is little wonder that in the second half of 1946 British policy makers began to look for ways out of their role in the military occupation. How they went about it, the tensions which developed in Japan between Robertson and a number of the senior British figures there, and Robertson's attempts to maintain the role and prestige of BCOF, are recurrent themes in the history of the force.

CHAPTER 7

THE OCCUPATION OF JAPAN: 1946-1947

The end of the Second World War not only left the British economically exhausted but meant a recasting of the relationship between Britain, the dominions and, as became increasingly evident, India. British aspirations in the wider world were no longer matched by British resources nor, it should be added, in all cases by British will. The process by which Australia had come to take the leading part in the conduct of the occupation force in Japan and as Commonwealth representative on the Allied Council for Japan was evidence of this shift. Despite the fact that American dominance in Australian security affairs during the Pacific war proved temporary — not least because the United States had no wish to extend its commitments to that part of the world after the end of the war — and that the Australians, in particular among the dominions, actively pursued a viable system of postwar Commonwealth defence cooperation within Commonwealth councils, relations between Australia and Britain after 1945 could never return to their pre-1939 status. This was neither accepted in all sections of Whitehall and Westminster, nor were the manifestations of Australian assertiveness in Commonwealth affairs appreciated by all those British officials in London and Tokyo who had to deal with them.

All this greatly reduced the chances for the success of BCOF, as became evident in the course of 1946 and 1947. The British *did* face enormous difficulties in the immediate postwar years and the fundamental changes to the status of India with independence and partition imminent made it unlikely that the Indian component of BCOF would remain long on occupation duties. But when due allowance is made for the real difficulties which London faced, there remains a sizeable body of evidence which indicates that what really grated with many key officials, especially in the Foreign Office, was the fact that British interests would not be allowed to predominate in what was a Commonwealth force, and that individual Australians would speak for their British counterparts, and indeed in the military sphere would command them. 'Britain' and 'Commonwealth' were no longer necessarily synonymous.

This chapter will concern itself principally with Anglo-Australian relations within the occupation force, although some attention will be paid to relations between the force and the Americans, since the right of access to MacArthur in particular was one bone of contention between London, its representatives in Tokyo, and Robertson. The key issues over which divisions in the Commonwealth organisation became apparent were the withdrawal of British and, to a lesser extent, Indian forces from Japan; the purpose and future role, if any, of BCOF; and the level of separate British representation in Japan. The duties of the occupation force itself did not vary much if at all in this period from those outlined already. Something more of the function of BCOF will be dealt with later, since from 1948 onwards, with the withdrawal of the New Zealand component also, the Commonwealth occupation became an almost entirely Australian show.

At the heart of disagreements between Robertson and British officials in Tokyo and London was the personality clash between the Commander-in-Chief, British Commonwealth Occupation Force and two British officials in particular, and this disharmony coloured much of the advice on and discussion of policy issues between London, Tokyo and Melbourne. At times too, differences in personalities very effectively covered fundamental disagreements in policy. So chronic did this situation become that one student of the occupation has described Anglo-Australian relations as 'generally a disaster'. And although Macmahon Ball and, by extension, Robertson, were seen to be touchy individuals in different ways, Buckley has noted that 'most of the senior Australian figures in the occupation were to feel aggrieved by British behaviour toward its Pacific ally'.[1]

The central problem in Japan, for Robertson, was the maintenance of the position of personal representative of the British prime minister on MacArthur's headquarters after the end of the Pacific war, and its incumbent, Lieutenant General Sir Charles Gairdner. A little needs to be said about the history of both this post and its occupant, because disagreements between Robertson and Gairdner run like a thread through the period until the final abolition of the position with Gairdner's retirement in 1948.

Churchill had first appointed Lieutenant General Herbert Lumsden as special representative to serve on MacArthur's staff in November 1943, in recognition of the need to maintain some sort of liaison in a theatre in which the British had virtually no role at all after the fall of Singapore and ABDACOM in early 1942. Because of the command arrangements which pertained in the South West Pacific Area Australian authorities were unable to supply much information on future planning and operational matters in the theatre, and MacArthur himself was constrained from communicating directly with British authorities by virtue of his position in the US chain of command as a subordinate of the Joint Chiefs of Staff — assuming of course that he had wished so to communicate with allied authorities. Lumsden's presence doubtless appealed to his vanity, and the former was able to keep his superiors informed of planning in this theatre which had obvious implications for activities in neighbouring South East Asia Command, and for the final campaigns against the Japanese in which Britain and the Commonwealth would play a part. Major General Adrian Carton de Wiart filled a similar position as Churchill's representative to Chiang Kai-shek in China.

Lumsden was killed in action in the Philippines on 6 January 1945 when the battleship *New Mexico* was hit by kamikaze strikes, and Churchill directed that a replacement be dispatched. Two names were put forward for consideration, and that of Major General Charles H. Gairdner selected. It was as splendid an example as one could have of the way in which a career might be revived. Gairdner had served as GSO1 on the headquarters of 7th Armoured Division during the first Libyan campaign. Although he had briefly commanded both the 6th and 8th Armoured Divisions in 1942 and 1943, the former had been in a training role only while the latter was in fact disbanded while under his command in January 1943; he thus had no real combat experience in the current war. Sent to India with Wavell in 1942, he returned to the Mediterranean theatre the following year and between February and May 1943 he was chief of staff to General Sir Harold Alexander at Force 141, the senior allied force headquarters engaged in planning for the invasion of Sicily. A recent distinguished historian of that campaign has described Gairdner at that time as 'woefully ill-equipped for a senior appointment of such critical importance. He was unfailingly courteous and well-meaning but otherwise out of his depth in the high-powered atmosphere of the Allied high command.' His tenure in the post was 'a bitter failure', and his performance of his duties there 'ineffectual'. When Montgomery refused to accept the plan for Sicily which he had drafted, Gairdner requested to be relieved of his position, and Alexander obliged him.[2] Some at least of the blame for the planning failure of HUSKY lay with Alexander himself, but Gairdner paid the price and returned to India and a succession of obscure postings, as Director of Armoured Fighting Vehicles, India from August 1943 to November 1944, and then as commandant of No 110 Lines of Communication Area in the Deccan District when he was picked for the job with MacArthur. It was a resurrection of Lazarus-like proportions.

Whether Gairdner was the best man for the job is another matter entirely. On the one hand, Britain had virtually no influence on MacArthur's planning and conduct of operations at any time, so that in one sense it really didn't matter who was sent as Churchill's representative. But Gairdner was the conduit for information on activities in the struggle against the Japanese and considerable judgement was required on the part of anyone required to work in MacArthur's 'court'; Gairdner very quickly became an uncritical enthusiast for the man. Writing to Ismay, Churchill's chief of staff, in May 1945, only a month after taking up his position, he felt able to say that:

> General MacArthur, in my opinion, stands head and shoulders above any other officer I have met here, in the breadth of his views, in the lucidity of his arguments, and in the unerring way he puts his finger on the essentials of a problem. For some reason which I cannot explain, and somewhat to my surprise, he has not behaved in a melodramatic or histrionic way in any meeting which I have had with him. Moreover, I believe him to be a sincere friend of the British Commonwealth. I think it would pay a very good dividend to back him whenever it is possible without imperilling paramount interests.[3]

His own commitment to British Commonwealth interests, and the manner in which he saw his task, may be divined from another observation to Ismay made later the same year. On that occasion he reported that MacArthur would have preferred the British liaison mission in Japan to have been 'a British Empire one but didn't feel too strongly about it . . . I raised this question in my original appreciation, but it was not accepted, and I am glad that it wasn't, as I believe that we would have difficulties with Australia, who would certainly want very strong representation on it, even if they didn't press that the head of the mission should be an Australian.'[4] And on another occasion still he used the opportunity provided by of one of his periodic return visits to London to inform the Foreign Secretary, Ernest Bevin, of

> the difficulty they were having in Japan owing to our being represented by Australia. The adoption of this method had reduced the prestige and position of Great Britain in Japan to a very low ebb . . . While the General commanding [ie, Northcott] was a good man the tendency was to forget there was a Great Britain at all and the whole bias with regard to our position was placed on Australia.[5]

Whatever the usefulness or otherwise of the position during the war itself, serious questions must be asked of the decision to maintain Gairdner in Japan after the Japanese surrender and the commitment to send a Commonwealth force to participate in the occupation. With the appointment of a commander-in-chief of the Commonwealth force, the continuing utility of Gairdner's position was examined by the Joint Planning Staff. Gairdner's mission 'deals with affairs of interest to the UK only, and has no authority to deal with matters of Commonwealth concern', they stated. Exactly so. But the report then went on to note that its authors,

> *do not think ... that if C-in-C BCOF were recognised as the channel for the presentation of British Commonwealth views on service matters to General MacArthur, this need necessarily affect the position of General Gairdner. It would have to be made clear that the C-in-C BCOF would be regarded as the channel only for questions affecting all members of the Commonwealth and on which a coordinated British Commonwealth view was required. General Gairdner would continue to act on matters of concern to the UK only, as he does at present.*[6]

JCOSA made it clear that the source of military advice to the British Commonwealth member on the Allied Council for Japan was the Commander-in-Chief, BCOF.[7] And because Gairdner's was not a service mission but a government one, he had no responsibility to the United Kingdom Chiefs of Staff.

The redundancy of Gairdner's position was made even clearer in mid-1946 with the dispatch of a new head for the United Kingdom Liaison Mission to Japan. This was a career foreign office official, Sir Alvary Gascoigne, designated as political representative and with ambassadorial rank. Gairdner was displaced as head of UKLIM but remained as prime minister's representative although it is unclear what exactly his function was now to be. Gascoigne became the means by which the British government sustained Anglo-American ties in Japan and sought to gain MacArthur's concurrence in British policy objectives, especially on trade and economic issues. Northcott and then Robertson was the source of Commonwealth military advice both to the Commonwealth representative on the ACJ and to MacArthur, the Supreme Commander, himself. Gascoigne's terms of reference made it clear that he was to work closely with Gairdner who was not subordinated to him, but did not specify what exactly it was that Gairdner was to do.[8] Gascoigne himself was no clearer. He understood clearly enough the antipathy which developed between Gairdner and Robertson, and wrote of it that:

> *Gairdner's sphere was quite different from Robertson's and the latter should in my opinion confine himself to ruling over his military zone in Western Japan and not try to usurp the authority which Gairdner and I wield in Tokyo. Robertson was essentially a military officer and Gairdner and I were essentially political and Robertson would not, or could not, understand that very simple fact.*[9]

The problem was that Gairdner did not understand it either. He outranked Robertson, at least substantively, and persisted in presenting himself publicly as the senior British Commonwealth officer in Japan. If his sphere was entirely political, as Gascoigne suggested, then he should not have concerned himself in any way with military affairs under the occupation, nor with any aspect of the Commonwealth occupation forces. Nor should London have used him to communicate military advice to MacArthur where that advice concerned aspects of the Commonwealth forces in Japan. None of these distinctions was to be observed. The real reason for maintaining Gairdner in Japan was made explicitly clear by Bevin in a minute to Attlee in late 1946, when the question of bringing him home was raised. 'I am against withdrawing General Gairdner for some time', he wrote. 'We must remember it is an Australian in command and [Macmahon] Ball is there as well. The General will be a source of strength to us.'[10] Gascoigne concurred, writing to Esler Dening at the Foreign Office when the question of Gairdner's appointment came up that 'with the Australian preponderance here it is, I think, doubly important that we should not remove our "biggest gun" at this juncture'. And he told Ismay that 'if this United Kingdom influence [with MacArthur] were removed, we (the United Kingdom) would suffer a severe blow which would probably redound to the benefit of Australia'.[11]

Robertson was alert to the difficulties which this situation posed for him. 'I see a little of Charles Gairdner', he wrote to his predecessor, Northcott, 'who, as you say, has a pleasant time [socially] and I fear that sometimes things happen from UK through him, instead of through JCOSA and myself.'[12] As he saw it, the situation was a simple one:

> as commander in chief of the British Commonwealth Occupation Force I must be senior to all service personnel from the British Commonwealth in Japan as I had never yet heard of a British commander in chief who was provided with a rival in the area of his own command . . . it was a military occupation and under the terms of the Far Eastern Commission decisions of September 1945 regulating the occupation the legal authority over all members of the British Commonwealth in Japan, no matter what their status, rested with me as commander in chief . . . With regard to Gairdner, I did not recognise his position at all for there was nothing in the Far Eastern Commission decisions or in the JCOSA organisation which provided for any other representation of the British Commonwealth in Japan other than BCOF and the Missions from the various countries accredited to SCAP.[13]

Since Gascoigne was now head of the United Kingdom mission and Robertson himself remained Commander-in-Chief BCOF, Gairdner's presumption of a role for himself as the senior British Commonwealth representative with MacArthur clearly was wrong. This did not stop him, in Robertson's words, from working 'constantly for UK's individual interests only in direct opposition to any question of British Commonwealth co-operation'.[14] Gairdner himself commented that 'our strange representation out here seems to go very well . . . [and] although there is little logical justification for it, I believe that UK interests are well served by it'.[15]

A perfect example of the way in which the British attempted to undercut the Commonwealth organisation to which they had agreed was provided by the issue of troop withdrawal late in 1946. The British had continued to press Robertson on the issue of extending the BCOF area to incorporate the port city of Kobe, which required MacArthur's concurrence, and in October Robertson informed Gascoigne that the moment was propitious, since American troop strength in Japan was continuing to decline and Eichelberger faced serious problems in spreading his available forces around Japan.[16] At a meeting on 22 October, however, the United Kingdom Defence Committee resolved to withdraw the British brigade from Japan and relocate it in Malaya as the first step towards building a strategic reserve in the region.[17]

No consideration was given to the likely views of the other Commonwealth governments concerned, even though the Joint Planning Staff report on which the decision was based made it clear that 'it might be held to be contrary to the spirit of this agreement [ie, the Northcott/MacArthur Agreement] if the United Kingdom informed the US government of their intention to withdraw the UK Brigade Group without previous consultation with the Australian government'.[18] And it made clear that this had implications for the Indian forces grouped with the British units in Brindiv, and hence for the future of BCOF as a whole, a point which the CIGS, Montgomery, had dismissed in the Defence Committee discussions but which was confirmed soon after by Auchinleck, the Commander-in-Chief, India.[19] The Secretary of State for the Dominions, Lord Addison, was not consulted on the decision and protested to Attlee that

> *on a purely practical point, the detailed arrangements for the establishment of the British Commonwealth Occupation Force were made direct between Australia and the United States. It is not for us to approach the United States with regard to the withdrawal of our force. The first step, if the decision is to stand, is for us to agree with Australia on the subject before any approach is made to the United States.*[20]

Attlee replied simply that 'with the exception of the small force in Japan [Australia and New Zealand] make no contribution to the burden of providing troops of occupation [elsewhere], but are quite prepared for us to pay the piper — for them to call the tune'. And he noted that 'we have a strong case'.[21]

The problem of course, as the Foreign Office well appreciated, was that the moves to extend the BCOF area which were then underway would be impossible with the withdrawal of the British and Indian forces. Approval was given for Gascoigne and Gairdner, but not Robertson or JCOSA or the Australian government, to be informed of the decision in order that 'some embarrassment in the situation' might be obviated.[22] Lord Tedder, the Chief of the Air Staff, was scheduled to visit RAF units in Japan in late November and it was suggested that he might use the opportunity to inform MacArthur of the decision, but Dening's view that the Supreme Commander should be told as soon as possible prevailed, and on 19 November Gairdner saw MacArthur and informed him of the decision to withdraw the British brigade.[23] The Australian government was informed but did not have sufficient time to pass this information on to Robertson in Japan, and may have assumed in any case that the C-in-C would be told about proposals which affected troops under his command. He was not, and the first he knew of it was when MacArthur asked him whether Australia intended to withdraw troops also. Gascoigne thought that 'it is a pity to cause his feathers to be ruffled unnecessarily', although Dening did not concur,[24] but Robertson made it clear privately that he was seriously affronted by the way in which the BCOF organisation had been bypassed, a fact confirmed for him by Tedder's visit. 'He is seeing the air force', he wrote to Northcott, 'but his real duties relate to the army.'

> *Monty is coming out to Singapore in December, but he is not coming on this far and Tedder is to do the work, short-cutting JCOSA completely. Most of us have believed that Australia or New Zealand might be inclined to diverge from the joint effort, but few of us would have guessed that UK would be the initiator.*[25]

The matter was referred finally to JCOSA on 19 December, and the British representatives likewise expressed dissatisfaction with the way in which the issue had been handled. The use of Gairdner as the channel of information to MacArthur 'not only caused affront to the Australians here but is very likely to upset the already delicate balance that exists *vis à vis* SCAP between the C-in-C BCOF and the Prime Minister's representative'. The procedural issues, while important, were secondary.

> *Having regard to what may become the accepted organisation for Imperial Defence it appears that an opportunity of demonstrating that the principles of regional defence and of executive agents in the various regions carry with them serious responsibilities, not only in theory but in practice too, has been allowed to slip ... a particularly suitable opportunity for demonstrating to the Australian government and Service authorities that the United Kingdom is sincere in delegating responsibility to Australia as executive agent in matters affecting the occupation of Japan has been missed. The regional conception of Imperial defence seems to have but slender hopes of flourishing unless the regional authorities are given full scope to exercise their responsibilities. Otherwise the Dominions may well feel that regional responsibility carries no more weight than a bubble which may be pricked whenever it is felt convenient to do so.*[26]

It was an old and troubling question, albeit in a new setting. Any hopes of a revived imperial or Commonwealth system of defence had to take cognisance of the fact that the events of 1942-45 had changed the Anglo-Australian defence relationship fundamentally. The issue was much bigger than the niceties of informing Robertson of changes to the forces under his command, or of smoothing egos over competing jurisdictions within the Commonwealth organisations in Japan. The failure of Commonwealth defence cooperation in Japan and the British refusal to treat JCOSA seriously as an organisation for the implementation of that ideal, regardless of any soothing noises from the Chiefs of Staff Committee, demonstrated what little chance there really was for a successful revival of imperial defence in the postwar years. And the attitudes of many British officials towards their dominion counterparts merely reinforced this. Gascoigne wrote later that 'the Australians lack any of these fine susceptibilities regarding courtesy and protocol. Only time will teach them these things, and, I fully realise that we must all be very patient.'[27] The Australians were fully alive to this, of course, Evatt having noted the tendency when he wrote to Chifley in 1945 that 'relationships with the United Kingdom ministers, especially Attlee and Bevin, are very satisfactory indeed, although officialdom is still inclined to attempt reduction of the Dominions to colonial status'.[28]

The announced withdrawal of the British brigade raised the twin issues of the related withdrawal of Indian forces and of the continued viability and purpose of BCOF as a whole. As CIGS, Montgomery told the Chiefs of Staff Committee that 'if we had to consider narrow UK interests only there would be some military advantage and no disadvantage in the dissolution of BCOF'. But he went on to note that realistically,

> *in the wider interests of British Commonwealth defence and lasting co-operation between the Americans, the other members of the Commonwealth and ourselves, we should not initiate proposals for the dissolution of BCOF.*[29]

Allied to the strain on army manpower, he felt, was the added consideration that 'from the operational point of view [BCOF] is no longer serving any useful purpose'. In fact, as the War Office recognised, reducing British forces in Japan was unlikely to ease the manpower problem, since 'the liquidation of this commitment would almost certainly entail an appropriate reduction in the manpower ceiling figures'.[30] On the basis of what he had seen while in Japan, Tedder believed that the British brigade could be withdrawn without affecting the area occupied or reducing the control of that area, but the major concern once the decision to scale down the British contribution had been made was the likely affect this would have on India. A token reduction of Indian elements in Brindiv was considered, in order 'to avoid a general crisis on the whole question of Indian troops overseas', since not only were Indian army units based in Japan but were engaged in imperial duties in Burma, Malaya and the Middle East also.[31] It was proposed to withdraw the 7th Indian Cavalry

Regiment, but there was never much likelihood that this would suffice to mollify Indian opinion, and in April the Australian government advised the Americans that all Indian forces would be withdrawn from Japan by 15 September 1947.[32] This was followed only days later by the announcement that the New Zealand government intended to reduce the size of its brigade to 2400 men, and the continued existence of BCOF was brought into question directly.[33]

This was much as Robertson had feared. Gascoigne reported that his reaction 'has not been quite so good'.

> *He ... seems to think that this 'defection' on our part will finally result in the whole of the British Commonwealth Occupation Force disappearing 'like melting snow', and he does not think that the melting will take long. He reckons that the other governments concerned (viz. Australia, New Zealand and India) will get tired of carrying out what is purely a 'police' job 'pour le plaisir des Americains'. If BCOF looked after its own military government and administered the Japanese, Robertson thinks it might be considered worth while to keep BCOF in being, but that is not the case.*[34]

The viability of the force was threatened further still with the decision to remove the entire remaining British contingent in October. The Australian Defence Committee had prepared a paper on the benefits of maintaining BCOF in April, and had circulated it to all relevant governments. They argued that Commonwealth prestige was enhanced by participation with the Americans, not least in the Pacific region, that it supported the claim to a role as principals in the formulation of the peace treaty, helped to underpin the position of the Commonwealth representatives on the Far Eastern Commission and the Allied Council for Japan, and afforded valuable experience in defence cooperation.[35] In a brief for Montgomery prepared before his visit to the Far East, the Foreign Office noted that involvement in BCOF had been intended to 'enhance British prestige in the eyes of the Japanese and demonstrate to the world in general, and the Far East in particular, that Great Britain was still a power to be reckoned with in this area'. Echoing a similar judgement made in the Chiefs of Staff Committee, it concluded that 'time has shown that the circumstances of the occupation have not produced the result desired ... [our] presence does not enhance British prestige or further British economic interests.'[36] And Dening took the initiative within the Foreign Office, noting that it had 'become increasingly clear for some time past that our occupation forces in Japan are serving no useful purpose'. He sought a coordinated approach which would result in the withdrawal of the whole force, not merely the British component, although he added that 'if their [Australia's] vanity persuades them that they alone should stay, then I do not think that this would do us irreparable harm, even though we should prefer that all should go together'.[37]

Once again, the decision to remove forces directly under Robertson's command was passed to MacArthur by UKLIM, with the Commander-in-Chief BCOF being informed after the event.[38]

Robertson, through the Australian government and indirectly through Gascoigne, requested that the British maintain certain key and specialist personnel in Japan, and that the withdrawal of remaining United Kingdom elements not be made precipitately, or else the future administrative and logistic operation of the force would be jeopardised. Gascoigne supported this plea, not least because all the rationing and administrative support for the Commonwealth missions, including his own, came through BCOF channels, and these were obviously placed at risk. The British Chiefs of Staff agreed to this, 'provided that the number retained in Japan was the minimum desirable'.[39] From an actual strength of 3800 (on an establishment of approximately 5000) the remaining British personnel in Japan would be reduced to 750 specialists who would then remain in Japan for some time.[40] But it was clear that by the end of 1947 the force, which had boasted an establishment of over 40,000 only eighteen months previously, was becoming more and more attenuated: actual strength on 4 December was 1623 officers and 14,459 other ranks, with most of the British personnel still to be withdrawn.[41]

The departure of the 5th Brigade had necessitated some reorganisation of BCOF. Revised manpower ceilings were set which emphasised further the Australian dominance of the force now that the British, Indians and New Zealanders had reconsidered their commitments. The Australian brigade now numbered 9500 in a total force of 14,300, and Robertson was advised both that no increase over these strengths would be permitted and, that with the reductions in hand, the basis on which BCOF ground components had been organised previously, as a field force, was to change. Henceforth the ground component would be a force able to render aid to the civil power. JCOSA felt that the aims and role of BCOF did not require radical alteration since, although the force was greatly reduced in size, the nature of the task in Japan had always differed from that anticipated at the war's end; and there was no likelihood by 1947 that BCOF would be called on to face opposition from armed forces.[42] There was even the suggestion that the Commonwealth area might expand further still to bring about the long-desired incorporation of Kobe. Major General W.J. Cawthorn, the Indian army representative on JCOSA, told Gascoigne that what he termed the 'Evatt school' of thought on Australian involvement overseas, which he characterised as 'the expansion of Australian representation abroad in terms of occupation forces, large diplomatic missions etc', seemed set to maintain its ascendancy in Australian thinking, and that an Australian commitment to the occupation was likely to remain for the foreseeable future;[43] elements of the Dominions Office argued in London that this continued presence was in fact a good thing.

In a strong response to Dening's advocacy of a mutual phased withdrawal from Japan by all Commonwealth elements, Holdgate of the Dominions Office stated that,

> *we cannot help feeling that the continued presence of forces in Japan from some part of the Commonwealth, even if not from the United Kingdom, is a matter of some importance and that the gradual dissolution of BCOF which you suggest as a happy solution, is hardly one which we could, if we are to be consistent, encourage . . .*[44]

But even if they remained in their current strength, the Australian component could not hope to cover the areas previously assigned to the force as a whole; the headquarters and base units were running down as a result of the withdrawals by other governments, and the continuing necessity of the joint chiefs organisation in Melbourne was questioned as the bulk of the remaining British and Indian forces were pulled out. Robertson received permission from Melbourne to approach SCAP with a view to handing back some of the areas taken over the previous year, while the removal of the RAF presence in Japan saw the command of a reduced British Commonwealth Air Force (BCAIR) pass to an RAAF officer.[45] Together with the proposals for the complete reduction of the United Kingdom component had come a request from London for the dissolution of JCOSA. Following consultations with the New Zealand government Chifley was able to advise Attlee that the Australian defence machinery would take responsibility for the control and administration of BCOF after 31 December 1947, on which date the Joint Chiefs of Staff in Australia would cease to exist. Britain was requested to provide an officer from the military liaison staff in Australia who might sit on the Australian Defence Committee when occupation matters of interest to the United Kingdom were discussed, while an Australian officer in London was detailed for the same task at that end. This latter function would be discharged infrequently, 'since Australia would in future take the initiative in considering the defence of the Pacific and such matters would comparatively seldom come on to the agenda of our Defence Committee in London'.[46] New Zealand likewise maintained an officer from its high commission to watch over New Zealand interests in the occupation force.

Thus ended for all intents and purposes the first attempt at a combined Commonwealth military endeavour on something approaching equal terms. It had been a less than resounding success. Several commentators have pointed to the formidable difficulties which faced British policy towards Japan, confronted as they were by the overwhelming strength of the American position in the occupation, itself a legacy of the dominant part which America had played in the defeat of Japan. It was to help offset this that Britain had pushed for a Commonwealth role in Japan in the first place, since in a time of economic and manpower stringencies the British needed the accretion of strength which the Commonwealth alone could provide. But British policy on the wider plane was inconsistent; 'having initially decided to take part in the occupation, [Britain] suddenly lost confidence in it and the reform programme associated with it. She changed policy radically in midstream in early 1947 [and] the British component of BCOF was withdrawn.'[47] That shift in policy may be attributed to several factors: Bevin's concentration on European affairs to the virtual exclusion of the Far East; a perceived inability on Britain's part to regain economic influence in Japan quickly as a benefit of participating in the occupation;[48] the serious manpower pressures facing the army in particular, made worse still by the loss of the Indian army as a source of manpower and the reduced term of national service enacted in 1947;[49] and resentment among British officials at the fact as well as the manner of Australian representation in the key Commonwealth positions in Japan.

At the level of BCOF this resentment focused principally upon Robertson, although as we have noted there was dissatisfaction expressed with Northcott as well which could not be put down in any way to alleged personality difficulties. Even when seeking to compliment the administration of the force, British officials found it difficult not to patronise the Australian effort. Having complained to Dening once again about Robertson ('although a good fellow in many ways, [he] suffers from a superabundance of egotism'), Gascoigne went on to note that 'I must at the same time pay warm tribute to Robertson's conduct of the business of BCOF. He has succeeded in "de-winkling" from the Americans, with whom he apparently gets on well, considerable amenities for his troops. We are, of course, dependent on him entirely for our rations, etc, and perhaps if you do see him you would consider saying a word of thanks for the services which he gives us.'[50] (But just a few months previously he complained of 'the antics of this fantastic Australian. Robertson suffers from la folie de grandeur, and his case is a pathological one.'[51])

To the problems of shifting policy imperatives in London was added a confused jurisdictional and personality conflict in Tokyo, from which all parties concerned emerged with little credit. The principal problem was Gairdner, whose own antics in Japan after Gascoigne replaced him as head of the United Kingdom Liaison Mission were no less 'fantastic' than Robertson's, and less easily justified. In March 1947 Robertson's promotion to substantive lieutenant general's rank was announced, backdated to January 1944. Gairdner attempted to have himself promoted to full general in response, an attempt resisted successfully in London on the grounds that 'General Gairdner is very low on the Lieutenant General list [and] it would be better not to pursue this question'.[52] Robertson was no less concerned with seniority matters, and his belief that the C-in-C should take precedence in military matters in Japan was supported by, among others, the Australian Minister for the Army after his visit in December 1946.[53] Gairdner continued to conduct himself like a figure out of the prewar Raj. He flew around Japan, and on trips as far afield as Hong Kong and Australia (to take in the Test matches and 'confer' with the Governor-General, the Duke of Gloucester, in early 1947) in an aircraft which he had named 'Eastern Monarch' and in which, from Robertson's viewpoint at least, he behaved very like one. Returning from Australia the plane crashed and Gairdner promptly indented to BCAIR for another, which just happened to be Robertson's own.

There ensued a long and acrimonious dispute in which Gairdner insisted that he should have first call on the aircraft, while Robertson instructed the air force that, in line with RAF instructions regarding the use of personal aircraft, Gairdner was to be given access only when on legitimate official business, and officials in the Cabinet Office in London looked on in exasperation. Even they were moved to describe Gairdner's complaints as 'rather querulous'.[54] All the while he sniped at Robertson in his letters and infrequent official dispatches to London,[55] although it is clear that not all those concerned in London were disposed to accept his version of events, and some at least, especially in the Dominions Office, were keen to avoid any open breach with Australia. When Gascoigne and Gairdner complained to the Foreign Office that Robertson had 'usurped' their prerogatives by trying to conduct a visiting parliamentary delegation within the BCOF area, Eric Machin pointed out to the Foreign Office that since the junior minister concerned was 'visiting RAF units overseas ... it could therefore be argued that the military C in C should look after him'.[56] And in a brief for the Secretary of State the Dominions Office noted, with admirable even-handedness, that while 'no doubt the personality of General Robertson makes him a difficult person to work with ... we cannot assume that the fault is all on one side'.[57] And even those within the Cabinet Office who supported Gairdner's retention baulked at some of his demands.[58]

While Robertson's disputes with Gairdner do not do him much credit, and reveal to the full on occasions that tendency to boorish egotism remarked on by some during the Second World War, he was nonetheless genuinely committed to making BCOF and the occupation work as a joint Commonwealth force. He never stinted in his assistance to the Commonwealth liaison missions which, as we have noted, were entirely dependent on BCOF resources for all their needs, even though, at least initially, he had been under no obligation to furnish them anything at all. Gascoigne too, in a difficult job, was committed to 'strengthening our local Commonwealth solidarity. This situation seems to provide an exceptional opportunity for a demonstration to the Americans, and also to the Japanese, of our complete unity as a family.'[59] Increasingly,

Gairdner seems to have viewed his position in Japan in self-serving terms. His career had been revived with his appointment to MacArthur's headquarters, and he devoted a considerable amount of his time in Japan to stressing his indispensability to those back in London while seeking always to have his term in Tokyo extended indefinitely. As he confided to his diary in mid-1947 when the question of his tenure had arisen again, 'Joe [Gascoigne] still seems very keen on it, and I don't mind but would like something more definite — such as until MacArthur goes or until peace treaty is signed. Another 18 months here would be boring enough but would save us £1000.'[60] His diary records a full round of social engagements, lunches, dinners, cocktail parties and rounds of golf, and numerous sour comments about Robertson and the Australians. ('Red Robbie was in good form, but of course as pompous as ever'; 'Brig Mackinlay, BGS at BCOF came to dinner. I didn't find him attractive but beyond pointing out some of the annoying pinpricks which I was always suffering from BCOF was reasonably moderate and kept my temper.')[61]

Gairdner seems to have seen MacArthur on a fairly regular but generally informal or even social basis, but as he admitted in his diary and as is clear from the content of his infrequent despatches to London, little of substance ever seems to have come from these meetings. Gascoigne saw MacArthur officially on 128 occasions between 1946 and 1951; Robertson met with him on 67 occasions in that time, and was the most frequently received non-American official after Gascoigne himself and the Prime Minister of Japan, Shigeru Yoshida, and much more frequently than senior American figures like Eichelberger.[62] To be sure, many of Robertson's visits were in the nature of courtesy calls, or to accompany visiting Australian political and military figures to see the 'great man'.[63] It is clear, however, that Robertson never experienced any difficulty in seeing MacArthur as and when he wished. It is clear also from Eichelberger's diary, that most of the hard work needed to maintain the BCOF organisation on a sound footing was conducted by Robertson through Eighth Army, with MacArthur functioning as a sort of court of last appeal, a fact of which Eichelberger was aware. 'I feel that Robbie plays General MacArthur off against me and vice-versa', he noted; but he testified to the former's success in full when he recorded elsewhere that 'in the polite vernacular of the day he is both a scrounger and a moocher'.[64] He got his way by an astute mixture of informality, personal charm and hard bargaining; Major General Clovis E. Byers, Eichelberger's chief of staff, wrote to him of how 'Robbie wanted to come down and talk a little business but the chief purpose of his trip was to have lunch and play golf'.[65] But after many such meetings, he came away with further concessions from Eighth Army in the form of facilities for his troops.

The fine hopes which surrounded the despatch of BCOF to Japan foundered internally on acrimonious disputes between senior military and

Robertson and MacArthur take the salute on the occasion of the arrival of the Australian Minister for External Affairs, Dr H.V. Evatt, Japan, 1947. *(AWM 44291)*

civil personnel in Japan and the growing divergence in policy aims between Britain and Australia in particular. Little if any of this was ever apparent to either the Americans or the Japanese, and so at one level the consequences of these arguments within the Commonwealth organisation were not too serious. Nor did they prevent the various Commonwealth armies from joining together in 1950 and 1951 to form combined units and formations in the face of military necessity during the Korean War. But this was to be the last such expression of Anglo-Dominion unity in the military sphere; after 1945 hopes for a revived system of imperial defence cooperation foundered on a lack of willingness in key areas of British officialdom, in particular, to recognise that such a defence relationship could not be conducted in pre-1939 terms. Relations between Robertson, Gairdner, Gascoigne and others in Japan and London in 1946 and 1947 demonstrated that clearly.

CHAPTER 8

THE OCCUPATION OF JAPAN: 1948-1950

As early as October 1946 the Australian Military Board had expressed dissatisfaction with the manner in which occupation affairs had been administered in general. As a first experiment in integrated empire forces BCOF, they felt, was not entirely a success. A better plan would have been for 'one nation to act as host assisted by self-contained national contingents'; as an instrument of control, 'JCOSA had proved to be overstaffed and unwieldy'.[1] With the withdrawal of British and Indian forces in the course of 1947 and the downgrading and eventual withdrawal of the New Zealand component in the first half of 1948, BCOF became a more or less completely self-contained national contingent in its own right, fielded and maintained entirely from Australia and overseen by the Australian defence machinery. The force was now engaged in long-term garrison duties, monitoring the reconstruction of Japan while the process of reaching agreement on the formal conclusion of a peace treaty was pursued by the former wartime allies among themselves. For Robertson this was perhaps the happiest period of the occupation, for although he now commanded a greatly reduced force his position was in no way reduced within Japan itself, many of the major irritants had been removed one way or another, and BCOF was by now well established in terms of amenities and resources. More so than before, he could enjoy his role as a senior military figure within both his own army and the wider Commonwealth military system.

Some recognition of his role in the latter was demonstrated in April with an invitation to attend the Chief of the Imperial General Staff's conference in Britain, scheduled for May. He had attended the previous year also, when the subject of Exercise SPEARHEAD had been a 'tactical discussion on overseas expeditions', and JCOSA had endorsed his participation. In 1948, Exercise BAMBOO was concerned with the staging and execution of mobile operations in an underdeveloped country in the Far East, and once again as 'the only commander of an integrated British Commonwealth force, his experience is likely to be of great interest to those present'.² Since in April 1948 he was in Melbourne for consultations with the Defence Committee and a spot of leave, the invitation was quickly considered and approved, and in mid-May he departed direct for London.

Such annual exercises are a regular feature of British pattern armies. On this occasion, Robertson's attendance was accompanied by a further string of missives between Gairdner and London and between concerned officials in London which was to contribute finally to a resolution of the Robertson-Gairdner standoff.

When he heard that the C-in-C was to attend the exercise, Gairdner wrote to the Cabinet Office to justify his position in the light of what he believed would be Robertson's criticisms of his use of resources and attempts to undermine BCOF. 'It is perhaps unnecessary to say that these accusations are entirely untrue', he wrote, '. . . and I wouldn't bother you about it except that Robertson is on his way to the UK and it would be a pity if he made unfortunate statements.'³ Hollis met Robertson later in the month, and reported that while 'he was superficially very friendly . . . it is just possible that [he] might plant some unpleasant little seed with reference to Gairdner', although clearly he had not yet done so.⁴ In fact, Gairdner's position in Japan was up for review as it had been periodically since the end of the war, and this time the decision was made to recall him.

The exact sequence of events is unclear. Robertson recorded that he spoke to the Chief of the Imperial General Staff, after remarks Montgomery had made at the exercise about the dominions assuming a greater role in the defence responsibilities of the empire. This was a subject, perhaps surprisingly, to which Montgomery attached considerable importance. Indeed he had emphasised it on various occasions in the Chiefs of Staff Committee, describing closer defence ties as 'vital' and noting that 'we cannot just go on relying on some vague friendly arrangements'.⁵ Whether Robertson's observations on the damage to Commonwealth cooperation inflicted by Gairdner's competing jurisdiction in Japan were the catalyst for his retirement cannot now be ascertained.⁶ But the matter was certainly under discussion within the Cabinet Office in June and July. Hollis minuted Attlee on the sorry state of relations between the two generals; 'I cannot help thinking that these differences can be doing no good to anybody, although they may by no means necessarily be a good reason for terminating General Gairdner's appointment.'⁷ Gairdner returned to Britain for his regular consultation in July, and was informed that he was to be retired. Hollis noted of the meeting that 'he did not refer at any length to General Robertson, but evidently there is a deep estrangement between them. No complaints about cars or aeroplanes this time'.⁸ In a draft note to Prime Minister Attlee two days previously, he had advised him that,

> *it is possible General Gairdner will ask if the termination of his appointment has any connection with the differences between himself and General Robertson. You can, of course, assure him that this is not the case, the real reason being that there does not seem to be any further need for this appointment in addition to the representative of His Majesty's Government, Sir A[lvary] Gascoigne.*[9]

In other words, the position was redundant. But then, even allowing for some settling-in period on Gascoigne's part, it had been for nearly two years. Gairdner returned to Japan in August to wind up his affairs and, after another querulous exchange with London in an attempt to convince the government to waive customs dues on a large consignment of cigarettes and alcohol which he proposed to bring back with him, departed Japan finally in November. He was retired the following year and, according to Robertson at least, spent some time angling for a vice-regal appointment in Australia. He was eventually successful, becoming governor of Western Australia from 1951 to 1963 and of Tasmania from 1963 to 1968, and there he continued from time to time to make remarks about the inability of Australians to run their affairs without guidance from Britain.

In the course of 1948 the declining strength of BCOF again became an issue, and the continuing purpose of the force was questioned in the Australian press on several occasions. The two issues were not necessarily linked. As Major General W. J. Cawthorn, Indian army representative on JCOSA, had noted to Gavin Long, 'all the adverse reporting in the Australian Press in the first twelve months of BCOF's existence was political and designed to embarrass the government of the day in Australia. It bore little if any relation to the facts and more often than not was either gross distortion or downright untruth.'[10] Of course, 1946 had seen the lead-up to a federal election in Australia, and in the second half of 1948 Chifley's government was increasingly embattled.

As noted, Robertson had returned to Australia for discussions on the future of the force. He visited New Zealand also to discuss that government's future plans for its contingent. While there, the New Zealand prime minister informed him that his government was uncertain that replacements could be found for the men then serving in Japan when their twelve-month enlistment period expired in July-August that year. The New Zealand CGS added that the deployment to Japan was of no military value to the New Zealand army. Robertson suggested that the New Zealanders might at least maintain a reduced battalion of 700 men in Japan for prestige reasons, but this was received coolly, since such a small force would be unable to maintain itself independently of the existing base organisation, as the New Zealand component had done formerly.[11] On 9 March 1948 the Minister for External Affairs proposed that notice be given of New Zealand's intention to withdraw its force and this was duly adopted by the cabinet. Nor was Robertson's suggestion of maintaining a weak battalion taken up. And on 29 June the New Zealand government gave notice of the withdrawal of the remaining RNZAF unit, No 14 Squadron, scheduled for October.[12]

The inability of BCOF to continue to administer and control an area of some 20,000 square miles (52,000 square kilometres) containing a population of about 10,000,000 people had been recognised already. In March, Headquarters, Eighth Army were advised that the 34th Australian Infantry Brigade would be withdrawing from Okayama and Fukuyama, and henceforth would be concentrated in the Hiro-Etajima area, the withdrawal to be completed by 1 June.[13] Robertson urged the Chiefs of Staff in Melbourne to maintain the Australian ground force component at 5000 other ranks since, with this, he believed that 'I should be able to further the purposes of BCOF and its maintenance on an ever reducing scale'; Japanese nationals would be used in increasing numbers to replace Commonwealth personnel in administrative and clerical roles in BCOF and further reductions would be effected in the Australian headquarters as its units were concentrated around Kure-Hiro-Etajima.[14] By this stage, the proportional contributions to BCOF were as follows:

Country	Establishments	Actual strengths	Percentage
UK	845	1351	11.25
Australia	11,049	8203	68.31
New Zealand	2763	2455	20.44
TOTALS	14,657	12,009	100.00[15]

But the remaining British personnel were being removed gradually, and the New Zealand presence was to be phased out entirely by the end of the year.

Yet further reductions were in hand, moreover, this time implemented by the Australian government. The Defence Council, meeting in Melbourne on 28 April, decided that the Australian contribution to BCOF should be reduced to a single infantry battalion and one fighter squadron of the RAAF, which with the necessary administrative and maintenance units would result in a manpower commitment of 2750 all ranks.[16] This had implications for American forces in Japan and Korea also: the total US force in Japan had been reduced with the arrival of BCOF in 1946, and although the US forces themselves had been run down in the ensuing two years, troop requirements in Far Eastern Command continued to place pressure on the US army and air force.[17] Congressional limitations on the size of the army meant that Washington could not oblige MacArthur with increases either in ground troop strengths or in additional anti-aircraft artillery units as he had hoped, and led to two requests from Washington to the Australian government for the latter to maintain a force equivalent to an infantry division less one regimental combat team (the American brigade group equivalent) 'until such time as it might be determined that a substantial reduction could be made in the occupation forces in Japan'.

Both requests were turned down, prompting the State Department to suggest the complete removal of the remaining Commonwealth force. MacArthur however turned this suggestion down flat, observing that although 'the strength of the Australian force is now so limited as to make it a negligible factor in strategic considerations', and despite the pertinent observation that 'insofar as reactions on the Japanese are concerned withdrawal or retention can be regarded as a matter of indifference', nonetheless:

> *The main consideration involved in suggesting the withdrawal would be the prejudice thereby occasioned to relationships with Australia and with the British Commonwealth of Nations. It is regarded as doubtful that any advantage which might accrue from the withdrawal would warrant the scars which might result from any possible action on the part of the United States in the initiation of such a movement.*[18]

The United Kingdom Chiefs of Staff, apprised of the US suggestion for an increased commitment from Australia, were appalled. Except on the grounds of continuing cooperation with the United States, 'it was not to our strategic advantage that Australia should continue to provide substantial forces for the occupation of Japan'. In any case, the British had hopes that 'Australian forces might be available in Malaya, and we had long term plans for their participation in the defence of the Middle East'. No pressure would be placed on the Australian government by London for an increased Australian presence in Japan; in any case, as the Chiefs of Staff Committee noted as well, 'it should be borne in mind that the peacetime Australian Army would only amount to one Brigade Group'.[19] And MacArthur was told to make do with what he had, since 'no increase in your US Army strength can be made at this time, and there is no evidence that an increase in British Commonwealth Forces will result from the intergovernmental negotiations thus far conducted'.[20]

The disbandment of the 34th Infantry Brigade and the relocation of two of its battalions to Australia was undertaken in partial implementation of the postwar plan for the army, which had been worked out gradually over the period since the end of the Pacific war. The two immediate needs which had faced the army in late 1945 were to furnish units for the occupation and to recruit men for service in the islands to Australia's north, to oversee the disarming and repatriation of surrendered Japanese personnel and to relieve 'hostilities only' men in that region. Having accomplished this, army planners turned their energies to shaping the postwar forces. The Defence Committee recommended to the government that the defence allocation should stand at £320,000,000 over a five year period commencing 1947-48, that a regular field force should be created within the army, and that peacetime national service should be introduced. The government refused the last, cut the defence estimates for the same period to £250,000,000, but agreed that the establishment of the Permanent Military Forces would allow for a field force of one independent brigade group of three infantry battalions and an armoured regiment with supporting units, with a projected strength of 4470 in a total regular establishment of 19,000. The army's share of the defence budget would be £15,000,000 per annum. The army also tried to obtain government agreement to members of the PMF being liable for service overseas in both peace and war, but for the time being the government baulked at this. With an eye to economy, the postwar army was to be equipped as far as possible with equipment already in stock, ie with Second World War surplus.

The 65th and 66th Infantry Battalions were returned to Australia to form part of the new 1st Infantry Brigade, and were based at Ingleburn, New South Wales, and Puckapunyal, Victoria, respectively. This left the under-strength 67th Battalion in Japan. Voluntary recruitment posed serious problems in a period of full employment in the civilian economy, and soon after the end of a major war there was little enthusiasm for military service. As a result, the fine intention of creating a regular field force was just that to a considerable extent. The structure existed, but all units were below strength and remained so for the rest of the decade. In 1948 the infantry units were redesignated the 1st, 2nd and 3rd Battalions of the newly formed Royal Australian Regiment, but there were few other changes to their circumstances.

In a very important sense these developments, half-formed though they may have been at this stage, marked a significant break with past practice. Implicit in the creation of a regular field force was an assumption that henceforth the regular army, not the CMF, would provide the first line of Australia's ground defences. By no means all those associated with the previous system opposed this, although they were alive to some of the problems. Blamey wrote to Robertson that 'the commanders I think have been very well chosen right down to the regimental commanders, and have good and enthusiastic teams of officers with them, but it is a strange thing that people are still deluding themselves with the idea that anything can make voluntary service in the army popular in prosperous times'. Blamey visited Japan at General MacArthur's invitation in September and October that year. Some wondered at Robertson's reaction to his old superior in the circumstances, but the two got on cordially during Blamey's visit. Blamey was now retired and very much in opposition to the Labor government, which, he felt, had treated him and many of his senior officers shabbily at the end of the war; perhaps the two were united in their view of the perniciousness of politicians and their ways. In his letter to Robertson Blamey had concluded by noting that 'you have lately been receiving some of the pinpricks that come with command. I am afraid that goes with democracy and what is called freedom of the press.'[21]

Such 'pinpricks' had been aimed at BCOF for several years. In October 1946 Robertson had written to Northcott that the press was 'chasing me hard at the moment on anything they can get and the next big distortion, which is already starting to burst, is the problem of fraternisation and as you know, whatever I say on that will be wrong'.[22] Again in 1947 he had cause to note that 'there has been criticism in the Sydney papers', although 'I do not see them and I do not worry very much about them'; with fine state parochialism he observed that 'most of the newspapers I get are only Melbourne ones and they seem to largely ignore BCOF'.[23] In truth, he could not afford to ignore hostile press criticism, because the military and political authorities in Australia were sensitive to it. As we have seen, one of the factors which had prompted Chambers' visit at the end of 1946 was the level of criticism of BCOF in the Australian press, and a few American papers.

In the course of 1948 the Australian press ran a number of adverse articles and reports regarding both the force and its commander, some prompted by the perception that BCOF fulfilled little useful function, some more mischievous. In response, Robertson went to some lengths to place favourable stories, and gave a number of lengthy interviews to journalists disposed to write favourably about the Commonwealth effort in Japan. How much real fruit this bore is anyone's guess, and on one occasion, noted below, an article which appeared under his name in an Australian newspaper got him into trouble with his political and military superiors by appearing to comment on current defence policy.

In January 1948 President McDonald of the Legion of Ex-Servicemen in Sydney described the Australian component in Japan as 'morally rotting', and went on to compare the attitude of 'high-ranking officers' in Japan 'to that of the German General Staff in wartime' on account of their allegedly debauched lifestyles and neglect of their men. The motivation behind this outburst is unknown, although reports of it were picked up and published as far away as Hong Kong, and Robertson declined to comment on either it or the related accusation that officers dealt extensively on the black market.[24] Perhaps it did no more than emphasise the general ignorance of the Australian people with regard to the force and conditions in Japan, a fact commented on by members of BCOF returning to Australia on leave.[25] But ignorance did nothing to stop the run of critical press comment. In April this reached a new peak with a former legal officer who had worked on the Tokyo war crimes trials charging that 'Australian troops in Japan were not a good advertisement for Australia', and that 'immorality and black marketing were widespread'.[26] The men were allegedly ill-trained and ill-disciplined 'by wartime standards', the incidence of venereal disease was high, 'black marketing was so general that it was impossible to control', and 'all our boys can do in Kure and Hiroshima is hanging [sic] around with prostitutes'. The officers were 'a special problem', and on balance BCOF's role was ineffectual and the force should be recalled. In addition, though one had to read well down the story to find it, the former legal corps captain complained about the Australian army rates of pay relative to the Americans with whom he had worked, and complained about being significantly out of pocket as a result of his service.

These were serious allegations, and led the army to despatch Major General C.E.M. Lloyd, formerly Adjutant General, on a fact-finding mission to Japan, accompanied by the three chaplains-general to the forces. The press made much of this mission, going so far as to claim that Lloyd had left Australia under an assumed name![27] The main focus of his investigations, it was reported, was black marketeering, hence the alleged secrecy attending his departure. The chaplains-general were to report on matters more closely related to the moral health and wellbeing of young Australians stationed in Japan, as an editorial in the Melbourne *Age* made clear a fortnight later. Noting that 'most people are inclined to treat with reserve sensational statements reflecting on the conduct of the troops', the editorial went on to argue nonetheless for a greatly reduced Australian presence in Japan given that 'no really worthwhile purpose is being served'. While disinclined perhaps to endorse the more outrageous charges levelled against BCOF, the *Age* subscribed to a general concern when it commented that 'an army of occupation anywhere is exposed to influences that only the faithful among Milton's archangels could resist ... it would be most undesirable to have the young men of the force exposed too long to the corrosive influence of idleness or lack of positive purpose about their service'.[28]

Robertson moved to counter these accusations, as he had done in the past. While in New Zealand in February he had given a long interview to a group of journalists there, emphasising the positive role of BCOF in Japan, no doubt in the hope that this might sway government and public opinion in favour of maintaining a New Zealand presence.[29] Now a favourable piece appeared in the *Sydney Morning Herald*, lauding the achievements of the troops under difficult conditions; 'amid the recent criticism of the behaviour of our troops ... little attention has been given to all that has been achieved', wrote Jack Percival, 'our correspondent recently in Japan'. While conceding that the Allied Council for Japan was 'as dead as a dodo', that BCOF played no military government function and, as a result, that 'BCOF is merely a super provost corps for General MacArthur's headquarters', he commented nonetheless that 'the morals of the troops are generally high, the majority of them are a good advertisement for the British Commonwealth, and most of them are keen on their assignments'.[30]

Lloyd's inspection revealed what Robertson and others had known, that the allegations concerning the moral degeneracy of the force lacked substance. Gascoigne thought that this press campaign was a rerun of that of 1946, 'a political stunt (the Australian elections are due in 1949)'. He reported to London that Lloyd and the chaplains 'would be able to put matters right' with their report, and that he himself thought that 'the general behaviour' of Australian soldiers in Japan 'had been extraordinarily good'. He also told Lloyd of 'how much I had admired the way in which Robbie carried out his liaison duties with the Americans during the past two years'.

> *Although Robbie and I have not always seen eye to eye, I do admire the way in which he has kept BCOF going, and I think it is just as well to let the top Australians know that we think so. Lloyd asked me whether he could say this to his Government on return to Australia, and I replied in the affirmative.*[31]

To further stifle criticism, the C-in-C himself weighed in with an article in the Australian press, stating clearly the importance of the force for the future of Australia's role in the Pacific. And ran foul of the Minister for Defence for seeming to comment on current policy outside his area of responsibility in Japan itself. The CGS, Sturdee, asked Robertson to explain his comments, and the latter justified his article on the grounds that there was nothing in it which he had not said publicly when in Australia at the beginning of the year or which had not been made by the minister himself in a statement to the House of Representatives in April. 'I submit', he concluded,

> *that it was most opportune that such an article ... under an authoritative name, should appear in the Australian press at a time when the status and integrity of the force has been seriously assailed by irresponsible statements which were published in the Australian press.*[32]

And, he might have added, which the minister had done little enough to counter. The reply did not fully satisfy Dedman, but the matter was allowed to drop, although Robertson felt that more could have been done officially to defend the good name of his command. Commenting on the attacks made on him by McDonald earlier in the year, he wrote to Northcott that 'why I should have to put up with unwarranted and untrue attacks from such a person, without someone in authority telling him when he gets off, is beyond me'.[33]

Several more favourable articles appeared in the second half of the year, and one long piece was published in early 1949 singing Robertson's praises and tipping him to succeed Sturdee as Chief of the General Staff at the end of that year: 'there may have been many personal misunderstandings about him, but Robbie has not once fallen down on any kind of assignment'.[34] The 'race' for CGS, if such there was, lay between three members of the 1914 graduating classes of Duntroon, Robertson himself, Frank Berryman and Syd Rowell. It was widely held in the army that if Labor was returned at the federal election in December 1949 then Berryman would have been made CGS,[35] a notion to which Berryman sometimes subscribed in later life. Rowell was VCGS to Sturdee, had been at Army Headquarters in Melbourne since assuming the position in 1946, and indeed was appointed by Labor late in 1949.[36] As one senior public servant in the Defence Department at the time has noted, 'in many ways ... it was unfortunate that Rowell, Robertson and Berryman were contemporaries and thus were worthy contenders for the CGS appointment in 1949. Each was quite capable of doing the job very successfully.'[37] How serious a contender for the top job Robertson was is now impossible to say; certainly in his last years in the army back in Australia he occasionally made it clear that he resented missing the appointment, since he felt that he had 'the score on the board in two world wars', and that while Rowell was 'a good staff general', he (Robertson) had both staff and command successes to his credit.[38] Later, he was to aver that 'luck is not so important as the day on which you are born', implying that Rowell got the job because he was slightly older and senior.[39] In fact, Robertson was the older by about six weeks, but in any case, the post of CGS is not filled on that basis. Relations between the two were never cordial, but as the first Royal Military College graduate to fill the post, Rowell's appointment further cemented the ascendancy of the regulars over the citizen soldiers within the army. Gascoigne had expressed the fear that Robertson's elevation to CGS 'would, indeed, be unfortunate from our point of view'; the Foreign Office thought, ironically perhaps, that it would pose 'a menace to Commonwealth cooperation'.[40] Neither eventuated.

In the second half of the year Robertson made a number of tours around what remained of the BCOF area, on one occasion accompanying the inevitable parliamentary delegation which seemed to be an annual fixture in the C-in-C's calendar.[41] The purpose of the tours was to reinforce the fact of the continuing British Commonwealth presence in the occupation upon the Japanese, and to enable Robertson to survey the progress made in the reconstruction of Japan and 'the acceptance of democratic methods by the Japanese people in our area', although quite how the latter was assessed is not clear.[42] The first trip lasted a week, from 22 to 27 September and, as Hopkins observed, resembled a royal progress:

Robertson and Menzies inspect a guard from the BCOF Signals Regiment, accompanied by the commanding officer, Lieutenant Colonel S. J. Greville, Japan, 1950. *(Author's collection)*

> at a large number of cities and towns of importance, as well as, very often, small wayside halts where the C-in-C's train stopped to take on water or to let another train pass on the single line, prefectural governors and mayors with their wives, chiefs of police and other officials of the community were ready to greet him and discuss their problems.

The second trip, a shorter one to Shikoku between 18 and 22 October, involved a similar progress viewing the reconstruction of a bombed-out country, making speeches to civil dignitaries while accepting the obligatory gifts, watching demonstrations of local crafts and performances by school children; in short, all the tedious and repetitive but highly necessary tasks which in Australia are usually the lot of state governors. On this occasion, the C-in-C's inspection received some coverage in the Australian press.[43]

The third tour, of two days duration, was of the areas around Okayama, Fukuyama and Mihara, areas formerly occupied by BCOF. Former BCOF facilities such as buildings and hospital equipment had been turned over to the Japanese here when the force had withdrawn, and Hopkins noted the way in which 'the Japanese seem to be keeping the place and equipment in reasonably good condition and remain enthusiastic as regards the value of the establishment'. Gascoigne commented to Dening that, despite Robertson's view that the Japanese appreciated fully the part played by the Commonwealth in the occupation of their country, he thought that 'as we know only too well, it is the Americans who administer the British area of occupation, and I doubt whether the Japanese have really any pronounced feeling of regard either for us or for [them]'.⁴⁴ While the tours no doubt did Robertson's morale and sense of self-importance no harm, it is difficult to disagree with Gascoigne's judgement, or with the view of Mr Patrick Shaw, head of the Australian liaison mission in Tokyo who, after a tour of his own earlier in the year, had written to his superiors in Canberra that 'the main and indeed only strong reason for the maintenance of this force in Japan [is] to demonstrate our continued interest and our readiness to assume responsibility in this area'.⁴⁵

In reviewing the year and the success or otherwise of British efforts in Japan, Gascoigne wrote to Bevin that 'the future outlook for Japan [is] not, in my opinion, a particularly rosy one. There seemed to be little hope for an early peace [while] the occupation had certainly reached its peak and appeared likely to become less and less effective as time went on.'⁴⁶ More than three years after the end of the war it was proving increasingly difficult to maintain the severity of the occupation regime. Discussions over a peace treaty foundered on Australian fears of a resurgent Japan and Anglo-Australian desires to limit Japanese financial and mercantile recovery, while the Americans, and not only MacArthur, desired an early peace on which to build a revived Japan as a political and economic bulwark against the Soviets and later, after 1949, the Chinese. But at a more mundane level than this, there was manifest within Japan itself a desire to normalise affairs with dispatch. Increasing numbers of Western civilians were now entering Japan on business and for other purposes, placing an additional administrative and logistic burden on BCOF's resources, and Robertson suggested to his superiors early in 1949 that responsibility for such matters be taken out of his hands, although he still carried responsibility for the Commonwealth liaison missions.⁴⁷

Another aspect of the softening of the occupation was the relaxation of the fraternisation order by MacArthur, which threatened to provoke a major clash between Australian and American policy. Occupation authorities henceforth were to be guided by a spirit of 'friendly interest and guidance towards the Japanese', and the order permitted free intermingling with Japanese in their homes and public places of entertainment, in sporting teams, and allowed soldiers henceforth to invite Japanese women to social activities in service establishments.⁴⁸ There was no consultation with Australian or British authorities in Japan before the order was issued. As will be recalled, the Australian attitude towards the defeated Japanese was still very uncompromising in 1949; only the year before, Robertson had made his Hiroshima day speech reminding the Japanese of their own responsibility for their defeat and the destruction of their country, and had been widely commended by the Australian press. Now, the Minister for Defence and the three service ministers in Australia recommended that the application of MacArthur's order to BCOF be resisted strongly. The closeness of a federal election played a part in their thinking; suggestions that the government was allowing Australian troops to fraternise with Japanese women would prove damaging during an election campaign. Robertson, on the other hand, was in an impossible position. Whatever his own views, MacArthur's directive was interpreted to apply to all occupation forces; even if he chose to disregard it, in all likelihood he would find enforcement of the existing order impossible in the new circumstances.

This was a policy dilemma. As the Department of External Affairs noted,

> *The only really honest argument is that the Australian people would not countenance any lifting of the ban on fraternisation at the present time. Even this is debateable, though admittedly it could be used to whip up a bit of a public outcry before the election.*[49]

American soldiers had always operated under a more relaxed set of rules covering relations with the Japanese, which was 'part and parcel of the United States tendency to allow the Japanese to slide into peace, which we have opposed all along. We do not consider that the Japanese should be treated on a friendly basis until the Peace Treaty is signed.'

Ultimately, the fraternisation ruling was relaxed within the BCOF area as well, although not without misgivings, and eventually Australians saw Japanese war brides returning home with their Australian soldier husbands. Realistically, circumstances had altered, and policy had to catch up. The men who had comprised the first Commonwealth units in Japan were veterans of the fighting in the Pacific, with little love for their newly-conquered hosts. One British officer recorded the attitude among some of his own seniors when he suggested that steps might be taken to alleviate conditions for the Japanese: 'A senior officer replied ... that he did not consider it mattered what the Japanese thought; they were "all — little —s, anyway"'.[50] But by 1949, veterans of the Pacific war were the exception in BCOF. In any case, attitudes on fraternisation had never been uniform between the occupation authorities. As one Foreign Office official, in self-congratulatory mode, recorded:

> *We feel that the British do not regard the Japanese with the blank hatred sometimes to be encountered amongst the Australians, or the even blanker incomprehension to be encountered amongst many Americans. By and large, our people seem to have a fairly reasonable appreciation*

of the merits of the Japanese and to be willing to help them to work their passage while remembering to keep a weather eye open ... What we lack in our dealings with Japan (and indeed with many countries, ex-Allies, as well as ex-enemies) is not magnanimity, but means, not good-will but surplus wealth.[51]

A willingness to establish normal relations with the Japanese on the individual level was a necessary precursor to any normalisation of relations internationally.

A change of government in Australia at the federal elections in December 1949 brought with it changed emphases in Australian defence and military policy, and finally spelt the end of Australia's direct military role in the occupation of Japan. In March 1950, cabinet resolved to give the Americans the requisite six months' warning of the withdrawal of all remaining Australian forces, by now amounting to base and headquarters elements, a single RAAF fighter squadron, No 77, and the severely understrength 3rd Battalion, the Royal Australian Regiment. Citing MacArthur himself in support of the decision, Eric Harrison, the new Minister for Defence, noted the changed nature of the occupation and the fact that the country was now completely demilitarised, that the necessity for surveillance no longer existed, and the 'social and political reformation' of Japan had reached a satisfactory stage.[52] The new Liberal government intended to introduce a national service training scheme and this, together with British pressure to play a part in the operations in Malaya against Communist insurgents and alongside a desire to build up the regular field force, which was still well below establishment, meant that there was little argument. Accordingly, on 31 March Cabinet resolved to inform the US government of the decision to withdraw.

Robertson returned to Australia for consultations in early April, and was informed of the fate of his force. In communicating its intentions to the US, the Australian government argued that its decision was taken 'not by any desire to weaken Pacific defences, but, rather, a desire to strengthen them by using the forces now in Japan as a nucleus around which to increase the armed strength within Australia itself'.[53] Robertson himself rather doubted the utility of sending Australian troops in their current state of preparedness to fight in Malaya,[54] but had few doubts about the need to use such forces as remained in Japan in order to build up the army in Australia. 'The regular troops in BCOF are part of the machinery for the expansion of the Australian army and, unless they are available in Australia for that expansion, the whole programme of build-up could be seriously interfered with. This applies with even greater effect to the air force.'[55] But he cannot have viewed the end of his command and return to Australia with complete equanimity; doubtless it was sweetened somewhat by the announcement in the King's birthday honours list of the award of a knighthood, an honour for which he had angled on and off for several years. To celebrate, he arranged for free drinks for all ranks in the canteens and leave hotels throughout the BCOF area.[56] However personally gratifying, he regarded it as recognition also for his command; 'I really feel now that the success of BCOF has been recognised', he wrote in reply to one congratulatory message, 'and that all those troops who have served uncomplainingly for over four years will feel that they have got a pat on the back'.[57] And to his sister he wrote that he expected 'to be home some time before Xmas but there is nothing definite yet'.[58] Five days later, the Korean War broke out.

A full assessment of the role of BCOF, and of Robertson's part in such success as it enjoyed, must take account of the role which the organisation played in the first twelve months of the Korean War, and will occupy part of the next chapter. But some interim judgements might be passed on the performance during the four years of that period of quasi-peace which is a state of occupation. Robertson faced an enormously difficult task in Japan, one which had proved too much for his predecessor, Northcott. In the chaotic state of immediate postwar Japan he managed to place the force on a sound administrative and organisational footing while establishing and maintaining excellent personal relations with the Americans at all levels. This latter achievement should not be underestimated; the character of the occupation was dictated entirely by the Americans and by MacArthur in particular and while no-one could have altered the conditions under which BCOF operated, especially in the area of responsibility for military government tasks which so irked British and some Australian officials, Robertson extracted a wide range of concessions from his American superiors to the ultimate benefit both of the force he commanded and the liaison missions for whose support he was responsible.

His relations with his British opposite numbers were less than satisfactory, but blame should be apportioned equally. There is no doubt that he had an exaggerated notion of his own importance, and that his arrogance and, on occasions, tactlessness, in his dealings with British officials unnecessarily aggravated a difficult situation. This applied particularly to his relations with Gascoigne. But there was more to it than a simple clash of personalities. While conceding Robertson's abilities and the excellence of his command and administration in Japan, the Foreign Office nonetheless revealed part of the cause of the disagreements when it noted that 'our decision to set up our Mission in Tokyo as virtually an Embassy was right, and with our past history and prestige in Japan it was inevitable (and in our view proper) that the United Kingdom should take the lead'.[59] In the pursuit of narrowly British interests this may well have been so, but what many British officials, especially in the Foreign Office, seemed incapable of understanding was that this was the first test of a genuinely Commonwealth approach to cooperation in the field, and that such an approach meant that British interests could not simply predominate in all circumstances and regardless of other views.

Gascoigne wrote later to Robertson to tell him:

> *how much I always admired your work in Japan and the manner in which you managed to get everything you wanted from the Americans, and yet keep on good terms with them. That was a fine job, Robbie, and whatever disagreements you and I may have had I always recognised the magnificent show that you were putting up for the Commonwealth.*[60]

One cannot imagine Gairdner writing such a letter, and indeed the sentiments expressed would have been foreign to him, given his oft-expressed views on the inability of the dominions to run things without guidance from London. Whatever successes Gairdner may have had in promoting British interests — and Buckley believes that he was largely responsible for laying 'the foundations of British occupation policies' in 1945 and 1946, and even that his demotion from head of UKLIM 'was probably a mistake'[61] — once Gascoigne had been sent out and with a senior dominion officer in command of BCOF there was no place for a competing centre of military authority within Japan. In the end, British commercial interests were not advanced significantly, certainly not at the level and with the speed that the Foreign Office and others desired, and the maintenance of Gairdner's position and the manner in which he discharged it needlessly offended the Australians and undercut much of what the Chiefs of Staff were saying in the early postwar years about the importance of regional roles in Commonwealth defence cooperation.

As restated in the directive issued to the Commander-in-Chief in March 1949, BCOF's role was 'to represent worthily the British Commonwealth in the occupation of Japan; to maintain and enhance British Commonwealth prestige and influence in the eyes of the Japanese and of our Allies; and to illustrate to, and impress on, the Japanese people as far as may be possible, the democratic way and purpose in life'.[62] The last objective, as Commonwealth authorities well knew, had little meaning while the Americans retained responsibility for military government. The first two are difficult to quantify. It seems probable that most Japanese were unaware of a separate Commonwealth identity within the occupation as a whole, and even those Japanese within the BCOF area retained little lasting impression of the force or of its commander. The effect on the Americans was another matter. MacArthur gave numerous expressions of regard for the presence and activities of the force. Other senior American officers likewise paid tribute to BCOF's role, often long after the event when there was nothing to be gained from effusive public declarations. General Edward M. Almond, MacArthur's chief of staff from 1946 to 1950, noted many years later that the Australians were useful partners in the occupation[63], while Eichelberger was grateful for the additional strength which BCOF supplied to Eighth Army at a time when the US was demobilising as rapidly as possible.

Overall, BCOF was a failure in that it was unable to realise most of the hopes held for it in 1945 and 1946. This was the fault neither of the troops who comprised it nor of the men who commanded it successively as commander-in-chief. Rather, the seeds of failure lay in heightened expectations of what the Americans would permit the Commonwealth to achieve, matched by confusion in and conflict between the policy aims of the contributing Commonwealth governments. The difficulties which BCOF faced initially were a consequence of the hasty and poorly thought-out manner in which the force was put together and dispatched to Japan. As an exercise in Commonwealth defence cooperation it fared badly in the face of British desires, in particular, to stress the primacy of individual national aims within a supposedly Commonwealth and co-operative context. Ironically, the greatest contribution which BCOF was to render to the furtherance of the Commonwealth ideal came not in the main phase of the occupation, but within the context of the first major armed clash of the Cold War.

CHAPTER 9

ROBERTSON, BCOF AND THE KOREAN WAR: 1950-1951

The Korean War appeared to many contemporary observers to result from aggressive behaviour similar to that of the European dictators in the 1930s and, as with the events of September 1939, came at the end of a series of clashes between the interests of two camps, this time the Soviet Union and the Western alliance. It is now appreciated generally that the outbreak of war on 25 June 1950 was the result of actions taken by the Soviet-backed regime in Pyongyang and not as a result of direct moves by Moscow. But at the time it seemed that the outbreak of war on the Korean peninsula (truly 'a faraway country of which we know nothing') presented the possibility of a general or world war perhaps only weeks or a few months away.

But it was not these events, nor the urgency of the early weeks of fighting during which the army of the Republic of [South] Korea (ROK), aided by under-strength and woefully inadequate US forces rushed in from occupation duties in Japan, were pushed down the length of the peninsula to a perimeter astride the Naktong River in the country's southeast, that ended Robertson's plan to be invested with his knighthood by King George VI in London. The circumstances of his award were slightly odd, in that the recommendation had been made by the British government, not by the Australian government as would have been normal with an Australian national.[1] It was customary nonetheless for Australians to be invested by the governor-general and the likely precedent of Robertson's trip to Britain, together with the cost of the visit, led the acting Minister for Defence, the acting Secretary of the department, and the Chiefs of Staff to oppose the idea.[2] By the time the decision was cabled to him in Tokyo, the situation in Korea had deteriorated considerably, leading the Australian Chiefs of Staff to note that 'in view of all the circumstances' the request had been turned down, and allowing Robertson to advise, his wife, who had returned to Melbourne from Japan the previous year, that 'in view of present excitements here [the government had decided that] I should not leave the country'.[3]

Within days of the war's outbreak, MacArthur began to pressure Robertson for the use of such Commonwealth forces as remained in Japan. A squadron of the British Pacific Fleet, which had never come under BCOF, had been made available on 28 June, and on the following day the Australian government made two ships of the RAN available also. Robertson wrote that 'there does not seem any likelihood of trouble here [ie, in Japan itself] but ... I have to remain in Tokio [sic] and keep my office in close touch with SCAP and all the other people so have both ADCs here and 24 hour phone'.[4] On 28 June, MacArthur had made his first request for the use of No 77 Squadron to provide air support to embattled US and ROK units,[5] and on 2 July the squadron flew into action over South Korea for the first time. On 3 July the Australian Chiefs of Staff instructed Robertson to provide them daily 'or more often if necessary' with a situation report on the fighting in Korea, together with information on the deployment of Australian forces,[6] and concurred in the proposal to attach selected Australian personnel to US units and to the basing of No 77 Squadron at Korean airfields when the situation permitted.[7] By 14 July the decision to withdraw BCOF from Japan was placed in abeyance.[8]

As the situation in South Korea deteriorated still further, Robertson came under strong pressure from MacArthur to deploy 3 RAR for combat duties there. Robertson knew full well that such a decision could only be made by his government, not least because the terms of the Defence Act still required that Australian soldiers volunteer for specific overseas duty, although such requirements did not pertain in the RAN or RAAF. From the beginning he made it clear that grave risks attended the too hasty despatch of the remaining under-strength, inadequately trained and ill-equipped Australian regular battalion in Japan. In his attempt to save as much of the outclassed ROK army as he could, Robertson thought that MacArthur:

> *has taken tactical and strategical decisions which I would not have risked. His overwhelming air superiority may prove that he was justified but I still feel that a major disaster to his forces cannot be ruled out. Because of the critical situation he may be compelled to commit the only remaining Div in Japan and he is already collecting single Bns from anywhere he can get them including the Okinawa garrison. I know where I stand if BCOF is not under any circumstances to be used but if a disaster occurs a call for help may be urgent and need a very quick answer ... I anticipate that he may ask me to explore the matter with you which would give time but I gravely fear there is a possibility that the position may become such that an urgent call may be made to anyone who has anything to offer. I saw General [J. Lawton] Collins [US Army Chief of Staff] on Friday and he appeared fairly confident but I know that SCAP would like Australians and would reason that if he got some he could expect more following his wartime experience.[9]*

SCAP did take enormous risks, and the early actions in the first weeks of the war saw some of the worst reverses to American arms in this century.[10] Consequently, pressure was placed on Britain and other members of the United Nations to supply forces also, and within ten days of the first intimation of MacArthur's need for ground troop reinforcement the Australian government agreed to the commitment of 3 RAR, but only after the battalion had been brought up to strength and undergone a short period of intensive training. As a result, it was not to arrive in Pusan until the end of September, a month after the first two British battalions of the 27th Brigade were dispatched from Hong Kong.

The creation of a United Nations Command and the decision by member nations of the Commonwealth to contribute ground and air forces to it raised a series of issues and problems which Robertson and his superiors in Melbourne were forced to face. Under the terms of the occupation, only those countries which had a role in the occupation were able to base forces in Japan; this was a considerable boon to the growing Commonwealth military presence in the region, because their logistic needs were quite different to those of the Americans and in any case the US army's logistic pipeline was fully stretched supplying its own formations and those of the ROK army. The British had hoped to avail themselves of some US sources of supply, but this quickly proved impossible and discussions then began on the level of support which BCOF might provide.[11] Robertson was ordered to consult with SCAP on the rapid rebuilding of a Commonwealth base organisation in Japan while the Australian Joint Administrative Planning Committee began work on a plan for the control, administration and logistic support of what was to be designated British Commonwealth Forces, Korea (BCFK).[12] Robertson stressed to his superiors the need for a joint Commonwealth organisation in the interests of both efficiency and economy. 'Whatever happens a base here is necessary and this implies a chain of supply right forward to the front line including some advanced base in Korea', he wrote. 'Any suggestion that each portion of the Empire should be separate and distinct must mean a large overhead to each with the establishment of separate bases and very distinct dollar commitments. The waste of effort in having all these separate bases and separate units appears to me to have nothing to commend it.'[13]

But as might have been predicted in the chaotic conditions which pertained, there was little time initially to lay down orderly procedures for the maintenance and support of Commonwealth units, which were thrust into the fighting almost as soon as they arrived in Pusan. 'BCOF is having more and more tasks loaded on to it by UK', Robertson signalled to Rowell, 'in spite of their insistence that the military force that they have sent to Korea is entirely on American maintenance and no concern of BCOF.'[14] Heavy demands were being made on BCOF medical and signals facilities by the British 27th Infantry Brigade, causing considerable problems for BCOF since 'our base troops had been already reduced materially in preparation for going home'.[15] If a peace treaty with Japan was to be concluded soon, then BCOF's capacity to support Korean operations would be at an end, in which case the Commonwealth governments concerned should begin building up a base area at Pusan; if BCOF was to be the base organisation for all Commonwealth forces, then some augmentation of strength would be necessary and some clear agreements and delineations reached between the Australian and British governments, and quickly.[16] 'I feel that we are just being made use of on the one hand and being insulted and slighted on the other', wrote Robertson.

> *The Americans also are somewhat bewildered and both their signals and medical branches cannot understand why the whole of this [support] is not done through BCOF. If UK is desirous of acting independently with her forces being maintained by the Americans then I consider this should apply to all her forces . . . [We can] then make very considerable reductions in BCOF and take some steps towards the withdrawal from occupation which appears likely in view of the persistent statements that a state of peace is to be given to the Japanese in the near future.*[17]

These circumstances led Rowell to despatch a long and very frank cable to his opposite number in London, Field Marshal Sir William Slim. In it, he expressed concern at the way in which Commonwealth cooperation appeared to be breaking down over the question of forces for Korea. 'We always talk very glibly about the way we cooperate', he wrote, 'but when it actually comes to the practical test we have a special facility for doing the opposite.' The 'sidetracking' of BCOF was a case in point, he felt. 'It may be that dislike in British minds of Robertson and his methods has persuaded you to set up a separate [logistic] channel of your own.' The only losers would be the troops, since Robertson was under no obligation to afford the 27th Brigade any assistance at all, and it was clear already that the American supply services could not hope to meet all the demands made of them.

> *In actual fact your people are compelled to use our signals and cipher staff and I have no doubt that very soon [you] will be asking for other facilities such as hospital accommodation. Under no circumstances would we refuse these facilities but we should very much prefer to have their use planned for and agreed rather than be put in the position of having to accept a fait accompli more particularly as any increase in the existing base facilities will have to be met from here.*

The alternative, he averred, was 'a bugger's muddle in which the only people to suffer will be the soldiers'.[18] Slim's response was prompt, and equally forthright. 'Hold your horses', he responded in similar tone; 'we are not trying in any way to cut out Robertson and the BCOF set-up.' The urgency of the dispatch of the 27th Brigade had led to *ad hoc* arrangements which needed to be put on a regular footing promptly, and in a separate cable to the head of the United Kingdom Services Liaison Staff in Melbourne Slim instructed that the future maintenance of British forces in the theatre 'will have to consist of all facilities which C-in-C BCOF can at present provide supplemented by increments in which of course we will take a share' if the Australian service authorities required it.[19] The Joint Administrative Planning Committee still thought that an advanced base in Korea would be sufficient for the needs of the Commonwealth force, since the JAPC operated still on the assumption that the deployment there would be shortlived and, since 'trained manpower is urgently required in the services in Australia, the withdrawal of BCOF should be authorised to commence forthwith'.[20] Events had now moved well beyond this point, however. New Zealand was also preparing to commit forces to Korea and the British now had agreed formally to the use of BCOF as the main supply point for their forces. As Rowell noted in response to the JAPC document, 'it would appear to be difficult to insist on a change of the policy which we ourselves proposed and endorsed', with the result that he recommended on behalf of the Australian Defence Committee that non-operational and administrative control of Commonwealth forces be exercised by the Commander-in-Chief, BCOF, but that once the real needs of those forces had been ascertained, that BCOF headquarters should be scaled down and all surplus elements returned to Australia.[21]

The result was the creation of a forward base area in Korea with responsibility for the maintenance and administration of units and formations in theatre, and drawing on the established organisation in Japan, which supplied hospital and signals support, training areas and leave and recreation facilities. BCOF assumed administrative responsibility for all Australian, New Zealand and British units in Korea on 24 October, although all Commonwealth forces continued to rely on American sources of supply for certain items which could not be provided from their own resources, such as engineer stores, POL [petrol, oil, lubricants] supplies, casualty evacuation and port operations.[22] This organisation, with some augmentation from British sources as the size of Commonwealth forces in Korea increased in late 1950 and the first half of 1951, continued to support BCFK for the rest of the war. When the peace treaty with Japan was signed at San Francisco in September 1951, provision was made for the continuation of support facilities in Japan until the end of hostilities. By then, of course, the organisation was functioning smoothly and well, and Robertson had long since departed Japan.[23] But his efforts in the first months of the Korean War had helped bring about that result, and for all that his reputation for being 'difficult' was known in London, his work in this phase of the war was appreciated by those in a position to know what was involved. 'Reports reaching us here show what great assistance and cooperation have been given by you and by the Australian staffs and units of BCOF to our brigade and base troops from the UK', wrote the Vice-Quartermaster General late in the year. 'I would like you to know how grateful we are for this help which has made all the difference in the difficult early stages of getting our force ashore and established in Korea.'[24] And of course, the new-found role for BCOF meant that the planned reduction and withdrawal of the force, and the return of its commander to Australia, was now postponed indefinitely.[25]

Had this been the sum total of Robertson's efforts in Japan and of his dealings with British authorities, all would have been well. Sadly, it was not, and circumstances conspired to revive all the old animosities and difficulties which had characterised relations between Robertson and Gairdner between 1946 and 1948 and in a manner which did the former little credit, although once again he was not solely to blame.

As instructed, Robertson had been sending back daily situation reports to the Chiefs of Staff in Melbourne, and had assumed that all information passed by him in this manner was then circulated to the interested chiefs of staff organisations in London and elsewhere.[26] Perhaps it was, but regardless of this the British Chiefs of Staff felt that they were not receiving sufficient information on the progress of the fighting nor, more particularly, on MacArthur's planning and thinking, and accordingly revived the appointment of a representative on MacArthur's staff. The post was now less ambiguously described as a senior British liaison officer, and to fill it the Chiefs of Staff appointed Air Vice Marshal Cecil Arthur Bouchier,[27] who had retired in 1949 after returning from three years as Air Officer Commanding British Commonwealth Air Forces in Japan, where he had deputised also as acting Commander-in-Chief during Robertson's occasional absences from Japan. The two men had got on well personally and professionally in that time, and it was a pity that the relationship was to descend into acrimony and backbiting in the course of 1950 and 1951.

Gascoigne recommended that Gairdner be brought out of retirement to fill the position, but thankfully this was not followed up.[28] The Foreign Office was alert to the potential for friction between Robertson and Bouchier, and advised Attlee that Robertson 'may resent the appointment, especially if the holder of it were to be someone who has recently served under him. General Robertson is a particularly "touchy" individual and we have had very many difficulties with him in the past.'[29] The Chiefs of Staff Committee were concerned that Bouchier not impinge on the work of the military members of the United Kingdom Military Liaison Mission; as their representative he would liaise with Gascoigne, but would not tender military advice to him since this would interfere with existing arrangements.[30] They did not agree that Robertson could or should exercise the function of representative of the United Kingdom

Robertson and Air Vice Marshal C. A. Bouchier, Japan, probably 1950. *(AWM DUNK 5049)*

chiefs of staff with MacArthur, although they instructed clearly that Bouchier was to have nothing to do with the administration or command of British forces in Korea and Japan 'and will concern himself entirely with policy matters'.[31]

Attlee had sought to allay the concerns expressed by the Foreign Office by speaking to Menzies while the latter was in London. In fact, the British Prime Minister had favoured recalling Gairdner, but both the Chiefs of Staff and the Foreign Office had preferred Bouchier's selection. Attlee had spoken to Menzies specifically in terms of sending Gairdner, and reported that the Australian Prime Minister 'would see that this was made all right' with Robertson.[32] Unfortunately, Menzies appears to have neglected to tell anybody about this. There were two other problems with the arrangement; the delineation between 'policy matters' and the command and administration of forces was blurred in the early weeks of the war, while the decision to appoint a special representative once again cut across the existing arrangements for Commonwealth representation by the Australians.

Major General A. J. H. Cassels, head of the British military liaison mission in Australia, pointed this out to the British Chiefs of Staff following a meeting of the Australian Defence Committee which considered the arrangements in October. Although there was no suggestion of disputing the appointment at the official level, privately the Australian Chiefs of Staff were very critical of it; 'they resented this and regard it as a retrograde step in Commonwealth cooperation', he wrote.

> *I... pointed out that Bouchier was your personal representative... and suggested that in similar circumstances they would also wish for an Australian representative of their own. They did not specifically answer this but implied that they had frequently not had such a representative in the past and referred continually to the initial charter of C-in-C BCOF where he was the representative of UK COS. They undoubtedly feel that this is similar to what they call 'the anomaly of Gairdner'. Would stress that whole discussion was perfectly amicable in spite of their views and when I suggested off the record that there would have been no trouble but for the personality of Robertson there was general nodding of heads.[33]*

This was less than just, and avoided the issue by cloaking it in a clash of personalities. Robertson recorded that 'there seemed to be many influences pulling in different directions in this matter',[34] and neither he nor the Australian Defence Committee can be blamed for being irritated at the way in which British authorities supplanted existing Australian representatives as soon as British interests appeared to require it. In this light, the British official historian of the Korean War has commented that 'while accepting that Australia and New Zealand were sovereign powers, the authorities in London continued to behave as if the old arrangements for imperial defence obtained'.[35]

Rowell made it clear that he wanted the organisation in Japan and Korea to work, 'but he feels that with the proposed directive to Robertson and however Bouchier's directive may be altered the show will not work so long as both remain. He has therefore instituted steps to withdraw Robertson by the end of the year.'[36] The Australian Chiefs of Staff concurred in this, cabling London that Robertson acted as representative of the UK Chiefs of Staff in his capacity as Commander-in-Chief BCOF, that Bouchier's appointment was anomalous, and that unless Bouchier was withdrawn or made subordinate to Robertson they would withdraw the latter from Japan.[37] Gascoigne was opposed strongly to any such move, emphasising the great value of Robertson's knowledge and experience of 'American psychology and local conditions'. In the light of this, officials in London sought a solution to 'this tiresome business', one which would avoid doing 'harm to our relations with Australia' while leaving Bouchier in place. The British High Commissioner in Canberra spoke to Menzies on the matter, but found little real interest in that quarter. 'In Robertson we are dealing with an inflated ego who has been a source of continuous embarrassment on the personal level', he wrote. 'Everyone seems to agree, however, that he has done an excellent job in Japan and we do not at this stage want him displaced. We can only hope that some action will be taken to ease the present tension.'[38]

In the end, Bouchier was instructed to confine himself to liaison with MacArthur's headquarters and to avoid interfering in operational or administrative matters, as he had done in July with the decision to rush the 27th Brigade to Pusan before the battalions were ready to depart and without most of their transport and heavy equipment. Robertson wrote of their relations that 'although the position was very difficult I treated him as I always had done, as a friend, and endeavoured to do what I could to help although I pointed out that his position would seriously embarrass me'.[39] Bouchier wrote in his daily report in October that he had 'had dinner and chat with General Robertson . . . He is very happy about the new BCOF arrangements . . . Everything is shaping well administratively here and soon when BCOF takes over many of my existing responsibilities I shall have more time to devote to the special duties of my appointment', ie, liaison with MacArthur.[40] In an earlier report he had claimed, like Gairdner before him, that 'British force going to Korea is purely United Kingdom force and therefore no concern of Robertson except by courtesy. He should be kept informed of events through me'.[41] The point, however, was that he had never had any responsibilities for either the 27th or the soon to arrive 29th Brigade. In these circumstances it is easy to appreciate Robertson's annoyance at the situation in which he found himself, since 'as a result of [Bouchier's] presence I did not hear as much as I should have heard of what was going on and UN command were never quite sure who they should refer to on British Commonwealth matters'.[42] After November Bouchier confined himself much more closely to his designated task of reporting on MacArthur's views and plans, although how closely he was taken into SCAP's confidence is difficult to judge. R. H. Scott in the Foreign Office thought that MacArthur was less than candid in his discussions with Bouchier, and that the latter was 'not in my view the possessor of a very sound judgement and . . . lends himself too readily to echoing the General'.[43] Unlike Gairdner or Robertson, he had no longstanding personal relationship with MacArthur on which to base his dealings with the Supreme Commander, and it seems unlikely, on the basis of his reports to his superiors in London, that he learnt much directly from MacArthur, although in a very rank-conscious headquarters his seniority was useful in gaining access to the views and opinions of those around the general. Following MacArthur's dismissal the following April, even this limited utility seems to have been questioned in London; after the ceasefire talks began at Kaesong in July 1951 his reporting was confined almost entirely to their progress. This was undoubtedly useful since civilians, even those in Gascoigne's position, were not permitted to attend SCAP briefings, but whether it required an additional special representative of senior military rank is another matter. Following American agreement to the appointment of a British deputy chief of staff to the SCAP headquarters in August 1952, Bouchier was recalled, and retired again the following year.[44]

Events surrounding MacArthur's dismissal provided Robertson's detractors with another opportunity for criticism and gave his superiors in Australia a further excuse to recall him if they were so minded; once again the cause was his inability to keep his mouth closed on subjects which were outside his areas of interest and responsibility. The day before MacArthur's relief by President Truman, Robertson called together a party of Commonwealth press correspondents and gave them the benefit of his views on MacArthur's conduct of the war, all 'off the record' and 'as a soldier'. The criticism which SCAP had attracted was unjustified, he claimed; MacArthur was merely trying to make the diplomats see the necessity of taking the war to the Chinese; 'if I were MacArthur and could not carry the war to the enemy, I would recommend the withdrawal of all Allied arms from Korea'. There was implied criticism of United Kingdom policy on Korea as well.[45] The timing could not have been worse, and the fact of the remarks, especially the alleged endorsement of the proposal to bomb north of the Yalu, was reported in some American newspapers. Small items appeared later in the Japanese and Australian press also, denying that he had made such statements and defusing speculation over his possible recall in consequence.[46] There was considerable consternation in London, not least because in some quarters in the United States the British were being blamed for engineering MacArthur's dismissal. The matter was even referred to the United Kingdom Chiefs of Staff Committee, who felt nonetheless that there was little they could do about it since 'our relations with General Robertson are already extremely difficult ... If possible, no action should be taken which would further embarrass these relations, particularly as we are not in a position to have General Robertson removed from his present post.' In any case, MacArthur had been removed since the remarks had been made, and 'statements by General Robertson of this sort in fact carry little weight', which was perfectly true.[47]

The occupation was winding itself up, and in any case occupation matters took a very secondary place to the conduct of operations in Korea under both MacArthur and his successor, Ridgway. Robertson was kept busy by the relief of the 27th Brigade and the intense fighting in April and May during the enemy's Fifth Phase offensive, during which the Australians were engaged heavily at Kapyong and an entire British battalion was wiped out on the Imjin, and by the formation of an integrated Commonwealth Infantry Division in July. During the Imjin battle Robertson was in Korea visiting the troops, and was consulted by the Americans as to the possible consequences of the loss of the Gloucesters; he advised the chief of staff of the US I Corps, under whose command the British 29th Brigade operated, 'not to endanger the remainder of the Corps line if that would be the result of attempting to extricate the trapped Gloster battalion'.[48] He had visited the brigade the day before, and recorded later that the situation 'was extremely dangerous at that time and very upsetting'.[49] The 29th Brigade suffered twenty-five per cent casualties in the battle, but there was never any suggestion, from the War Office or anywhere else, that Robertson's advice or the American decision not to risk further forces in the attempt to extricate the trapped battalion was other than the right one.

By the middle of the year the Australian Chief of the General Staff had resolved to bring Robertson home and make him Director General of Recruiting. The Joint Administrative Planning Committee recommended downgrading the position of Commander-in-Chief to the rank of brigadier, a clear recognition that the occupation duties involved had dwindled almost to nothing.[50] There was also a suggestion that Major General Cassels, now commanding the Commonwealth Division in Korea, should combine that post with responsibility for occupation matters, while delegating his administrative functions for the occupation elsewhere. Objections were raised from several quarters. The New Zealanders made it clear to Canberra in August that they did not want Robertson removed at that time while the negotiations for the Anzus pact were in train; 'it is undesirable that any step should be taken which might prejudice contact by Australia and New Zealand with the United States service authorities on the highest levels. The most valuable direct point of contact is in Tokyo.'[51] The New Zealanders were opposed also to placing all Commonwealth forces in the theatre under British control. Having agitated for Robertson's removal for so long, the British too now raised objections on the grounds that Cassels could not be expected to command a division in the line and attend to duties in the rear areas in Japan. If Robertson was to be recalled, another Australian general officer should replace him.[52]

Rowell was particularly irritated by this, since he had discussed the change with Slim when the latter had visited Australia in June and July, and had thought that agreement had been reached. 'You will appreciate that a lot of personal considerations have been brought into this matter', he wrote, 'the chief of which is Robertson's desire not to come back here. He himself has raised no objection but has seen that Cassels and Stewart [the New Zealand representative] do so on his behalf.'[53] And he concluded by noting that should the Australian government decide to recall Robertson, 'I am afraid it will be quite out of the question for us to provide a Lieutenant General to succeed him'. These observations were almost certainly unfair, to Cassels and Stewart and probably to Robertson as well, while the implied threat not to replace the latter with an officer of equal rank was almost petulant. In any case, blocked by the fundamental objections of two of the three other Commonwealth countries with major ground forces in Korea, Rowell was forced to accept the situation. The British chiefs of staff were informed that Robertson would be left in place for the present, an outcome far from welcome to the Foreign Office; 'from other than the military point of view this decision is unwelcome and we are so informing the Chiefs of Staff'.[54]

These complaints proved premature, for on 6 October 1951 Robertson was advised formally that he was to be recalled to Australia and his place taken by Lieutenant General William Bridgeford, until then Quartermaster General of the army. The Foreign Office representatives in Tokyo were delighted, although unhappy about the possibility of further difficulties with a high-ranking Australian officer jealous of the prerogatives of his rank and position. 'Bridgeford may not be so touchy or pretentious as Robertson', wrote Clutton in Tokyo,

> *but there are occasions when difficulties are bound to arise ... the appointment will prolong locally the inevitable difficulties experienced by the Heads of Commonwealth Missions in Tokyo in having in their midst a high-ranking Commonwealth Commander-in-Chief whose precedence and status in relation to themselves can be subject to such widely differing interpretations.*[55]

But he consoled himself with a feeling of 'very welcome relief to know that Robertson is really going'.

Robertson returned to Australia on 17 November, having handed over to his successor and taken his leave of his commands in Japan and Korea. He had been tipped in the press to take over as Director General of Recruiting as early as the previous August, and returned now to generally favourable comment in the Australian newspapers and a round of civic receptions.[56] He reported to members of both houses of parliament on the conduct of the occupation and the course of the fighting in Korea, and made a number of radio broadcasts as a preliminary to the recruiting campaign which he was to direct, and in which he stressed the serious nature of the fighting in Korea and its implications for Australia; 'some might be of the opinion that it was only a small affair, but there were more troops engaged than were at El Alamein'.[57]

With the exception of a couple of short visits, Robertson had been away from Australia for nearly five and a half years. In that time the

Robertson and General Matthew B. Ridgway take the salute before Robertson's departure from Japan, 1951. *(AWM DUNK 5043)*

government had changed, and with it had come some wide-ranging alterations to defence policy, themselves influenced by international events and the deepening of the Cold War between the two great power blocs. The recruitment campaign and the national service scheme which were to occupy his time for the next year were expressions of this. The fighting in Korea would continue until the ceasefire in July 1953, and Australian troops would remain there until 1955 monitoring the truce, but henceforth Robertson's interest would be taken up with concerns closer to home.

A partial assessment of his command in Japan has already been made. The period between the outbreak of the Korean War and his final recall at the end of 1951 saw him devote all his considerable energy and organisational ability to solving some potentially intractable problems of supply and administration in the face of competing demands from both the Americans and the service authorities in Britain and Australia. That the early Commonwealth contingents in Korea were able to take the field and be maintained there for any length of time owed a very great deal to his considerable knowledge of local affairs and personalities coupled with his ability to get things done. It was a pity therefore that a record of achievement should be marred by personal disagreements with British officials, especially with Bouchier with whom he had enjoyed good relations previously. That the problem was not one simply of personalities, however, was illustrated by the objections voiced by the Australian Defence Committee and by the way in which Bouchier attempted to interfere in matters which had nothing to do with him, much as Gairdner had done earlier.

The years immediately after the Second World War were difficult ones for Anglo-dominion relations at several levels. Attlee and other British ministers objected from time to time that the dominions, especially Australia, were truculent in their dealings with London and wished to obtain the benefits of a Commonwealth position while at the same time going their own way in foreign policy. Especially this was felt to be the case with Evatt between 1945 and 1949, and there was some truth in the criticism. But the British were perfectly capable of playing the same game; indeed, they were past masters at it. In the aftermath of the war Britain's financial and strategic position was desperately difficult, and successive British governments needed the added economic and military strength which the empire, and the dominions in particular, could provide in order that Britain's claims to world power status and ability to deal on a basis of rough equivalence with the United States might be maintained. The desire to devolve tasks in Commonwealth defence cooperation to the dominions was an important aspect of this process, one however doomed to failure by the attitude of many British officials, especially in the Foreign Office, who could not accept, if indeed they recognised, that Britain's power was declining irrevocably and that the world had changed since 1939, not least in terms of the role and aspirations of countries like Australia.

The occupation of Japan might have been a great and successful demonstration of these new principles of regional defence responsibility within the Commonwealth. At one level, as in Korea too, the experiment was relatively successful, in that armies and air forces derived from a British pattern demonstrated that they could combine effectively on the operational and administrative levels. But in a far more fundamental way the occupation demonstrated decisively to officials in Australia, and to the more sensitive Britons in the Commonwealth Relations Office and on JCOSA, that a postwar revival of imperial defence would be attended with little success. It is doubly ironic that the man who for many in London epitomised some of the worst features of Australian assertiveness in postwar affairs, the Commander-in-Chief, British Commonwealth Occupation Forces, was known to his Australian contemporaries as a pronounced Anglophile who genuinely sought to strengthen the basis of Commonwealth military cooperation in peace and war within the context of postwar realities.

PART THREE

Peace hath so besotted us that as we are altogether ignorant, so are we much the more sensible of the defect, for we think if we have men and ships our kingdom is safe, as if men were born soldiers.

Sir Edward Cecil *(1628)*

CHAPTER 10

THE FINAL YEARS: 1952-1960

'Humility is not an occupational disease of successful military commanders', wrote Blamey's biographer, John Hetherington.

> Nearly every military commander is an intensely ambitious man governed by an instinct to impose his will on those about him as well as on the enemy in front of him. If he were not, he would not be a military commander. The exceptions who temper their masterful qualities with humility — the only one from the Second World War who comes readily to mind is Wavell — are so rare as to be all but unbelievable.[1]

The tribalism and factionalism of the Australian generals during the war years carried on into the peace, despite the fact that the majority of those who had held high commands during the war were retired or returned to civilian life soon after the war's end. The animosities continued just below the surface, to be resurrected over an issue such as the appointment of a successor to Sturdee as Chief of the General Staff and professional head of the army.

With Rowell as one of the chief contenders for the post it was natural that Blamey should favour one of the others, and logical that this should have been his wartime chief of staff, Berryman. At a dinner for senior AMF officers at Victoria Barracks, Sydney, before the announcement had been made formally, Blamey told him that 'he thought Chif[ley] had made the appt of Sid [to CGS] but with a change of Govt it would NOT necessarily hold as Vernon [Sturdee] remains till April'.[2] Sturdee in fact seems to have been above the factions, both during the war and thereafter, and Rowell's appointment was made on his recommendation. There was never any likelihood that it would be overturned, and those concerned deluded themselves if they really thought so. But this still left three senior lieutenant generals in the army, all accomplished and ambitious men, and all conscious of their prerogatives. It did not make for an easy time in the conduct of the army's affairs. There is some evidence even that Berryman hoped to succeed Rowell in 1953, assisted by at least one government minister.[3]

After the appointment was made public, Rowell wrote a gracious letter to Berryman, and we must assume to Robertson also, although no copy of it has survived, commenting on his appointment. It could 'just as easily have gone to yourself or Robby as it has to me', he wrote, 'and I'm sure the Army would have got on as well with any of us at the top'.

> *As it happens it has come to me. But I would be more than a mug if I felt that I had gotten on without the help of a lot of people over the years, or that I could succeed in holding the job down without the cooperation of my colleagues... This letter will, I am afraid, do little to temper what naturally will be a keen disappointment to you. But I do hope it will assure you of my highest regard for all you have done for the army and my pleasure to have you as a colleague for the remaining years of our service.*[4]

But relations between the three were not always easy, especially between the CGS and Robertson once the latter was appointed to Southern Command in 1953 and found himself 'sharing' Melbourne with his senior. As one senior officer, himself later CGS and at that time Director of Military Operations and Plans under Rowell has observed, 'I am glad that I had no Red Robbies lurking in the background when I was CGS.'[5]

The post of Director General of Recruiting had been created by the Menzies government in August 1950 as part of the Liberal-Country Parties' emphasis upon boosting the defence of Australia. As Blamey had noted shrewdly, voluntary military service held little attraction in a time of economic boom and full employment. The national service scheme which the government introduced in 1951 was as much a political gesture as anything, since the period of full-time service obligation was just six months in total, there was no overseas service obligation for national servicemen, and the actual military value of the training imparted in this time was nugatory. It was popular with the electorate, however, perhaps for precisely those reasons. Lieutenant General Sir Edmund Herring had been persuaded to take the recruiting job on a temporary basis on leave from his duties as Chief Justice of Victoria, and had laid the foundations for a more rational approach to army manpower policy in that time. In February 1951, for example, he noted in a paper on Australia's defence problems that 'there is an all-too-prevalent idea amongst those who know little of the history of the 1st and 2nd AIF that these Forces were raised quickly, and because of the inherent fighting qualities of the Australian, were ready for battle almost at once. This is a dangerous misconception.' And he noted with concern the way in which 'responsible citizens [were] still talking about pushbutton warfare', when the fighting in Korea demonstrated that 'it is still the man on the ground that matters'.[6]

While the shape of postwar defence and military policy was formulated, Australia had been served by the Interim Army, formed on

1 October 1945. Its function was to maintain a force in being, comprised of all those still on full-time duty on that date, until a more permanent force was formed, and for a time all recruiting was into its ranks. It was disbanded on 14 August 1952 and its members transferred to the Australian Regular Army (ARA) or to the Regular Army Supplementary Reserve (RASR). The Australian Regular Army, on the other hand, was formed out of the old Permanent Military Forces in September 1947. In many cases these changes were merely administrative, at least as they affected individuals. But in the period between the demise of the old system and the creation of the ARA, some fundamental questioning of previous policy went on within the senior ranks of the army, certainly in so far as the role and function of its component parts was concerned.[7] Considerable thought was given to the basis of postwar planning also. As VCGS, Rowell had written in March 1946 that in neither world war had the expeditionary force been raised 'on the basis of the army organisation then existing for our peace time forces. There is no doubt that in future the peace time force — whatever its composition — must be the basis on which the raising of the forces for war is effected.'[8] This led naturally to consideration of a standing regular army, as we have seen. And the principal tasks of such a force, as expressed in the army postwar plan of March 1947, were to be cooperation in empire defence, local defence of the Australian mainland, and the maintenance of the Australian ground component in BCOF, in which role Robertson had encountered it.[9]

But for the reasons suggested already, the attempts to bolster the regular forces had not met with great success thus far, and in any case Herring was anxious to return to the bench. His services in fact were extended beyond the original term while attempts were made to find a suitable high-ranking officer to take over the task, and following on discussions with Menzies, the Minister for Defence, P.A. McBride, resolved on Robertson, who was duly advised in late July.[10] It was intended that Herring should return to his judicial post after 31 August 1951, and McBride requested that Robertson arrange an early return to Australia in order to spend a fortnight's handing-over period with his predecessor. 'The government attaches the highest importance to building up the Permanent and Citizen Forces to their planned strengths as quickly as possible and to the recruiting campaign as a means to this end', he cabled. 'We consider it essential to have as Director-General of Recruiting an officer of wide experience possessing the confidence of the government, the services and the public.' Robertson replied that 'throughout my service I have avoided long handovers and I feel I can grasp all that is necessary in one week', but in any case his return was delayed well beyond that as a result of objections voiced by the British and New Zealand authorities to his removal from Japan at that time. As an interim measure, since Herring was now insistent on returning to the bench on 1 September, Major

General W.M. Anderson was appointed to the duties of the position pending Robertson's eventual return.[11]

Anderson was on leave prior to retirement, but his choice would not have displeased Robertson. He had been Adjutant General of the Australian Military Forces from 1947 to 1951, but his greatest recommendations in Robertson's eyes were that he had served with the light horse in Palestine, had been Robertson's AA & QMG on the Armoured Division's headquarters, and had served him again as brigadier in charge of administration in BCOF from 1946 to 1947. As Robertson prepared to return from his long period of command in Japan, Anderson continued to oversee the recruiting campaign for the forces in Korea; in the second half of 1951 the Australian government came under strong pressure from the United States to increase its force commitment to the war, a decision which was made reluctantly and in the knowledge that the strength of the regular army was such that an additional battalion could not be despatched immediately. In the period from January to June 1950 only 136 recruits had enlisted in the AMF; between 28 June and 19 July this figure had increased by only ninety-eight.[12] Since its inception in October 1950, the recruiting campaign had cost the government £385,182.[13]

It is perhaps moot whether the recruiting campaign boosted the army's strength, or whether involvement in the Korean War would have done this in any case. As figures for the strength of the forces demonstrate, by 1952 both the regular and citizen components had grown appreciably. The latter of course was now processing large numbers of national servicemen under the 1951 scheme.

Date	Permanent forces	Citizen forces	Total
June 1950	14,543	18,236	32,779
June 1951	19,443	20,981	40,424
June 1952	27,572	42,858	70,430
June 1953	27,180	69,061	96,241
June 1954	24,414	82,893	107,307

Between 1957 and 1960, with the battalion group on operational duty against the insurgency in Malaya, the regular army maintained a strength of 21-22,000, and this was to remain fairly constant until the sizeable expansion brought about by involvement in Vietnam in the mid-1960s.

Robertson returned to Sydney on 14 November amidst considerable publicity. Herring had been right when he commented that he would bring 'some of the glamour he carried by virtue of his recent return from Japan and Korea' to the position, although it should be added that with an eye as ever to the possibilities, Robertson had dispatched his public relations officer ahead of him to orchestrate the press coverage which attended his arrival.[14] He had made it clear that he would 'use my arrival to get maximum recruiting publicity', and although he was advised not to speak 'on more detailed matters relating to the recruiting campaign until he has acquainted himself... with the local position', he spoke happily to groups of reporters from the morning and evening papers and various radio stations, and his arrival was the occasion for several lengthy articles in the press.[15] Within a month of his return, he was advising bodies such as the Red Cross 'to embark on a large-scale plan for dealing with a world war', saying that if there was not a war, the preparations for one would not go amiss'.[16] Robertson, the Prime Minister told parliament, 'can speak with authority on the needs of the services for recruits to build up the objectives in strengths which have been laid down by the government for attainment by June 1953'.[17]

The recruiting campaign was overseen by a sub-committee of the Cabinet, to which the Director General was answerable directly. There was a recruiting secretariat at the national level, on which the services were represented by the Second Naval Member, the Adjutant General and the Air Member for Personnel, together with representatives from ex-services groups and the Assistant Director General, who reported direct to Robertson. There was a small staff at the national level also, concerned mostly with publicity, finance and general policy, but much of the routine work was carried out by state recruitment committees, on which again sat the local service commanders, representatives of the Returned Services League and other ex-service organisations, and leading citizens, and each of which was chaired by a prominent citizen with military ties; in the case of New South Wales, for example, Sir Iven Mackay was chairman from 1950 to 1952. In general terms, the manner in which recruitment for the services was approached had not changed much since the First World War. For all the emphasis which the government placed upon the recruiting campaign, the Cabinet sub-committee directly concerned never met, and in practice the Director General worked through the Minister for Defence.[18]

At the time of Robertson's appointment, service manpower in general still lagged badly behind establishments, and the introduction of the national service scheme, contrary to what many may think, merely exacerbated the situation. Considerable resources had to be diverted from other tasks to provide the training and administrative support which the scheme required, and this at a time when all three services, but the army in particular, were being called on to maintain forces in an active war zone in Korea. Both the army and the air force had recourse to recruiting in the United Kingdom in order to make up the shortfall in regular enlistments.[19] But as late as 11 January the following year Robertson was forced to ask Shedden for copies of any papers which might give him 'an overall picture of the present defence policy and plans', and in particular any statements on the approved service establishments in peace and war.[20]

The position of Director General involved rather more than Robertson perhaps had imagined. Rather than a week's handover, as he had confidently advised the Minister would be all that he needed, he found himself retaining Anderson's services well into the new year. As he explained now to the Minister,

> he knows everyone, whereas I have hardly been in Australia for 12 years and, quite apart from not knowing the people, I do not know much of what has been going on in Australia and very little indeed of what has been taking place in the Australian Army — I have been too busy elsewhere.[21]

Part of the problem, in addition to his lack of familiarity with personalities, was that although, as we have noted, service representatives sat on certain of the committees there were no service personnel in the recruiting organisation as such; 'that being so, I am rather out of touch with what takes place in those Services'. This lack of detailed knowledge of policy was exemplified by his proposals for the creation of new Citizen Military Forces units as a spur to recruiting, a proposal strongly and successfully opposed by the CGS who, in concert with the CMF member of the Military Board, pointed out to the Minister for the Army that 'all the ground covered by General Robertson has been gone over in great detail since we commenced the raising of the CMF in 1948'. Recruiting for the CMF had failed 'in the great centres of population, where we already have established units ... and it is in these centres rather than the smaller country centres that attention should be concentrated'.[22] Robertson's proposal for the re-establishment of an Inspector-General's Branch to oversee all three services was no more successful.

Whilst enlistments for the permanent forces were generally satisfactory by 1952, not least because of the Korean involvement and the attraction of overseas service, recruitment for the CMF lagged badly: although 13,000 men joined the citizens' force in the twelve months to January 1952, a low retention rate meant that the actual net increase in the size of the force over the same period was little more than 2000 personnel. The competing demands of the regular forces and the national service scheme starved the CMF of resources and made the outcome more or less inevitable, given the government's attitude to increasing the defence allocation. Robertson found his time in charge of recruiting a frustrating experience. He felt he was surrounded by apathy on the part of the general public and many politicians, the state recruiting organisations were cumbersome and ineffective, and he complained of hostility towards the directorate on the part of the individual services, which resented any attempt to encroach on their jurisdictions while blaming it for any shortcomings in overall manpower policy.[23] In his public statements he warned of the consequences of lack of preparedness given the threatening international situation — 'We must be prepared, and must get down to the job of holding this country. If we don't, it will not be ours for long.'[24] And like many before and since, he wondered at what he perceived as the apathy of the young and the 'inability' or 'unwillingness' to see the necessity of a defence obligation; 'life has been too easy for the post-war youngster', he asserted.[25] In September 1952 the government announced a review of the recruiting organisation, and while publicly the government considered the campaign 'a source of satisfaction', Robertson himself must have welcomed his departure from the position to take up the post of General Officer Commanding Southern Command in January 1953.[26]

He carried over his concern with preparedness to his new post, and in typical fashion was soon out and about inspecting the units in his command, correcting deficiencies, reproving and encouraging those under him. The presence of Army Headquarters, and the CGS, in Melbourne undoubtedly grated. There was little love lost between himself and Rowell by this stage, and relations were characterised by pettiness and aggravation on both sides. They had never been especially close, and animosities which had developed during the war were aggravated for Robertson by his failure to get the top job. That there were two senior three-star generals in Melbourne tended to diminish the status of both. The military assistants to the two generals concocted a ploy whereby when the two spoke on the phone, they would be connected simultaneously so that neither would have to wait on the other![27] Much of this was petty in the extreme, and there can be little doubt that Robertson on occasions went out of his way to irritate Rowell, who was forced to reprove him in writing on a number of occasions over such matters as direct approaches to the minister on matters which were the prerogative of the CGS, and on the question of promotions.[28] Relations reached their lowest point in late 1953, with Rowell upbraiding Robertson for a memorandum 'the general tone of [which] . . . is offensive. In particular, in the last paragraph it makes accusations against the integrity and honesty of purpose of myself as head of the Service, which can not be tolerated.'[29] There was similar acrimony over the question of a successor as CGS when the matter arose in mid-1954.[30]

His sixtieth birthday fell on 29 October 1954, and Robertson was placed on the retired list the following day, after forty-three years in the army including 3985 days on active service in two world wars, Japan and Korea. The Melbourne newspapers covered his departure at length, and continued to report his views and public statements.[31] He was appointed honorary Colonel of the Royal Australian Regiment, in which he took a keen and active interest and which maintained his association with the regular army of which he had been a part for most of its existence, and occupied himself with various boards and organisations, including a period as President of the Victorian Branch of the Royal Empire Society and the committee of the Metropolitan Golf Club. Retirement found him active, fit, engaged, and as opinionated as ever.

On 16 August 1956 Jessie died in hospital, two days after suffering a cerebral haemorrhage. Her death certificate gave her age as sixty-four, but she was in fact eighty, and had been in failing health and a semi-recluse for some years. She was buried with Presbyterian rites four days later at Springvale cemetery . They had been married for forty-two years. Although he was always unfailingly loyal and caring towards her, she had been a difficult woman and, it has been suggested, a professional as well as something of a personal burden to him. Whatever other impact it had upon him, and that can only be surmised, her death gave him the opportunity to develop closer relations with his sister's children then living in Melbourne, and with their young families whose company he enjoyed enormously as he did that of all young people. He took a delight also in the children of the younger officers who worked for him. In his last years he mellowed somewhat, although he was capable, as always, of some outrageous piece of bombast which would irritate his detractors and delight his many friends and admirers. One such occurred on the premises of the Metropolitan Golf Club where Robertson, while on the committee, had seen to the installation of marble floors in the change rooms. These became slippery when wet, and one day Robertson encountered a senior member sitting and nursing a swollen ankle, the consequence of a fall on the wet and slippery surface. 'Precisely', pronounced Robertson. 'I slipped myself and had I not been an excellent ice skater in my youth I might have hurt myself.'

On 28 April he suffered a ruptured aorta, and died soon after at Heidelberg Repatriation Hospital at the relatively early age of sixty-five. He had been in good health, although he smoked heavily, and his death came as a considerable surprise to most. His funeral, with full military honours, was held at Scots Church, Melbourne and was conducted by the Moderator General of the Presbyterian Church and the Protestant chaplain general. Eight generals acted as pall bearers — Herring, Rowell, Clowes, Boase, Simpson, Beavis, Edgar and the current CGS, Sir Ragnar Garrett, while Major General Sir Frank Kingsley Norris bore his honours and decorations, and guards of honour were provided by the 2nd Battalion, Royal Australian Regiment and the 1st Armoured Regiment. It was the largest military funeral since Blamey's in 1951.

Afterwards, Robertson was interred with his wife at Springvale; on the stone his brother had inscribed: 'Reason resigns, faith gives thanks, but

Robertson's coffin leaves Scots Church, Melbourne, 3 May 1960. (By permission of The *Age*, Melbourne.)

instinct and affection mourn'. The Melbourne press carried articles on his life and career, but obituaries appeared around the country and officers and men who had served under him wrote of their experiences to their local papers. 'Always a soldier's general', said the Sydney *Bulletin* in its obituary, 'whatever his faults, and however hard he was sometimes to live with, he was a fine soldier, a fine leader and trainer of men and a fearless propagandist whenever he had a purpose to serve.'[32] 'It is said of modern generals that they must also be good politicians', wrote the *Sydney Morning Herald*. 'Red Robbie ... never learnt to be a good politician. But he leaves his own personal memorial in the minds of the men who served with him.'[33] But perhaps the Adelaide *News* provided the best summary of his life and career: '"Red Robbie" made a number of powerful enemies during his tumultuous career. But he made more true friends. He was that all-too-rare phenomenon in modern armies — a true personality, a character, and a grand leader of men.'[34]

CHAPTER 11

'RED ROBBIE': A SUMMATION

Few who knew him were ambivalent about Robertson. Throughout his career, but especially as a senior officer, he inspired great affection and admiration and almost equal detestation among superiors, contemporaries and juniors alike. 'By nature Robertson was tough,' wrote one such who had served under him in Western Australia in the latter part of the war, 'a strong personality, sure of himself and sure that there was only one way to go about anything — the right way. He was forthright in speech and act and contemptuous of half-measure and compromise. As a result he made a few bad friends both above and below him'.[1] But on the personal side, 'in his rare "off-duty" moments, he was a courteous, kindly, amusing and charming man'.

One's opinion of Robertson depended very much on the perspective one adopted, on the position from which one observed him. Discord leaves a stronger impression than harmony, but it must be wondered if there has ever been a more discordantly competitive and ambitious group of senior officers than that which led Australia's armies in the Second World War, and the fact of personal rivalry and sometimes poisonous feuding between individuals obviously coloured the accounts we have of the rivals themselves. That the animosities in many cases were based on the previous twenty years of defence cutbacks and stymied career opportunities for the regulars in particular, explains, but hardly excuses. In many instances, it required the viewpoint of a junior or outsider to present any sort of balanced picture of the senior generals and their abilities. C. M. L. Elliott, a wartime Brigadier, General Staff at Land Headquarters and on Headquarters, Second Australian Army, senior enough to know the individuals well during the war but junior enough in rank not to be seen as a rival, asserted later that the best officers he had ever served under were 'Red Robbie (as a commander) Rowell (as a senior staff officer and as a commander) and Gaffer Lloyd (as a senior staff officer and as AG)'. And he noted that Lloyd and Robertson were 'two shining examples of true delegation' of authority to their subordinates. 'Whilst Red Robbie would always uphold the delegate's right to make decisions within the delegation, the General would well and truly tell the delegate privately what he thought of a bad decision. Rowell would do the same.'[2] For many, as a result, he was the ideal senior, concerned to educate and bring on his subordinates in the tasks and duties of their position but keen also to develop them for other and hopefully higher posts: 'a firm, stimulating and exacting mentor, but a kind one too . . . I remember him with respect, admiration, and above all, affection.'[3] This goes a long way to explaining the high regard in which the majority of those who served him still hold him to this day.

An outsider's perspective could be equally illuminating. Gavin Long, official historian of Australia in the Second World War, spent much of the period 1939-45 visiting Australian units and formations, talking with soldiers and officers of all ranks and conditions, and constantly taking notes on these for the great task which would occupy him until his death in 1968. Few men knew the wartime army as well and as intimately as he. His judgement on Robertson is lengthy, and is worth quoting in full.

> *In the first war and again in the second Robertson had his crowded hour . . . He was still 'Red Robbie' in 1941, though his hair was grey rather than red. In 1940 he was given the bde formed as a result of reducing the 6 Div bdes from 4 bns to 3. Menzies had announced in 1939 that all comds would be given to militia offrs, and it was said at the time that Robertson was given the comd only because the Govt was bewildered by conflicting claims from several states, each with their candidate and solved the problem by bringing Robertson from no state as he was comdg at Darwin.*
>
> *There can be no doubt that R. trained his brigade well, and in action was a forceful and learned leader. It is doubtful whether there was another leader in the Australian Army with greater devotion to his job of training and comdg soldiers, or with more military learning or a more complete and carefully worked out doctrine of war.*
>
> *Those who admired him — and they included most of the keener and abler offrs who worked under him — ranked him as Australia's ablest soldier.*
>
> *What were his defects? His detractors said that his egotism was insufferable. He was an egotist, but an egotist of the least insufferable kind. Not one of those vain, and therefore touchy egotists who cannot avoid interposing themselves between their audience and the subject under discussion (like so many critics of art and books) but a hearty, honest egotist, and a grand talker.*
>
> *He was ambitious, but few soldiers lack ambition. With R. this quality took the form of frequent detraction of his seniors and of offrs of equal rank. This was done not as part of a well thought-out plan of intrigue the object of which being to unseat his seniors and put him in their place, but because he was honestly convinced he was the better man. He was no less cutting of offrs serving under him than of offrs senior to him, if he considered they lacked drive and the intellect he demanded in a soldier. His mistake, from a worldly-wise point of view, [was] that he*

> *made his disapproval of certain of his seniors no more of a secret than his disapproval of some of his juniors.*
>
> *Soldiers under him who he admired he admired greatly. He had nothing but praise from the beginning for Dougherty (but not for Mitchell or Louch) and Onslow, and any good man from 6 Div Cav. Mitchell 'thought he had nothing to learn about war'; R. thought he had much to learn, and would, I think, have been happier with subordinates who had* not *served in the last war.*
>
> *He was conscious of his own weaknesses (if weaknesses they be) but his intense interest in his profession left no room for the cultivation of diplomacy. He did not drink much. In the field he lived simply and took no leave his men could not share.*
>
> *... In all affairs he admired English standards — discipline, military doctrine, equipment — often to the detriment of Aust. After a fortunate beginning in this war R's ambition and outspokenness led to his removal from the field of battle.*[4]

That same bombastic egotism which Long identified could make him a figure of fun, even ridicule, and serve to obscure his abilities. Several jokes at his expense went the rounds during the jockeying for position in 1942. One had him writing a memoir entitled 'Great Men Who Have Met Me'; another had St Peter greeting a psychiatrist at the pearly gates with the words 'You've come just in time. You must see God, He thinks He's Robertson.' Yet he could be remarkably considerate and fair to those around him, especially those in more junior positions. On the annual report of one young officer who had served as his ADC in Japan he wrote, 'A likeable officer whom I took as ADC to give him a wider view and experience than he had had in the past. I believe he has benefitted.'[5] Another time an officer on the headquarters of the Armoured Division asked the GOC if he was to be replaced because of his age; the general 'looked up at him quizzically and said "Every court needs a jester", and the officer concerned stayed on'.[6] And as honorary colonel of the RAR he made a particular point at regimental functions of spending time talking to the subalterns and junior officers, and not merely to the seniors.

A shrewd observation in an article published soon after his death noted of him that he was 'the "Red Robbie" of many admirers and few friends',[7] and this was especially so as he grew older and became more senior in rank. In the opinion of one of his oldest friends, the reason for this was not far to seek. Jessie 'was still, throughout their married life, an obstacle to her husband's possible friendships. Robbie himself had no illusions and was always alert to the possibility of press or other gossip building up which concerned her, and always he had to take into account her outspoken habits.'[8] Once, when answering questions from a Japanese women's group about life in Australia, she described the Country Women's Association as 'a pack of thieves'. On another occasion, she made a public fuss over the appearance of gifts presented to her and another senior officer's wife by a Japanese delegation. On several occasions she caused incidents with visiting groups of journalists which had to be headed off by Robertson.[9] An increasingly cheerless match, the lifelong deception concerning its origins must have had an adverse effect on his personal relations with many of his contemporaries.

As a soldier he was the complete professional. Even those within the army who disliked him, for whatever reason, conceded his very considerable abilities as a field commander, a trainer of troops, and an administrator. If he drove his subordinates hard, he drove himself harder still. He would not tolerate half-measures or shortcuts; he had an unerring ability to master the detail of even unfamiliar subjects, which made his tours of inspection an education for those around him and a source of discomfort for those who failed to meet his exacting standards. And yet, as Rowell noted, 'he possessed, to an outstanding degree, the capacity to inspire the loyalty and affection of those who served under him. No military commander can ask for more.'[10]

Robertson is now a largely forgotten figure outside the small closed world of the army which he inhabited for so many years. His life and career are worthy of comment and study for a number of reasons, however. On the one hand, his service career parallels the development of the professional officer corps almost from its foundation until the displacement of the citizen soldiers by the regulars in the aftermath of the Second World War. The manner in which Australia created and maintained its military forces for the first half of the present century had its equivalent in other Anglo-Saxon countries, especially Canada in the same period.[11] In both cases, the small, long-service professional military strove, ultimately successfully, to have government accept that they and not the amateur soldiers should be the principal source of military advice and policy formulation. It was an argument accepted implicitly in the case of the RAN and the RAAF, but one long resisted in the case of the army. Its implementation after 1945 altered fundamentally the basis on which Australian defence was organised, and its legacy is with us still.

But Robertson's stage was wider than that. For over five years he occupied the post of Commander-in-Chief of the British Commonwealth Occupation Force in Japan, only the second Australian to hold such a position and to command British and Commonwealth troops in a multinational force. The broader intentions of the occupation, or at least of the Commonwealth role within it, were never realised, but this was in no way his fault or that of his force. The roots of BCOF's failure lay in the manner in which the force was committed, together with the lack of agreement between London, Canberra and the other Commonwealth capitals on the policy goals to be achieved. Robertson's disagreements with his British counterparts in Tokyo and with officials in London did nothing to alter that state of affairs, but certainly helped to obscure it on occasions.

Robertson and his generation were unique. Their kind does not inhabit the Australian army today, and indeed there is probably little room for them in that modern, high technology and intensely bureaucratised organisation. But their example should not be forgotten, especially among those who aspire to success in the profession of arms. For whatever their failings as men, they were an astonishingly successful generation of soldiers, and Australia and its army owes them much.

BIBLIOGRAPHIC ESSAY

In the decade before he died Robertson was at work on his memoirs. He began them in Japan in the late 1940s, dictating for an hour or so at a time each morning to his personal assistant, Lieutenant Mavis Lay, who then typed them up for correction. Referred to only half-jokingly as 'the million-pound libel', they were completed substantially at the time of his death. And at that point, together with such other personal papers as the letters he had written to his brother from Gallipoli, and which he had borrowed back to assist in the writing, they disappeared.

I have reconstructed his papers as far as is possible from a disparate range of sources, but these are not really a substitute for the originals nor for the tantalising autobiography. Robertson was never paper-shy, and wrote extensively both privately and for publication. A list of his published writings will be found at the end of this essay, and the endnotes should be sufficient to lead the interested reader to the source for any specific point made in the body of the text. The purpose of this essay is to outline the sources used in general and to offer a few observations on their difficulties.

Published sources on the army in the twentieth century are highly variable in quality and usefulness, and there is still as yet no history of the Australian army proper. Biographies of its leading personalities range from the barely competent to the outstanding. And the treatment of different periods is uneven as well; the First World War is probably the best-served of all, while the interwar and postwar periods are still marked by a dearth of good literature and the Second World War yields fewer works of scholarship than one might think.

The standard work on the Royal Military College, Duntroon, and which takes in much else besides, is Chris Coulthard-Clark, *Duntroon: The Royal Military College of Australia, 1911-1986,* Sydney, 1986 which supersedes the older but occasionally still useful J.E. Lee, *Duntroon: The Royal Military College of Australia, 1911-1946,* Canberra, 1952. The foundation years at RMC are dealt with also in Chris Coulthard-Clark, *A Heritage of Spirit: A Biography of Major General Sir William Throsby Bridges,* Melbourne,

1979. The Staff Corps *versus* Militia conflict which is so important to my account is dealt with in passing by many authors but has been the subject of direct study only by David Horner, whose 'Staff Corps versus Militia: The Australian Experience in World War II', *Defence Force Journal,* 26, January/February 1981 is the single most important contribution. Still lacking is any study of the social function of the militia in Australia in any period, or any social history of life and conditions in the regular army at any level.

The operational experience of the Australian army, and of the First and Second AIF in particular, is dealt with at great length in the official histories associated with their principal editors, C. E. W. Bean's *Official History of Australia in the War of 1914-18,* Sydney, 1921-42 (12 volumes), and Gavin Long's *Australia in the War of 1939-45,* Canberra, 1952-76 (22 volumes). In general, however, this is not the place to look for detailed comment on the internal workings of the army during either world war, nor is there much in Long's history on the activities or organisation of the army in Australia during the Pacific war. In addition, both must be supplemented by the British official series in order to provide necessary strategic context, especially for the First World War. Both Bean and Long knew the army of their day intimately, and their papers are replete with observations on personalities and conflicts within the forces. In neither case did much of this find its way into the final work, although in Long's papers especially there are numerous lengthy analyses of the state of the wartime army and its leading figures and speculation on the implications for the postwar service.

Biographies of Robertson's contemporaries are not numerous, and some of the most significant of them, such as Sturdee and Northcott, have received no study at all. John Hetherington, *Blamey: Controversial Soldier,* Canberra, 1973 is defensive in its tone and superficial in its coverage. Ivan Chapman, *Iven G. Mackay: Citizen and Soldier,* Melbourne, 1975 is a useful book spoiled by inadequate references. Stuart Sayers, *Ned Herring,* Melbourne, 1980 is an authorised life with all its pitfalls, while W.B. Russell, *There Goes a Man: The Biography of Sir Stanley G. Savige,* Melbourne, 1959 makes no attempt at either analysis or impartiality. G.H. Fearnside and Ken Clift, *Dougherty: A Great Man Among Men,* Sydney, 1979 does not do its subject justice, while S.F. Rowell, *Full Circle,* Melbourne, 1974, the only published memoir by a former Chief of the General Staff, is frustrating at all the points where one most wants enlightenment and a clearly stated personal view of events. Far and away the best study of this generation is A.B. Lodge, *The Fall of General Gordon Bennett,* Sydney, 1986; his PhD thesis on Lavarack awaits publication. A good collective portrait of the Second World War generals in action is given in David Horner, *Crisis of Command: Australian Generalship and the Japanese Threat, 1941-43,* Canberra, 1978.

The occupation of Japan has generated an extensive literature, almost entirely concerned with the American side and generally failing to notice

Commonwealth participation. The best single treatment of MacArthur and his role as Supreme Commander for the Allied Powers is D. Clayton James, *The Years of MacArthur. Volume III: Triumph and Disaster 1945-1964*, Boston, 1985, which takes in the Korean War as well. Roger Buckley, *Occupation Diplomacy: Britain, the United States and Japan 1945-1952*, Cambridge, 1982, is the only significant treatment of the Commonwealth role, but is limited by its focus on British affairs and by the fact that it tends to stop short on many issues in 1947. Although more limited in scope, Ann Trotter, *New Zealand and Japan 1945-1952: the occupation and the peace treaty*, London, 1990, is an excellent study of many of these problems seen from the perspective of the smallest dominion involved. There is some good recent work on British attitudes to MacArthur's imperium; in addition to the articles cited in the notes, see Peter Lowe, 'British Attitudes to General MacArthur and Japan, 1948-50', in Gordon Daniels (ed.), *Europe Interprets Japan*, Tenterbury [Kent], 1984, and 'An Ally and a Recalcitrant General: Great Britain, Douglas MacArthur and the Korean War, 1950-51', *English Historical Review*, July 1990. On the Korean War, see Jeffrey Grey, *The Commonwealth Armies and the Korean War: an alliance study*, Manchester, 1988. Robertson's role receives slight coverage in Robert O'Neill, *Australia in the Korean War. Volume I: Strategy and Diplomacy*, Canberra, 1983 and Anthony Farrar-Hockley, *The British Part in the Korean War. Volume I: A Distant Obligation*, London, 1990. There is nothing published on the Australian army in the early years of Menzies' postwar administration.

Scholars are well served, in general, by the archival sources and by their guardians. The principal keepers of the services' records are the Australian War Memorial and the Australian Archives, chiefly in its offices in Mitchell, ACT and Middle Brighton, Melbourne. The War Memorial is concerned primarily with operational records generated by units and formations and boasts also an extensive collection of private papers from both ordinary soldiers and their leaders. The war diaries for the wars of 1914-18 [AWM 4] and 1939-45 [AWM 52] should in all cases be supplemented by the operational policy files of the written records collections for those wars [AWM 25 and 54 respectively and in AWM 114 for the occupation of Japan and the Korean War]. Higher military policy, especially in peacetime, can be followed in the collections in Mitchell and Middle Brighton, although many of the records for the army in the interwar period have been destroyed, especially those concerning the administration of militia affairs. It is still necessary, and desirable, to supplement Australian records with material generated or retained by United Kingdom authorities. In addition to the records of higher headquarters under which Australian formations operated, and which are held in the UK at the Public Record Office, Kew [WO 95 for 1914-18 and WO 201 for 1939-45], it is worth consulting the collections amassed by the British official historians in the compilation of their own official series [CAB 45 for 1914-18 and CAB 106 for 1939-45]. These contain a great deal of correspondence with Australian service personnel on aspects of the fighting relevant to the UK, as well as with Australian official historians, and are well worth a look.

The disinclination of Australian service leaders to write much for publication has been noted already. Fortunately a number of those important to my purposes deposited collections of personal papers in public institutions, usually but not exclusively the Australian War Memorial. Of particular value were: the Blamey papers [3DRL 6643], Savige papers [3DRL 2529], Berryman papers [PR84/370], Stevens papers [3DRL 3561], Allen papers [3DRL 4142], Mackay papers [3DRL 6850], and Antill papers [3DRL 3607]. At the National Library are the Vasey papers [MS 3782] and Brudenell White papers [MS 5172]. The Mitchell Library in Sydney holds the Bennett papers [MS 807] and the Northcott papers [MS 1431]. The Shedden papers [CRS A5954] held at Australian Archives, Mitchell, although they offer little or nothing of a personal nature, contain much important official and demi-official correspondence. Also at the War Memorial are the papers of Mackay's biographer, Ivan Chapman [3DRL 6433], and Blamey's biographer, John Hetherington [3DRL 6224]. In a class of their own are the diaries, notebooks and correspondence of Gavin Long [AWM 67], which also contain some of Chester Wilmot's papers relating to the early Mediterranean campaign.

A list of Robertson's principal published writings follows.

'Horse Racing in Australia', *Cavalry Journal*, XX, 1931.
'Simplicity in Fire-Plans', *Army Quarterly*, 24, 2, July 1932.
'Hill 60: 10th Light Horse Attack', *Reveille*, 6, 2, 1 August 1932.
'The Empire and Modern War', *Army Quarterly*, 26, 2, 1933.
'The 10th Light Horse Attack at Magdhaba', *Reveille*, 7, 4, 1 December 1933.
'Mena and Moonlight', *Reveille*, 7, 10, 1 June 1934.
'A Modern Sheep Station in Southern Queensland', *Cavalry Journal*, XXIII, 1934.
'A Spy Story', *Cavalry Journal*, XXIV, 1935.
'The Defence of Australia', *Army Quarterly*, 30, 1, April 1935; repr. Department of the Army, Canberra, 1942.
'Some Light Horse Christmases', *Reveille*, 9, 4, 1 December 1935.
'The 10th Australian Light Horse Attack at Magdhaba, 23rd December 1916', *Cavalry Journal*, XXV, 1936.
'The NZs at Rafa', *Reveille*, 11, 8, 1 April 1938.
'Cooperation', *Journal of the Institute of Engineers of Australia*, 10, 12, December 1938.
The First Forty Days: 1914, Department of the Army, Melbourne, 1950 [a military training pamphlet].

NOTES

Abbreviations

AWM	Australian War Memorial
CARO	Central Army Records Office
CPD	Commonwealth Parliamentary Debates
DAFP	Documents on Australian Foreign Policy
FRUS	Foreign Relations of the United States
ML	Mitchell Library, Sydney
NLA	National Library of Australia

All series with the prefixes WO, CAB, FO, DEFE, PREM, AIR, DO are held in the Public Record Office, Kew, London; records with the prefix CRS are held by Australian Archives at either their Mitchell, ACT or Brighton, Victoria offices.

Introduction

[1] Geoffrey Elton, *The Practice of History*, Sydney, 1967, 134-35.

[2] Robert Skidelsky, 'Exemplary Lives', *Times Literary Supplement*, 13-19 November 1987.

[3] Jacques Le Goff, 'After *Annales:* the Life as history', *Times Literary Supplement*, 14-20 April 1989.

[4] Geoffrey Serle, *John Monash: A Biography*, Melbourne, 1982.

[5] *See* D. M. Horner (ed.), *The Commanders: Australian Military Leadership in the Twentieth Century*, Sydney, 1984; A. J. Hill, *Chauvel of the Light Horse*, Melbourne, 1978; P. A. Pedersen, *Monash as Military Commander*, Melbourne, 1985; A. B. Lodge, *The Fall of General Gordon Bennett*, Sydney, 1986.

1 Foundations: 1894-1915

[1] Details of his schooling are taken from a memorial address by Brigadier J. D. Rogers in 1962, copy in the author's possession; letter, Ewen McLean, Geelong College archivist, to author, 7 December 1988.

NOTES

[2] The standard histories of the Royal Military College Duntroon, are Chris Coulthard-Clark, *Duntroon: The Royal Military College of Australia 1911-1986*, Sydney, 1986, and J. E. Lee, *Duntroon: The Royal Military College of Australia 1911-1946*, Canberra, 1952.

[3] Details of his cadet performance are taken from his personal file, RMC Duntroon archives.

[4] Information from Mr Bruce Robertson of Sydney. The account of this by R. N. L. Hopkins in D. M. Horner (ed.), *The Commanders: Australian Military Leadership in the Twentieth Century*, Sydney, 1984 is in error.

[5] See Coulthard-Clark, *Duntroon*, appendix 5.

[6] *AWM* 182.

[7] Diary, Lieutenant Colonel N. M. Brazier, 19 November 1914. AWM 1DRL 147

[8] C. E. W. Bean, *The Story of Anzac*, volume I, Sydney, 1921, 138.

[9] C. E. W. Bean, *The Story of Anzac*, volume II, Sydney, 1924, 617.

[10] The appointment of officers as described here was not confined to the light horse. T. S. Louch, a brigadier in the Second World War, joined the 11th Battalion, 3rd Infantry Brigade as a private in 1914. His officers 'were mostly from the Militia or the Senior Cadets; some had been Area officers and others school teachers. Two had been at the Boer War, but few, if any, had ever served in the ranks'. Louch, *In the Ranks*, privately published, n.d., 9.

[11] AWM 40, box 3, file 'M'. *See also* N. W. H. Beaven, 'With the Machine Guns', *The Kia Ora Coo-ee*, vol. 2, August 1918.

[12] Brazier, diary, 20 November 1914. AWM 1DRL 147.

[13] Interview, Corporal Evan Bain, A Squadron. Peter Liddle collection, Leeds University.

[14] 3rd Light Horse Brigade War Diary, appendix May 1915. AWM 4, 10/3.

[15] C. E. W. Bean, *The Story of Anzac*, volume I, 600.

[16] 3rd LH Bde, Brigade order No 54, 8 May 1915. AWM 4, 10/3.

[17] 10th Light Horse Regiment War Diary, 23 July 1915. AWM 4, 10/15.

[18] Brazier diary, 16 May, 23 July 1915. AWM 1DRL 147.

[19] *Infantry Training Manual (4 Company Organisation)*, London, 1914, 202.

[20] Lieutenant H. C. Foss, 10th ALH (later 28th Battalion), typescript, 10. AWM 1DRL 298.

[21] New Zealand and Australian Divisional Orders, appendix, 1 June 1915. AWM 25, 515/367/233.

[22] A. C. N. Olden, *Westralian Cavalry in the War: The Story of the 10th Light Horse Regiment AIF in the Great War, 1914-1918*, Melbourne, 1921, 46.

[23] 3rd LH Bde War Diary, 28 July 1915. AWM 4, 10/3.

[24] Interview, Private C. H. Williams, A Squadron. Liddle collection, Leeds University.

[25] 3rd LH Bde War Diary, 18 August 1915. AWM 4, 10/3.

[26] *Ibid.*, 20 August 1915.

[27] 'This officer's work has not been satisfactory and in interests of Regt do not consider his services be retained.' 3rd LH Bde War Diary, 29 October 1915. AWM 4, 10/3.

[28] *Ibid.*, 23 August, 26 August 1915.

[29] Notebook, Lieutenant Colonel N. M. Brazier, 'Episodes of HQ treatment detailing disputes with Antill', and diary, 22 August 1915. AWM 1DRL 147.

[30] The account of Hill 60 is based on: H. C. H. Robertson, 'Hill 60: 10th Light Horse Attack', *Reveille*, 1 August 1932; manuscript account of the Hill 60 action written by Robertson for Bean, July 1931, AWM 3DRL 7953, item 28; letter, Robertson to Major General G. F. Wooten, 30 August 1954, Robertson papers; C. E. W. Bean, notebooks 216-225, AWM 3DRL 606; typescript account by Lieutenant H. C. Foss, AWM 1DRL 298; and unit and brigade war diaries.

[31] Remarks relating to the account of the Hill 60 action in the British official history, 29 July 1931. AWM 3DRL 7953, item 28.

[32] Letter, H. C. H. Robertson to C. E. W. Bean, 29 July 1931. *Ibid.*

[33] Foss, typescript account, 26. AWM 1DRL 298.

[34] 3rd LH Bde War Diary, 8 and 26 September, 1915. AWM 4, 10/3.

[35] *Ibid.*, 30 November 1915. *See also* letter, Antill to Headquarters New Zealand & Australian Division, 22 November 1915. AWM 25, 515/367/233.

[36] H. C. H. Robertson, 'Some Lighthorse Christmases', *Reveille*, 1 December 1935, 92.

2 A good war: 1916-1919

[1] 3rd LH Bde War Diary, 1 January 1916. AWM 4, 10/3.

[2] *Ibid.*, 3, 5, 6, 20, 28 January and 4 February 1916.

[3] Letter, Antill to R. H. Antill [brother], 5 January 1916. AWM 3DRL 3607.

[4] *Commonwealth Parliamentary Debates*, vol. 87, 22 November 1918, 8259-61. *See also CPD*, vol. 82, 1290, 1364; vol 91, 22 April 1920, 1423-24; 5 May 1920, 1751.

[5] Coulthard-Clark, *Duntroon*, 64.

[6] H. S. Gullett, *The Australian Imperial Force in Sinai and Palestine 1914-1918*, Sydney, 1923, 116. *See also* Olden, *Westralian Cavalry*, 73-6; AWM 40, box 3, 53/16 file 'R'; 3rd LH Bde War Diary.

[7] Gullett, *Sinai and Palestine*, 116.

[8] H. C. H. Robertson, 'Mena and Moonlight', *Reveille*, 1 June 1934, 20.

[9] 3rd LH Bde War Diary, 5 August 1916. AWM 4, 10/3; Olden, *Westralian Cavalry*, 88-9.

[10] Olden, *Westralian Cavalry*, 90-3; brigade and unit war diaries.

[11] Hill, *Chauvel*, 80.

[12] Gullett, *Sinai and Palestine*, 157.

NOTES

[13] Olden, *Westralian Cavalry*, 95.

[14] The unit marching out state was rather less than this suggests, through the necessity in mounted units of detailing men for foraging and related duties, together with the brigading of the machine gun sections which took place officially after the battle of Romani. The three regiments left Romani on 23 November in the following strengths: 8th ALH — 21 officers, 387 men, 458 horses; 9th ALH — 20 officers, 388 men, 456 horses; 10th ALH — 21 officers, 387 men, 449 horses. 3rd LH Bde War Diary, 23 November 1916. AWM 4, 10/3.

[15] Letters, Wiggin to HQ Desert Column, 1 December 1916 and Chaytor to HQ Desert Column, 4 December 1916. WO95/4471.

[16] Anzac Mounted Division General Staff War Diary, Order No 66, 20 Dec 1916. AWM 4, 1/60; George MacMunn and Cyril Falls, *Military Operations: Egypt and Palestine*, volume I, London, 1928, 252-3; Gullett, *Sinai and Palestine*, 214-15.

[17] Letter, Timperley to ?, n.d., AWM 3DRL 6294.

[18] 3rd LH Bde, Order no 1, 20 December 1916. AWM 4, 10/3.

[19] Letter, Timperley, *op. cit.*

[20] Anzac Mtd Div War Diary, 23 December 1916. AWM 4, 1/60.

[21] H. C. H. Robertson, 'The 10th Light Horse Attack at Magdhaba', *Reveille*, 1 December 1933, 3.

[22] 3rd LH Bde War Diary, appendix D, December 1916. AWM 4, 10/3.

[23] Signal, Divisional Headquarters to all Brigades, 23 December 1916, Anzac Mtd Div War Diary. AWM 4, 1/60.

[24] Robertson, 'The 10th Light Horse Attack at Magdhaba', 3.

[25] 10th ALH War Diary, 23 December 1916. AWM 4.

[26] Letter, Major G. Birkbeck, 2nd ALH, to Director, Australian War Memorial, 15 July 1927. AWM 93, 13/1/28.

[27] Chauvel, 'Operations December 20th to December 24th, including the occupation of El Arish and the attack at Bir el Magdhaba', and despatch, Chetwode to HQ Eastern Force, 2 January 1917. WO95/4471. *See also* Chauvel's letter to Birdwood on the operations in this period, 7 January 1917. AWM 25, 519/1.

[28] MacMunn and Falls, *Egypt and Palestine*, volume I, 257.

[29] Robertson, 'The 10th Light Horse Attack at Magdhaba', 26.

[30] Recommendation forwarded to HQ Anzac Mtd Div by Brigadier General Royston, 24 December 1916. AWM 28. The recommendation was written by Todd and approved and forwarded by Royston.

[31] Memorandum, A & NZ Mtd Div, 2 January 1917, AWM 25, 941/1.

[32] Robertson, 'The 10th Light Horse Attack at Magdhaba', 27; letter, Robertson to Director, Australian War Memorial, 17 September 1935. AWM 93, 419/87/5.

[33] AWM 40, box 3, 53/12, 'M'.

[34] H. C. H. Robertson, 'The NZ's at Rafa', *Reveille*, 1 April 1938, 42.

35 The 6th and 22nd Brigades had served in Egypt as part of Western Force against the Senussi, and were transferred across to Eastern Force after that threat had been removed.

36 Note on record of active service, personal file, Central Army Record Office; DSO recommendation, AWM 28.

37 Hill, *Chauvel*, 97-8.

38 Gullett, *Sinai and Palestine*, 256.

39 Letter, Gullett to Chauvel, 30 December 1920. AWM 40, box 3, 53/40.

40 Letter, Major General W. Malcolm, General Staff Branch, Headquarters Fifth Army, to Birdwood, 17 May 1917 and reply, 18 May 1917. AWM 25, 515/1.

41 Circular instruction, GOC I Anzac Corps, 14 December 1916. AWM 25, 515/3.

42 Minute, R. H. Brade, War Office to Secretary of State for the Colonial Office, 6 August 1917. AWM 25, 721/89.

43 Casualty form, personal file, CARO.

44 Gullett, *Sinai and Palestine*, 354.

45 Yeomanry Mounted Divison War Diary, June 1917-March 1918. WO95/4504.

46 Sir George de S. Barrow, *The Fire of Life*, London, 1942, 167.

47 The composition of a divisional headquarters was as follows: the general officer commanding, three general staff officers, two administrative staff officers, an assistant director of medical services and his deputy, the aide-de-camp to the GOC, an intelligence officer, gas warfare officer, assistant provost marshal, a Royal Air Force liaison officer, one staff trainee in the G Branch, a camp commandant, and fifty-seven other ranks. Mounted divisions would have an assistant director of army veterinary services and his deputy also.

48 Lieutenant C. H. Perkins, Bucks Hussars, undated recollections. Liddle collection, Leeds University.

49 H. C. H. Robertson, 'A Spy Story', *Cavalry Journal*, XXIV, 1935.

50 H. C. H. Robertson, notes on the British official history *Egypt and Palestine* for Cyril Falls, n.d. [?1929]. CAB 45/80.

51 Yeo Mtd Div War Diary, 13 November 1917. WO95/4504.

52 Robertson, notes. CAB 45/80.

53 Yeo Mtd Div War Diary, 23 November 1917. WO95/4504.

54 Aside from the works of Falls and Barrow and the divisional war diary cited above, the activities of the Yeomanry Mounted Division in this period may be followed in: *The Advance of the Egyptian Expeditionary Force — July 1917 to October 1918*, London, 1919; General Sir George de S. Barrow, *Two Cavalry Episodes in the Palestine Campaign of 1917-1918*, London, n.d. [1937]; Barrow, *Action of 6th Mounted Brigade at El-Mughar*, Cairo, 1918.

55 Major General R. N. L. Hopkins, letter to the author, 3 March 1987; General Staff, Delta Force War Diary, March-April 1918. WO95/4439.

56 Headquarters, Force in Egypt War Diary, April-September 1918. WO95/4455.

NOTES

[57] There is no satisfactory account of the repatriation of the AIF in 1919. For the AIF in Egypt see Hill, *Chauvel*, 194-96, 244 note 18; Suzanne Brugger, *Australians and Egypt 1914-1919*, Melbourne, 1980.

[58] Coulthard-Clark, *Duntroon*, 60-2.

[59] *Ibid.*, 62.

[60] *Report in connection with the Royal Australian Naval College, Jervis Bay and the Royal Military College, Duntroon by Professor Sir Edgeworth David, Major General C. B. B. White and Captain G. F. Hyde*, 6 July 1923, 4. National Library of Australia MS5172, folder 20, Brudenell White papers.

3 Between wars: 1919-40

[1] 'Report on the Military Defence of Australia by a Conference of Senior Officers', 1920, volume II, 31. AWM OW84/5, A1.

[2] *Ibid.*, volume I, 3.

[3] 'Retrenchments in the Armed Services', n.d. CRS A1945, 19/1/19.

[4] 'Report of the Inspector-General of the Australian Military Forces, part I, 31 May 1922', *Parliamentary Papers*, 1922, vol 104, 6-7. Emphasis in original.

[5] Gavin Long, *To Benghazi*, Canberra, 1951, 11-12.

[6] 'A brief narrative of the organisation, strength, and training of the Australian Military Forces since Federation', 31 December 1929. Military Board Proceedings, 1928, volume 1, folder 18, CRS A2653.

[7] Claude Neumann, Australia's Citizen Soldiers 1919-1939: A study of Organisation, Command, Recruiting, Training and Equipment, MA thesis, Department of History, Faculty of Military Studies, University of New South Wales, 1978, 90-1.

[8] *Ibid.*, 99-101.

[9] The definition is borrowed from Robert Hyslop, *Aye Aye, Minister: Australian Naval Administration 1939-1959*, Canberra, 1990, 61-2.

[10] *Australian Military Regulation and Orders*, regulation 33.

[11] Neumann, 84, 108-11.

[12] David Horner, 'Major-General George Alan Vasey: Commander, 7th Australian Division', in Horner (ed), *The Commanders*, 263.

[13] '"Red Robbie" — He grew up with Duntroon', *Daily Telegraph*, 26 February 1949.

[14] Major A. V. T. Wakely, *Notes on Working for the Examination for Admission to the Staff College*, Melbourne, n.d. [1922], 4.

[15] Robin Higham, *Armed Forces in Peacetime: Britain, 1918-1940, a case study*, London, 1962, 87.

[16] Alun Chalfont, *Montgomery of Alamein*, London, 1977, 96.

[17] Philip Warner, *Auchinleck: The Lonely Soldier*, London, 1982, 37.

[18] Brian Bond, *British Military Policy Between the Two World Wars*, Oxford, 1980, 62.

[19] David Fraser, *Alanbrooke*, London, 1982, 86-7.

20 Chalfont, *Montgomery*, 111.

21 'Staff College course 1923 — senior division', courtesy of the Staff College library, Camberley. The lack of a serious study of the staff colleges and military education generally in this period is explained by the almost total absence of records for the 1920s.

22 Bond, *British Military Policy*, 37.

23 'Better to know one's associates in advance than learn their good or not so good points from bitter experience'. S. F. Rowell, *Full Circle*, Melbourne, 1974, 27; 'Half-Track', 'Frank the Florist', etc., *Bulletin*, 22 March 1961, 47.

24 Rowell, *Full Circle*, 64.

25 Confidential report, Staff College, 1924. AWM 182, Military Secretary's records.

26 White, notes for the new CGS, n.d. [July 1923]. NLA MS 5172, folder 25, White papers.

27 Report of the Inspector-General of the Australian Military Forces, Part I, May 1922, *Parliamentary Papers*, vol 104, 16.

28 Letter, Lt Col C. W. Frizell, Directorate of Military Training to Military Representative, Imperial General Staff (Australian Section), 20 April 1925. AWM 182, Military Secretary's records.

29 Letter, as above, 4 April 1925. *Ibid.*

30 Letter, Brigadier T. H. Dodds, Military Representative, to Secretary, Military Board, Melbourne, 6 April 1925. *Ibid.*

31 Confidential report on officers, March 1926. The Australian army refused access to Robertson's reports on grounds of confidentiality. I was fortunate that several of his reports were among the papers and photographs held by his niece, Mrs R. G. O'Shea of Melbourne, who kindly allowed me access to them.

32 See the Inspector-General's reports for 1926 and 1927.

33 R. N. L. Hopkins, *Australian Armour: A History of the Royal Australian Armoured Corps 1927-1972*, Canberra, 1978, 15-23.

34 Confidential report, 1929. Robertson papers.

35 'Allotment for duty', 24 January 1930. AWM 182, Echelon Register, Military Secretary's records.

36 For example, reporting on the training status of the 1st Light Horse Regiment's camp 1928-29. 2nd Miltary District file registers, CRS SP 1879, 491/2. Unfortunately, the reports themselves have not survived.

37 Inspector-General's report, Part I, April 1930, 8. *Parliamentary Papers*, vol. 133.

38 Interview, Major General R. N. L. Hopkins, Adelaide, 11 May 1987.

39 *Ibid.*

40 Confidential report, June 1930. Robertson papers.

41 *RMC Journal*, April 1934, 27.

42 Echelon Register, December 1933. AWM 182, Military Secretary's records.

NOTES

[43] *RMC Journal,* April 1934, 27.

[44] Lavarack (CGS) to Montgomery-Massingberd (CIGS), periodical letter, 7 August 1935. CRS A6828, 3/1930.

[45] 'I gave many speeches in factories, lunch-rooms and town halls in the years 1935-39, seeking recruits for my battalion [57/60th]. It was a time when the numerical strength of the CMF — then purely a voluntary force — was at a low ebb and all unit commanders were seeking recruits. At our lowest ebb we went into one annual camp at Seymour only 120 strong, making training almost impossible.' Major General Sir Jack Stevens, unpublished MS, 18. AWM 3DRL 3561.

[46] *RMC Journal,* April 1936.

[47] Minute, Lavarack to Secretary, Military Board, 10 May 1934. CRS A2623, Military Board Proceedings, 1934, volume 1, agenda 5.

[48] *Army Quarterly,* 24, 2, July 1932.

[49] *Army Quarterly,* 26, 2, 1933.

[50] *Army Quarterly,* 30, 1, April 1935, and republished in booklet form during the Second World War.

[51] Australian Military Forces Gold Medal Essay, CRS MP927, A67/1/25.

[52] Paul Hasluck, *The Government and the People 1939-1941,* Canberra, 1952, 47.

[53] See especially the series of articles in the *Sydney Morning Herald* between 23 November and 1 December 1937, the last of which specifically picks up the arguments in Robertson's 1935 article.

[54] 'Cooperation', *Journal of the Institute of Engineers of Australia,* 10, 12, December 1938, 444.

[55] G. D. Solomon, *A Poor Sort of Memory,* Canberra, 1978, 84-5.

[56] Letter, Brigadier Ralph Eldridge, RMC class of 1940, to the author, 6 August 1990.

[57] Undated notes [1950s?]. Robertson papers.

[58] *Ibid.*

[59] Quoted in Neumann, pp. 181-82.

[60] Squires report. AWM 54, 243/6/58.

[61] 'The increased war planning activity of the last two years, together with the expansion of the Militia Forces has created a demand for more Staff Corps officers; there is in consequence a serious shortage of such officers.' Squires to Gort (CIGS), periodic letter, 7 August 1939. CRS A6828, 3/1939.

[62] Neumann, 120.

[63] File registers, Headquarters 2nd Military District. CRS SP1879, 491/1. Again, the report itself has not survived.

[64] There is no satisfactory account of this remarkable early regular unit. See K. H. Trevan, 'The Darwin Mobile Force', *Army Journal,* April 1972.

[65] *The Northern Standard,* 14 April 1939.

[66] Memorandum, Robertson to Military Board, 3 May 1939. CRS MP729/6, 38/401/23.

[67] *The Northern Standard,* 9 June 1939.

[68] 'Coordination of Defences at Defended Ports', Defence Committee minute 22/1939, 10 February 1939. CRS A816, 14/301/81.

[69] 'Supply of war garrison at Darwin', memorandum, Robertson to Military Board, 17 June 1939. CRS MP729/6, 24/401/24; 'Water supply Darwin', memorandum, Robertson and Lt J. H. Walker, RAN [District Naval Officer], n.d. [June? 1939]. CRS MP 1049/5, 2017/2/12. Early defence measures at Darwin are discussed in Alan Powell, *The Shadow's Edge: Australia's Northern War,* Melbourne, 1988. I am grateful to Professor Powell for copies of these two documents.

[70] *The Northern Standard,* 11 August 1939.

[71] *Ibid.* See also the issue of 25 August 1939.

[72] Correspondence between Senator H. S. Foll, Minister for the Interior and G. A. Street, Minister for Defence, 17 August and 8 September 1939. CRS [Northern Territory] F1, 40/478.

[73] Fortress Combined Operational Headquarters War Diary, 28 August 1939. AWM 124; Headquarters 7th Military District War Diary, 1 September 1939. AWM 52, 1/7/46.

[74] Darwin Mobile Force War Diary, September 1939-August 1940. AWM 52, 1/5/44.

[75] Minute, 14 September 1939. FCOH War Diary, AWM 124.

[76] Robertson, president; Wing Commander C. Eaton and Lieutenant Commander J. H. Walker, DNO, Captain E. P. Thomas, RN, members; Lieutenant Commander A. E. Fowler, Major J. H. Thyer and Flight Lieutenant W. J. Duncan, staff officers.

[77] FCOH War Diary, 21 September, 29 September 1939. AWM 124; Headquarters 7MD War Diary, 21 September 1939. AWM 52, 1/7/46.

[78] *The Northern Standard,* 3 November 1939.

[79] FCOH War Diary, 5 November, 8 November 1939; minutes Darwin Defence Coordination Committee, 1 April, 5 April 1940. AWM 124.

[80] Although the official historian accepts the tale that Menzies announced a monopoly of commands for the militia without reference to anyone else, Blamey's biographer notes that neither Menzies nor the cabinet were concerned with appointments below the divisional level, and that the story arose from a misunderstanding between the prime minister, Squires and Lavarack. Hetherington, *Blamey,* 88-9.

[81] Gavin Long, *To Benghazi,* Canberra, 1951, 45-6.

[82] 7MD War Diary, 8 April 1940. AWM 52, 1/7/46.

[83] Major General Sir Jack Stevens, unpublished memoir, 27. AWM 3DRL 3561.

[84] Letter, Vasey to Jessie Vasey, 25 March 1940. NLA MS 3782, box 2, Vasey papers.

4 'His crowded hour': 1940-1941

[1] 'Account of attack on Tobruk by Lt Col A. P. Fleming, ex 2/8th Bn', n.d. AWM 54, 521/3/11.

[2] 'I do not consider the behaviour any worse if as bad, as the AIF in 1914-15. We are aiming at a much higher standard. I can assure you that I am using every power at my disposal to improve the standard of discipline.' Letter, Allen to Blamey, 23 March 1940. AWM 3DRL 4142.

NOTES

[3] Signal, HQ Ausforce to Army HQ, Melbourne, n.d. [29 May 1940]. AWM 3DRL 6850.

[4] Letter, Vasey to wife, 12 April 1940. NLA MS 3782, box 2.

[5] Ken Moses, 'Legend of "Red Robbie"', [Melbourne] *Sun,* 20 April 1946.

[6] Long, *To Benghazi,* 83.

[7] Moses, 'Legend of "Red Robbie"'.

[8] Letter, Lieutenant Colonel A. P. Fleming, 2/8th Battalion to author, 28 January 1989.

[9] Letter, Robertson to sister, 12 [June?] 1940. Courtesy of Mrs Nanette Clutterbuck, Robertson's niece, of Perth.

[10] Berryman papers. AWM PR84/370, folder 1.7.

[11] 19th Infantry Brigade War Diary, 4-6 December 1940. AWM 52, 8/12/19.

[12] 'It is proving very hard to make a team — particularly without a captain.' Letter, Vasey to wife, 19 October 1940. Vasey papers.

[13] Letter, 9 April 1940. Vasey papers.

[14] Letters, 17 November, 23 August 1940. Vasey papers.

[15] 'Everything followed the same pattern. Pre-attack conferences were run like order groups with no whiff of a bloody committee meeting. Orders were short and clear with everything there that ought to be there and nothing that oughtn't. Above all there was an aura of complete calm and courtesy round HQ. In the month or so I was with them I never had a cross word from or to anyone.' Letter, Brigadier R. M. Jerram, CO 7th Battalion, Royal Tank Regiment to Ivan Chapman, 3 March 1968. AWM 3DRL 6433.

[16] On Savige's views see Russell, *There Goes a Man: The Biography of Sir Stanley G. Savige,* Melbourne, 1959, 206-07; Vasey wrote on several occasions that Savige should be removed: 'The one snag is Stan. He's hopeless. Quite unfitted for his job and I'm trying to work up Iven to do something about it', and 'Had Iven any real go Stan would get a bowler hat.' Letters, 1 March and 6 January 1941. Vasey papers.

[17] Neumann, 116.

[18] Letter, John Hetherington, Blamey's biographer to W. R. Lancaster, Director, Australian War Memorial, n.d. [mid-January 1971]. Hetherington papers.

[19] Notebook 96, 56. AWM 67, Long papers. The story is recounted also in S. Wick, *Purple over Green: The History of the 2/2 Australian Infantry Battalion 1939-45,* Sydney, 1977, 39-41.

[20] 19th Bde War Diary. AWM 52, 8/2/19.

[21] 'How that damned old school tie sticks with the Staff out here, and how they are using it . . . it was a damned black day for the 8th Bn and myself in particular when we left your command, we have been in trouble ever since and had a cow of a run, just means to an end for the Staff to climb at the expense of a damned fine Bn.' Letter, Mitchell to Savige, 7 October 1940. AWM 3DRL 2529, 87/10. Savige papers; letter, Lieutenant Colonel A. P. Fleming to author, 28 January 1989.

[22] Stevens, unpublished MS, 20. AWM 3DRL 3561; letter, Vasey to wife, 17 March 1941. Vasey papers.

23 'Strain of recent campaigns has been intense and do not think they could stand strain of further similar experience.' Letter, Blamey to Forde, Minister for the Army, 2 June 1941. AWM DRL 6643, 6a (1). Blamey papers.

24 Mackay wrote to him afterwards of his appreciation for 'the excellence of your arrangements and the success which attended the attack . . . I feel that 19th Bde has now been fully "blooded" and may be relied upon to give a good account of itself always'. AWM 3DRL 6850, item 100. Mackay papers.

25 Conversation with Major B. H. Travers, formerly ADC to Mackay, notebook 61. Long papers.

26 Russell, *There Goes a Man*, 205.

27 Bardia lecture. Berryman papers.

28 Notebook 39, 45-50; diary, 20 July 1944. Long papers.

29 '19th Australian Infantry Brigade diary of events. Libyan campaign', 3-4. AWM 54, 521/2/2.

30 Notebook 61, 27. Long papers.

31 19th Bde diary of events, 7. AWM 54, 521/2/2.

32 Interview, Major General Sir Ivan Dougherty, Sydney, 17 October 1986.

33 Chester Wilmot, *Tobruk 1941: Capture — Siege — Relief*, Sydney, 1944, 33-4.

34 The surrender of Tobruk and Robertson's comments are covered in various places. Chapman, *Iven Mackay*, 201-02; *White over Green: The 2/4th Infantry Battalion*, Sydney, 1963, 75; letter, Robertson to Chester Wilmot, 12 February 1943, and 'Report on the capture of Tobruk' by Brigadier I. N. Dougherty, n.d., both AWM 54, 521/3/11.

35 Letter, Brigadier Ken Wills, then GSO3 I Australian Corps, to John Hetherington, 20 November 1970. AWM 3DRL 6224 , folder 2, item 15. Hetherington papers.

36 19th Bde diary of events, 12. AWM 54, 521/2/2.

37 Wilmot, *Tobruk 1941*, 51.

38 AWM DRL 6850, no 107. Mackay papers.

39 Report by XIII Corps commander [O'Connor] on capture of Tobruk, 23 January 1941. WO201/345. See also 'Summary of the Battle of Tobruk', n.d. CAB 106/834.

40 Travers, Mackay's ADC, noted in his diary for 23 January 'All three brigs looking very tired. Iven sick tonight.' Notebook 61, 31. Long papers.

41 G. H. Fearnside and Ken Clift, *Dougherty: A Great Man Among Men*, Sydney, 1979, 39-40.

42 17th Brigade War Diary, 3 February 1941; Brigadier's private war diary, 3 February 1941. Both AWM 3DRL 2529, 89/1 and 87/10. Savige papers.

43 17th Bde War Diary, 4 February 1941.

44 Brigadier's private war diary, 3 and 4 February 1941. Savige papers.

45 Russell, *There Goes a Man*, 211-12.

46 Letter, O'Connor to GOC 7th Armoured Division, 26 January 1941. XIII Corps War Diary. WO169/1107.

NOTES

47 Notebook 90, 21-2. Long papers.

48 Menzies' overseas trip diary, 11 February 1941. NLA MS 4936/13/3, Menzies papers.

49 John Hetherington, *Blamey: Controversial Soldier*, Canberra, 1973, 124-25; Chapman, *Iven Mackay*, 211.

50 Letter, Field Marshal Lord Harding of Petherton, chief of staff XIII Corps, to author, 8 July 1986. O'Connor, commanding XIII Corps, wrote that Robertson 'was a swashbuckler whom I did not have much use for', but a paragraph later was able to add that the Australian commanders' 'plaint that senior [British] officers did not understand them ... was a fair criticism'. Letter, O'Connor to Long, 23 November 1950. CAB 106/727.

51 Wilmot, *Tobruk 1941*, 14.

52 Diary 5, 20 July 1944. Long papers; letter, Brigadier R. R. Vial, Intelligence Officer, 6th Div HQ, to author, 28 November 1987.

53 Hetherington, *Blamey*, 144; Chapman, *Mackay*, 213;

54 Letter, Vasey to wife, 17 March 1941, Vasey papers; letter, Rowell to Hetherington, n.d. folder 2, item 15, Hetherington papers.

55 Letter, Brigadier C. E. M. Lloyd to Hetherington, n.d. 'I certainly have no recollection of hearing or being told such a statement by Robbie. If I had heard it, or of it, it would have stuck in my mind ... In my experience Robbie would argue strongly for his own view, but given an order he carried it out.'

56 Medical records, personal file, CARO.

57 Interview, Major General Sir Ivan Dougherty, Sydney, 17 October 1986.

58 *Ibid.* One of their number in the 2/8th Battalion has written that 'for reasons not known to the troops our Brigade commander in the desert campaign had remained in Palestine'. Roland Griffiths-Marsh, *The Sixpenny Soldier*, Sydney, 1990, 156-57.

59 Rowell, *Full Circle*, 48.

60 AWM 54, 839/3/2.

61 Lieutenant General Sir Francis Tuker, *Approach to Battle: A Commentary. Eighth Army, November 1941 to May 1943*, London, 1963, 185.

62 Minutes, DDMS, CRE, CRA, 1 Australian Corps to Headquarters Australian Imperial Force Middle East, July 1941. AWM 54, 839/1/2. Respondents were commenting on the standard of reinforcements for the period ending March 1941.

63 Letter, General Sir Arthur MacDonald, 2/15th Battalion, to author, 9 April 1987.

64 AIF (Middle East) Reinforcement Depot War Diary, April 1941. AWM 52, 29/3/39.

65 'Robertson felt humiliated, and after that I do not think that he ever gave the General [Blamey] complete loyalty.' Norman D. Carlyon, *I Remember Blamey*, Melbourne, 1980, 61. Carlyon was Blamey's ADC for most of the war, a staunch defender of his chief and a harsh critic of his foes.

66 Minute, Robertson to HQ AIF Middle East, 25 April 1941. AWM 52, 29/3/39.

67 Letter, Robertson to Blamey, 15 May 1941. AWM 3DRL 6643, 5A(4). Blamey papers.

68 Letter, Blamey to Robertson, 22 May 1941. *Ibid.*

69 HQ AIF Reinforcement Depot General Staff Instruction No 28, 21 June 1941. AWM 52, 29/3/39.

70 *Ibid.*

71 'Objects of the Reinforcement Depot', July 1941. AWM 54, 941/6/9.

72 General Staff Instruction 31, 26 June 1941. AIF (ME) Rft Tng Depot War Diary. It read in part, 'No society of men whatever can preserve its unity and continue to exist if the criminal element is not punished, since, if the diseased member does not receive proper treatment, it causes all the rest . . . to share its affliction.'

73 'Visit of liaison officer to AHQ Melbourne', 20 July 1941. AWM 54, 839/1/2.

74 Letter, Robertson to Long, 4 December 1942. Personal records, Long papers.

75 Letter, Robertson to Ernest White, 14 June 1941. I am grateful to Ivan Chapman for a copy of this document.

76 Letter, Sergeant L. M. Long to Gavin Long, 3 September 1941. Long papers.

77 Wilmot, *Tobruk 1941,* 14.

78 'Organisation and Training AIF (ME) Reinft Depot' and 'Syllabi of the Tng Units', August 1941. AWM 54, 839/3/2.

79 Letter, General Sir Arthur MacDonald, G3 HQ Reinforcement Depot, to author, 9 April 1987.

80 Letter, Robertson to mother, 28 November 1941. Robertson papers.

81 Letter, Robertson to White, 14 June 1941.

82 Signal, Army HQ to Blamey, 13 July 1941. AWM DRL 6643, 6a (1).

83 Signal, Blamey to Sturdee, 20 October, and reply, 23 October. *Ibid.*

84 Chapman, *Iven Mackay,* 240.

85 Signal, Sturdee to Blamey, 11 December 1941. AWM DRL 6643, 6a (1).

86 'Notes on War Cabinet agendum 443/1941'. AWM 54, 9/2/14.

87 Hetherington, *Blamey,* 193.

88 Notebook 1, 24. Long papers.

89 George Weller, *Singapore is Silent,* New York, 1943, 44-5.

90 Letter, Robertson to Ernest White, 14 June 1941.

5 'A turbulent subordinate': 1942-1946

1 Rowell, *Full Circle,* 99.

2 Paul Hasluck, *The Government and the People: 1942-1945,* Canberra, 1970, 12-19; Dudley McCarthy, *South-West Pacific Area — First Year: Kokoda to Wau,* Canberra, 1959, 29-31.

3 Letter, Major General J. D. Richardson to Headquarters, Eastern Command, 12 January 1942. AWM 61, C2/1/400.

NOTES

[4] Neumann, 116.

[5] Minute, Richardson to HQ Eastern Command, 6 January 1942. *Ibid.*

[6] Notes on Berryman interview, n.d. [September 1956?]. AWM 93, 50/2/23/331.

[7] Interview, F. M. Forde, 4 March 1971. NLA TRC121/8. *See also* letter, Forde to Hetherington, 29 September 1970. Folder 2, item 15, Hetherington papers.

[8] Letter, Rowell to Hetherington, n.d. *Ibid.*

[9] Letter, Herring to Hetherington, 25 November 1970. Folder 4, item 20, Hetherington papers.

[10] Stuart Sayers, *Ned Herring: A Life of Sir Edmund Herring,* Melbourne, 1980, 198-99.

[11] Letter, Lavarack to Blamey, 5 November 1942. 170 D, Blamey papers; Berryman interview. AWM 93, 50/2/23/331.

[12] Letter, Garrett to Hetherington, 17 November 1970. Folder 4, item 20, Hetherington papers.

[13] Diary 9, 5 October 1942. Long papers.

[14] Letter, Rowell to Vasey, 19 May 1941. Box 2, Vasey papers. 'The lord is established in Cairo with his son as personal assistant. We are rarely consulted. I prefer it this way, as we are now not tuned to the same wave length and are never again likely to be.'

[15] Rowell, *Full Circle,* 105.

[16] Letter, Rowell to Hetherington, 5 July 1971. Folder 4, item 4, Hetherington papers.

[17] The 'revolt of the generals' is treated briefly in a number of accounts. See D. M. Horner, *Crisis of Command,* 57-60; Carlyon, *I Remember Blamey,* 89-90; Chapman, *Iven Mackay,* 261-62; and the biographies of Herring and Blamey.

[18] Hopkins, *Australian Armour,* 94-5.

[19] Draft War Cabinet Minute, November 1941. 8A(1), Blamey papers.

[20] 'Mobility in Relation to Plans for the AMF', n.d. [April 1941]. AWM 61, S18/1/834.

[21] Memorandum, Lieutenant Colonel R. H. Nimmo to Army Headquarters, Melbourne, 5 April 1942. *Ibid.*

[22] Memorandum, GOC 1 Cav Div to HQ Eastern Command, n.d. [16 January 1942]. *Ibid.*

[23] Memorandum, GOC 1 Cav Div to HQ Eastern Command, n.d. [29 January 1942]. *Ibid.*

[24] Letter, Robertson to Dougherty, 31 March 1942. I am grateful to Major General Sir Ivan Dougherty for a copy of this letter.

[25] Memorandum, GOC 1 Armd Div to HQ Home Forces, 27 January 1942. AWM 54, 44/1/4.

[26] Interview, Major General R. N. L. Hopkins, GSO1, 1 Aust Armd Div, Adelaide, 11 May 1987.

[27] 1st Australian Armoured Division War Diary, 22 April, 24 April, 26 May 1942. AWM 52, 1/5/31.

[28] Order of the day, 23 June 1942. 1 Aust Armd Div War Diary, AWM 52, 1/5/31.

[29] 'Preparedness for War', Brigadier R. H. Nimmo, 1 Aust Armd Bde, to HQ 1 Aust Armd Div, 27 June 1942. AWM 54, 44/1/4.

[30] 'Combat efficiency of units', 19 July 1942. CRS MP729/6, 42/401/142; memorandum, GOC 1 Aust Armd Div to LHQ (CGS), 23 July 1942. AWM 54, 44/1/4.

[31] Memorandum, GOC 1 Aust Armd Div to LHQ, 6 August 1942. AWM 52, 1/5/31.

[32] Hopkins, *Australian Armour*, 102-04. The manufacture of armoured fighting vehicles in Australia was one of the few failures in munition supply policy during the war, and armoured units were equipped eventually with American tanks. See D. P. Mellor, *The Role of Science and Industry*, Canberra, 1958, 301-22.

[33] Training instruction No 8, 16 July 1942; divisional exercise, 29 September 1942. AWM 52, 1/5/31.

[34] Diary 9, 14-16 August 1942. Long papers.

[35] *Sydney Morning Herald*, 28 October 1942.

[36] Diary, 5 September 1942. Long papers.

[37] *Ibid.*, 5 October 1942.

[38] Combat efficiency report, 30 September 1942. AWM 54, 44/1/44.

[39] Letter, Major General R. E. Wade, CO 10 Aust Armd Regt, to author, 13 December 1987.

[40] David Dexter, *The New Guinea Offensives*, Canberra, 1961, 17-18.

[41] Hopkins, *Australian Armour*, 105.

[42] 1 Aust Armd Div War Diary. AWM 52, 1/5/31.

[43] Notes on 'G' conference, 23 March, 1 April 1943. *Ibid.*

[44] 'I became an NCO in that magnificent yet frustrated division ... Many others tried to transfer out of the division, and some gained their wish, but I was kept there until discharged at the end of the war, embittered.' John Barrett, *We Were There: Australian Soldiers of World War II Tell Their Stories*, Melbourne, 1987, 7-8. Alec Hill, training with his brigade of the 9th Division on the Atherton Tableland in 1944-45, notes that the drafts from the armoured division received at that time 'were considered to be the best we had in the war'.

[45] Wade, letter to author, 13 December 1987.

[46] Forde, transcript, NLA TRC 121/8.

[47] Chapman, *Iven Mackay*, 262.

[48] Diary 3, 31 October 1943, diary 4, 19 March 1944. Long papers.

[49] Dexter, *The New Guinea Offensives*, 18.

[50] F. W. Perry, *The Commonwealth Armies: Manpower and organisation in two world wars*, Manchester, 1988, 167.

[51] Stevens, MS, 61. AWM 3DRL 3561. 'There are more reasons than one imagines for individual postings.'

[52] Hetherington, *Blamey*, 338.

[53] Letter, Garrett to Hetherington, 17 November 1970. Folder 4, item 22, Hetherington papers.

NOTES

[54] Letter, Elliott to Hetherington, 18 November 1970. *Ibid.*

[55] Letter, Bennett to Blamey, 28 August 1943. 170 D, Blamey papers; 2 Australian Division War Diary, 10 September 1943 and October 1943. AWM 52, 1/5/3.

[56] Letter, Bennett to Blamey, 5 September 1943. Mitchell Library, MSS 807/3, Bennett papers; and reply, 13 September 1943, 170 D, Blamey papers.

[57] Letter, Bennett to Blamey, 17 September 1943, Bennett papers; letter, Blamey to Bennett, 13 March 1944, MSS 807/4, Bennett papers.

[58] Letter, Gorman to Hetherington, 10 November 1970. Folder 4, item 20, Hetherington papers.

[59] Telegram, Forde to Curtin, London, 1 May 1944. AA, A5954, box 655, file 17. *See also* A. B. Lodge, *The Fall of General Gordon Bennett,* Sydney, 1986, 220-43.

[60] Letter, J. M. Fraser, acting Minister for the Army, to Northcott, CGS, 5 April 1944. 85.12, Blamey papers.

[61] Letter, Northcott to Fraser, 13 April 1944. 170 D, Blamey papers; 3rd Australian Division War Diary, 1-3 February 1944. AWM 52, 1/5/4.

[62] Philip Thomas, *Army Doctor: the reminiscences of a West Australian Army medical officer during the World War 1939-1945,* Perth, 1981, 102-03.

[63] Letter, Robertson to Berryman, 3 January 1944. PR84/370, series 2, item 13. Berryman papers.

[64] Blamey to Adjutant-General, 13 February 1943. 98.4, Blamey papers.

[65] Medical records, CARO, and Echelon register, AWM 182.

[66] Letter, Northcott to Vasey, 21 October 1944, box 3, Vasey papers; Coulthard-Clark, *Duntroon,* 161.

[67] A copy is in box 7, Vasey papers.

[68] Sol Encel, *Equality and Authority: a study of class, status and power in Australia,* Melbourne, 1970, 455.

[69] Diary 3, 31 October 1943, Long papers. He made similar observations in the last volume of the official history, Gavin Long, *The Final Campaigns,* 75.

[70] Notebook 27, Long papers.

[71] Berryman notes, AWM 93, 50/2/23/331; letter, Rowell to Vasey, 11 April 1944, box 9, Vasey papers. I. G. McNeill, General Sir John Wilton as GSO1, 3rd Australian Division, Queensland and New Guinea, 1942-43, B. Litt. thesis, ANU, 1984.

[72] General Staff Western Command War Diary, 20 April, 27 April 1945. AWM 52, 1/7/36.

[73] Letter, Jessie Vasey to Robertson, 25 March 1945. Robertson papers. 'On another occasion George Alan was saying how sad your employment made him when some of those present pointed, rather tersely, to certain "characteristics" which annoyed them. GAV turned on them and said "I know he thinks he is Christ and if you made him Christ tomorrow he would be Christ. I know he brags but so does Montgomery and I think Robbie quite as able".'

[74] Commonwealth Parliamentary Debates, volume 181, 28 February 1945, 128-29.

[75] Long, *The Final Campaigns,* Canberra, 1963, 70-1.

[76] Berryman, notes on draft chapters for David Dexter, September 1956. AWM 93, 50/2/23/331.

[77] 5th Australian Division War Diary, 21 April 1945. AWM 52, 1/5/10.

[78] *See,* for example, article in the [Melbourne] *Herald,* 22 August 1945, reproduced in John Robertson and John McCarthy, *Australian War Strategy 1939-1945,* St Lucia, 1986, 414-16; Peter Charlton, *The Unnecessary War: Island Campaigns of the South-West Pacific 1944-45,* Melbourne, 1983; 'examples of splendid fortitude, but whether they should have happened seems likely always to be in dispute', Gavin Long, *The Final Campaigns,* 387.

[79] Long, *Final Campaigns,* 265.

[80] 5th Div War Diary, May–June 1945. AWM 52, 1/5/10.

[81] *Ibid.,* 25 July 1945.

[82] Minutes of War Cabinet meeting 11 July 1945. CRS A2673, volume 16; 6th Australian Division War Diary, 28 July 1945. AWM 52, 1/5/12. Major General H. W. Lloyd had been recommended for command of the 5th Division, but War Cabinet ruled that at sixty-one, a younger officer should be appointed 'in view of the desirability of his experience in an active field command being conserved to the AMF during the postwar period'. Brigadier K. W. Eather, a citizen soldier aged forty-four, was sent instead. *See also* signal Forde to Blamey, 8 March 1945, 85.12, Blamey papers.

[83] 6 Div War Diary, 21 July 1945. 6 Div War Diary, 21 July 1945. AWM 52, 1/5/12. Battle casualties were 442 all ranks killed, 1141 wounded, and 16,203 hospitalised through disease in the ten months to August 1945. Long, *The Final Campaigns,* 385-86.

[84] Letter, Fraser to Chifley, acting Prime Minister, 2 June 1945. CRS A5954, box 2313.

[85] Stevens, MS, 89-91; 6 Div War Diary 2 August 1945; Robertson medical records, CARO.

[86] Letter, Lieutenant Bruce Flude, 2/8th Battalion, to author, 21 November 1988; Long, *Final Campaigns,* 559; 6 Div War Diary 7 September, 12 September 1945.

[87] Letter, Berryman to Mackay, 17 September 1945. PR84/370, series 2, item 13, Berryman papers.

[88] 'Handling of Japanese PW' and summary of operations, 6 Div War Diary 15 September. *Ibid.*

[89] Signal, Sturdee to Blamey and Northcott, 20 October 1945. Item 3.9, Berryman papers.

[90] Signal, Coleman to Quealy, Army Headquarters, 4 September 1945. CRS A816, 52/301/222; Long, *The Final Campaigns,* 581-82.

[91] Signal, Robertson to Sturdee, 19 October 1945. 3.9, Berryman papers.

[92] 'Statement showing personnel returned from abroad and discharged', CRS A816, 58/301/165A.

[93] G Branch First Army War Diary, 18 November, December 1945. AWM 52, 1/3/2.

[94] Weekly report No 13, 18 January 1946. *Ibid.*

NOTES

[95] Chief of the General Staff: Sturdee, Vice Chief of the General Staff: Rowell, Adjutant-General: Clowes, Deputy Chief of the General Staff: Milford, Quartermaster-General: Bridgeford, Master General of the Ordnance: Beavis, Northern Command: Boase, Eastern Command: Berryman, Southern Command: Robertson.

[96] Diary 10, 23 February 1946. Long papers.

[97] Letter, 11 May 1946, [Melbourne] *Sun;* in draft AWM 3DRL 357. Savige papers.

6   The occupation of Japan: 1945-1946

[1] Military Board Instruction, 23 May 1946. AWM 54, 721/27/1.

[2] Minute, F. M. Forde, acting Minister for Defence to Cyril Chambers, Minister for the Army, 20 June 1946. CRS A816, 52/301/246.

[3] Military Board Agendum 27/1946.

[4] Letter, Chifley to Forde, 12 April 1946. CRS A816, 41/431/43.

[5] Letter, Sturdee to Blamey, 25 September 1945. AWM 3DRL 6643, 61/170. Blamey papers.

[6] Signal, Sturdee to Shedden, 2 April 1946. *Ibid.*

[7] Letters, Robertson to Latham, 23 April, 29 April 1946. NLA MS 1009, 1/5801, 1/5802. His position as GOC Southern Command was filled by Major General Cyril Clowes.

[8] Roger Buckley, *Occupation Diplomacy: Britain, the United States and Japan 1945-1952,* Cambridge, 1982, 102.

[9] Signal, HQ 6 Div to subordinate commands, 26 July 1945. AWM 52, 1/5/12, appendix 51.

[10] Draft memorandum for the State-War-Navy Coordinating Committee, 11 October 1945. *Foreign Relations of the United States, volume VI: The British Commonwealth, The Far East,* Washington DC, 1969 744-45. Earlier it stated, 'General MacArthur considers, and the Joint Chiefs of Staff concur, that if the United States is to maintain the controlling voice in the occupation of Japan, US participation in the occupation forces must be at least equal to that of all other nations combined.'

[11] Buckley, *Occupation Diplomacy,* 87.

[12] Geoffrey Bolton, 'Australia and the Occupation of Japan' in Ian Nish (ed.), *The British Commonwealth and the Occupation of Japan,* International Studies, 1983/78, London, 1983.

[13] Minutes of the Chiefs of Staff meeting, 30 August 1945; letter, Stephenson to Ismay, 30 August 1945; minutes of the Defence Committee, 31 August 1945. AIR 8/1116.

[14] Minutes, Chiefs of Staff meeting, 12 September 1945. *Ibid.*

[15] W. J. Hudson and Wendy Way (eds), *Documents on Australian Foreign Policy 1937-49. volume VIII: 1945,* Canberra, 1990, 428-32. See also 432-3, 474-5, 487, 511-13.

[16] Signal, Chiefs of Staff, London to Chiefs of Staff, Melbourne, 1 November 1945. AIR 8/1117.

[17] Secretary of State to Australian Minister, Washington, 7 December 1945. *FRUS*, volume VI, 879-80.

[18] A copy of the cable was dispatched to London on 15 December. Hudson and Way (eds), *DAFP* VIII, 708-10.

[19] Text of the Northcott/MacArthur Agreement is to be found in Hudson and Way (eds), *DAFP* VIII, 728-31.

[20] Cable, British High Commission, Wellington, to Dominions Office, 30 September 1945. AIR 8/1116.

[21] Minute, ACAS (P) to CAS, 20 December 1945 and cable, British Military Staff, Melbourne, to Chiefs of Staff, London, 24 December 1945. AIR 8/1117; note by CAS to Chiefs of Staff Committee, 3 January and 8 January 1946. FO371/54078.

[22] Alternatives offered by MacArthur were the northern island of Hokkaido, rejected because of the extreme cold it experienced, and Kyushu, which was considered too small and lacked a major port.

[23] Cable, Foreign Office to UKLIM, Tokyo, 5 July 1946. FO371/54099.

[24] 'Dispatch by Lieutenant General John Northcott', 25 July 1946, copy to the UK Chiefs of Staff. AIR 8/1118.

[25] Robertson, unpublished MS, 11. Copy in the author's possession.

[26] *Ibid.*, 40.

[27] Letter, Gascoigne to Dening, 3 February 1947. FO371/63671; Robertson, unpublished MS, 17-21.

[28] Buckley, *Occupation Diplomacy*, 91-2.

[29] Chiefs of Staff Committee minute COS (45) 288th meeting, 24 December 1945. AIR 8/1117.

[30] Cable, B[ritish] I[ndian] E[lement] JCOSA to Chiefs of Staff, 4 May 1946. AIR 8/1118; Buckley, *Occupation Diplomacy*, 91.

[31] Brindiv intelligence review for the fortnight ending 7 October 1946. Brindiv War Diary, WO268/768.

[32] In addition to Buckley and Hopkins, see Major J. M. Walsh, 'British Participation in the Occupation of Japan', *Army Quarterly*, LVII, 1, October 1948; 'The British Commonwealth Occupation Force', *Stand-to*, 1, 3, March 1950; Lieutenant Colonel F. J. C. Piggott, 'Occupying Japan', *Army Quarterly*, LIV, 1, April 1947; F. C. Hutley, 'Our Occupation of Japan: A Memoir', *Quadrant*, January-February 1984; Frank Clune, *Ashes of Hiroshima: A Post-War Trip to China and Japan*, Sydney, 1950. The activities of the Australian infantry battalions are outlined in D. M. Horner (ed), *Duty First: The Royal Australian Regiment in Peace and War*, Sydney, 1990, 24-48.

[33] RMO's monthly report for November 1946, 10 December 1946. War diary, 65th Battalion, AWM 52, 8/3/102.

[34] War diary, 65th Battalion, 11 July; RMO's monthly report, November 1946. *Ibid.*

[35] *Ibid.*, 4 July 1946, 11 March 1947.

[36] BCOF HQ, Operational Order 4, 18 March 1947, Operational Order 8, 12 January 1948. AWM 114, 417/1/27.

[37] Buckley, *Occupation Diplomacy*, 92.

[38] Rowell, *Full Circle*, 161-2.

[39] Alan Rix (ed.), *Intermittent Diplomat: The Japan and Batavia diaries of W. Macmahon Ball*, Melbourne, 1988, 70. Macmahon Ball's powers of observation occasionally let him down: he convinced himself on their first meeting that Robertson neither drank nor smoked!

[40] *Ibid.*, 96, 90.

[41] Robertson, unpublished MS, 8.

[42] 'Those who served with BCOF in the early stages will recall that conditions left a great deal to be desired — accommodation was sub-standard, food monotonous and amenities virtually non-existent.' Philip M. Green, *Memories of Occupied Japan*, Sydney, 1987, 77.

[43] Hopkins, 'Australian Occupation in Japan', 105.

[44] JCOSA memorandum, 30 July 1946. CRS A5954, Box 1698.

[45] Letter, Robertson to Chifley, 2 July 1946. CRS A5954, Box 1886.

[46] 'High incidence of venereal disease within BCOF', appendix to JCOSA agendum 61, 30 August 1946. CRS A5954, Box 1886.

[47] Hopkins, 'Australian Occupation of Japan', 107.

[48] A. G. Butler, *The Australian Army Medical Services in the War of 1914-18. Volume II: The Western Front*, Canberra, 1940, 410n, 502.

[49] 'Despatch by Lieutenant General John Northcott', 25 July 1946, copy for UK Chiefs of Staff Committee. AIR 8/1118, 9.

[50] For Northcott's order *see* Robin Kay (ed.), *Documents on New Zealand External Relations. Volume II: The Surrender and Occupation of Japan*, Wellington, 1982, 1366, and discussion of it, 1367-9. For unfavourable press comment on the continuation of the policy, 1437-8.

[51] *Herald Tribune*, 7 August 1948; *Washington Post*, 7 August 1948; *Newsweek*, 16 August 1948.

[52] Correspondence on this issue between Headquarters BCOF and SCAP, August 1946. MacArthur Memorial, RG5, SCAP Official Correspondence.

[53] Robertson, unpublished MS, 47-8.

[54] Eichelberger diary, 5 August 1946. Perkins Library, Duke University.

[55] Robertson, unpublished MS, 49-50.

[56] *Ibid.*

[57] Eichelberger diary, 25 December 1946.

[58] *Chicago Tribune*, 20 November 1946.

[59] Robertson, unpublished MS.

[60] Letter, Chambers to J. J. Dedman, Minister for Defence, 15 January 1947. CRS A816, 19/304.388.

[61] 'Visit of Minister to Japan', n.d. [January 1947]. CRS A816, 19/304/388, 6-7.

[62] Letter, Gascoigne to Dening, Foreign Office, 4 January 1947. FO371/ 63671.

[63] Letter, Haydon to P. E. Coleman, Assistant Secretary, Department of Defence, 7 February 1947. CRS A816, 19/304/388.

[64] Rix (ed.), *Intermittent Diplomat,* 96.

[65] Northcott, 'Despatch', 6. AIR 8/1118.

7 The occupation of Japan: 1946-1947

[1] Roger Buckley, 'Working with MacArthur: Sir Alvary Gascoigne, UKLIM and British Policy towards Occupied Japan, 1945-52', in Ian Nish (ed.), *Aspects of the Allied Occupation of Japan,* International Studies 1986/4, London, 1986, 3.

[2] Carlo D'Este, *Bitter Victory: The Battle for Sicily 1943,* New York, 1988, 75, 122-23.

[3] Letter, Gairdner to Ismay, 30 May 1945. CAB 127/51.

[4] Letter, Gairdner to Ismay, 28 November 1945. CAB 127/51.

[5] Memorandum of conversation, Bevin, 13 June 1946. PREM 8/969.

[6] Joint Planning Staff report to the Chiefs of Staff Committee, 23 April 1946. FO371/54095.

[7] Memorandum, F. G. Shedden, Secretary, Department of Defence to John Burton, Secretary, Department of External Affairs, 27 November 1946. CRS A1067, P46/10/ 33/14. None of this stopped Gairdner from trying to create a role for himself as a source of military advice to Macmahon Ball. Chiefs of Staff Committee minutes COS (46) 54, 5 April 1946. FO371/54091.

[8] Letter, Foreign Office to Gascoigne, 23 May 1946. FO371/54095.

[9] Letter, Gascoigne to Sir Esler Dening, Foreign Office, 1 March 1947. FO371/63674.

[10] Minute, Foreign Office to Attlee, 7 November 1946. PREM 8/969.

[11] Letter, Gascoigne to Dening, 17 October 1946; letter, Gascoigne to Ismay, 17 October 1946. FO371/54111.

[12] Letter, Robertson to Northcott, 28 November 1946. Mitchell Library MSS 1431/18, Northcott papers.

[13] Robertson, unpublished MS, 53-4.

[14] *Ibid.,* 64.

[15] Letter, Gairdner to Attlee, 11 December 1946. FO371/63670.

[16] Cable, Gascoigne to Foreign Office, 23 October 1946. FO371/54109.

[17] Defence Committee minutes, 22 October 1946. AIR8/1118. The committee had discussed the matter previously, at a meeting on 3 October, but deferred a decision while the implications of the proposal were considered further.

[18] 'BCOF. Withdrawal of UK Brigade Group', Joint Planning Staff report, annex II, 2. FO371/54109.

[19] Signal, VCIGS to DSD, 20 December 1946. WO216/786.

[20] Minute, Addison to Attlee, 23 October 1946. FO371/54109.

NOTES

[21] Minute, Attlee to Addison, 24 October 1946. *Ibid.*

[22] Minute, MacDermott, Foreign Office to Haddon, Cabinet Office, 6 November 1946. FO371/54109.

[23] File note, Dening to Cabinet Office, 13 November 1946; cable, Gascoigne to Foreign Office, 19 November 1946. FO371/54111.

[24] Letter, Gascoigne to Dening, 3 December 1946 and reply, 7 January 1947. FO371/63670.

[25] Letter, Robertson to Northcott, 28 November 1946. Mitchell Library, MS1431/18, Northcott papers.

[26] 'Memorandum by the representatives in Australia of the United Kingdom chiefs of staff on the procedure for handling major matters concerning BCOF', 21 December 1946. AIR8/1118. The Chiefs of Staff Committee paid the memorandum little attention; see Chiefs of Staff Committee minutes (47) 5. DEFE4/1-4.

[27] Letter, Gascoigne to MacDermott, Foreign Office, 12 February 1948. DO35/2812.

[28] Cable, Evatt to Chifley, 26 September 1945. Evatt papers, overseas trips 1945, cables — London. Thanks to Professor Peter Dennis for this reference.

[29] Chiefs of Staff Committee minutes COS (47)175(O), 27 August 1947. DEFE5/5.

[30] Chiefs of Staff Committee minutes COS (47) 101, 8 August 1947. DEFE4/6.

[31] Cable, Chiefs of Staff to British representative, JCOSA, 7 December 1947. AIR8/1118. Cable, Robertson to Shedden, n.d. [early December]. CRS A816, 481/1/2.

[32] Cable, War Department to MacArthur, 19 April 1947. MacArthur Memorial, RG9, blue binder series.

[33] Chiefs of Staff Committee Joint Planning Staff report, 27 May 1947. DEFE4/1-4.

[34] Letter, Gascoigne to MacDermott, Foreign Office, 9 January 1947. FO371/63671.

[35] 'An appreciation of the value of BCOF', 22 April 1947. CAB106/834; [Australian] Defence Committee minutes, 17 April 1947. CRS A816, 52/301/309.

[36] 'Memorandum on Japan for the CIGS', 23 June 1947. WO216/786. In the Chiefs of Staff Committee Sir Rhoderic McGrigor 'recalled that the object in suggesting a British Commonwealth Occupation Force in Japan had been to further Commonwealth interests and influence in Japan. In fact, this object had not been achieved ... [and no] advantage to British Commonwealth trade interests resulted from the presence of BCOF'. Chiefs of Staff Committee minutes COS (47) 24 (final). DEFE4/1-4.

[37] File note, Dening, 13 March 1947. FO371/63675.

[38] Cable, Gascoigne to Foreign Office, 5 October 1947. CAB 106/834.

[39] Chiefs of Staff Committee minutes COS (47) 126, 10 October 1947. CAB 106/834; cable, Gascoigne to Foreign Office, 10 October 1947. FO371/63689.

[40] Cable, Chief of Staff of the Army to MacArthur, 14 December 1947. MacArthur Memorial, RG9, blue binder series.

[41] Cable, MacArthur to Department of the Army, Washington, 17 December 1947. *Ibid.*

[42] JCOSA memorandum, 'Proposed reorganisation of BCOF', 30 May 1947. CRS A816, 52/301/309.

[43] Letter, Gascoigne to Dening, 8 February 1947. FO371/63674. 'I was able to speak very frankly to Cawthorn because, although he is an Australian, he is well-known to be a particular friend of the United Kingdom, and a man of great discretion and tact.'

[44] Letter, Holdgate to MacDermott, Foreign Office 28 February 1947. FO371/63674.

[45] Cable, JCOSA to Robertson, 5 December 1947. CRS A816, 52/301/309; cable, Robertson to Sir John Slessor, CAS RAF, 7 October 1947. CAB 106/834.

[46] Cable, Chifley to Attlee, 9 December 1947; minute, Wilson Smith to Sir John Stephenson, 17 December 1947. DEFE11/50.

[47] Ian Nish, 'The Occupation of Japan: Some British Perspectives', in Ian Nish (ed.), *The East Asian Crisis, 1945-1951: The Problem of China, Korea and Japan*, International Studies 1982/1, London, 1982, 69. *See also* Buckley, 'Working with MacArthur'.

[48] One Foreign Office official minuted of the 'faint hope we may still have for an early return of our businessmen'. File note, 3 July 1946. FO371/54099.

[49] On this latter *see* Frank Myers, 'Conscription and the Politics of Military Strategy in the Attlee Government', *Journal of Strategic Studies*, 7, 1, March 1984.

[50] Letter, Gascoigne to Dening, 20 April 1947. FO371/63678.

[51] *Ibid.*, 6 February 1947. DO35/2813.

[52] Minute, Rowan to Hollis, Cabinet Office, 5 March 1947. PREM8/969.

[53] Minute, John Dedman, Minister for Defence, to Cyril Chambers, Minister for the Army, 2 May 1947. CRS A816, 52/301/345. Dedman did not agree that this necessitated further formal action, noting that Robertson's position in regard to command of BCOF and the provision of advice to SCAP was safeguarded in the MacArthur/Northcott Agreement, and that any intrusions in these spheres by Gairdner should be taken up with Attlee direct. This was small comfort in view of Gairdner's role in the troop withdrawal issue.

[54] Letter, Hollis to Helsby, Prime Minister's Office, 3 November 1947. CAB127/52. The correspondence is at PREM8/969. Gairdner described the dispute as 'all very irritating and petty, but unfortunately inevitable, owing to the character of Robertson . . . one must occasionally hang on to one's own end of the bone, or there wouldn't be a bone to hang on to!'

[55] To give but one further example, Gairdner to Attlee, 23 April 1947. PREM8/969.

[56] Minute, Machin to Orme Sargent, 13 March 1947. DO35/2813.

[57] Minute for Secretary of State, 11 March 1947. *Ibid.*

[58] *See* minute, Hollis to Attlee, 26 February 1947, in which Gairdner's requests for another private aircraft and British motor car so that 'his status in Japan would be greatly improved' are discussed. CAB127/52.

[59] Dispatch 264, Gascoigne to Bevin, 27 November 1947. DO35/2813. He went on to note that although 'the friendship between this mission and BCOF generally is not as close as it should be . . . I can truly say that our differences have been, and will I hope always be, completely concealed from foreign eyes.'

[60] Gairdner diary, 11 July 1947. I am grateful to Mr Walter Scott of Perth, Western Australia for granting me access.

[61] *Ibid.*, 12 June, 2 May 1947.

[62] D. Clayton James, *The Years of MacArthur. volume III: Triumph and Disaster 1945-1964*, Boston, 1985, appendix, 693-4. Gairdner does not appear at all on this list of those who had most contact with MacArthur, compiled from his official appointments diary.

[63] A full list of Robertson's appointments with SCAP and the occasion for each meeting is contained in MacArthur Memorial, RG 5, Memos to the CINC [1945-1951]. For example: 'He [Robertson] is planning to leave for Kure on Thursday and hopes to come in and have a "yarn" with you about the elections.' Memorandum, 28 November 1949.

[64] Eichelberger diary, 7 January, 3 August 1947.

[65] Letter, Byers to Eichelberger, 10 October 1947. Eichelberger papers, box 18 (personal) — letters.

8 The occupation of Japan: 1948-1950

[1] Report on CGS Conference, 10-11 October 1946. Military Board proceedings 1946, volume 1. CRS A2653.

[2] Minute, F. G. Shedden to Minister for Defence, ? March 1947. CRS A816, 11/301/610; minute, Shedden to Minister for Defence,. 9 April 1948. CRS A816, 58/301/174.

[3] Letter, Gairdner to Hollis, Cabinet Office, 12 May 1948. PREM8/969.

[4] Minute, Hollis to Helsby, 21 May 1948. *Ibid.*

[5] Letter, Montgomery to VCIGS, Simpson, 22 February 1947. WO216/204; CIGS memorandum to the Chiefs of Staff, 3 March 1947, *ibid;* notes on CIGS' meeting at Dominions Office, 10 June 1947. WO216/195; Chiefs of Staff Committee minutes COS (47) 97, 30 July 1947, COS (47) 103, 13 August 1947. DEFE4/6.

[6] Robertson, unpublished MS, 69-70.

[7] Minute, Hollis to Attlee, 29 June 1948. CAB127/52.

[8] Hollis, file note, 14 July 1948. *Ibid.*

[9] Draft, Hollis to Attlee, 12 July 1948. *Ibid.*

[10] Cawthorn to Long, 'Comments on draft of history of the Indian contingent in Japan', 2 September 1952. AWM 93, 50/2/2/28.

[11] 'Report of a Cabinet meeting attended by the Commander-in-Chief, British Commonwealth Occupation Force', 7 February 1948. Robin Kay (ed.), *The Surrender and Occupation of Japan*, 1474-80. *See also* minute, CGS to Minister for Defence, 5 February 1948. *Ibid.*, 1481-84.

[12] *Ibid.*, 1484-89. Prime Minister, Wellington to Prime Minister, Canberra, 9 March 1948. CRS A1838, 481/1/3. *See also* Ann Trotter, *New Zealand and Japan 1945-1952: the occupation and the peace treaty*, London, 1990, 66-70.

[13] Memorandum, Shea [?] to Chief of Staff, Eighth Army, 18 March 1948. Eichelberger papers, box 17 (official) — letters.

[14] Cable, Robertson to Chiefs of Staff, Melbourne, 12 April 1948. CRS A816, 52/301/309.

[15] 'Strength of BCOF', 19 April 1948. *Ibid.*

[16] Minute, Council of Defence, 28 April 1948. CRS A1838, 481/1/2.

[17] Cable, MacArthur to Department of the Army, Washington, 28 May 1948. MacArthur Memorial, RG9, blue binder series; letter, Major General Paul J. Mueller, Chief of Staff, GHQ FEC to Eichelberger, Eighth Army, 1 June 1948. Eichelberger papers, box 17 (official) — letters.

[18] Cable, MacArthur to Department of the Army, Washington, 4 December 1948. See originating signal, Chief of Staff to MacArthur, 29 July 1948, D/A to MacArthur, 3 December 1948 and MacArthur to D/A, 4 December 1948. All MacArthur Memorial, RG9, blue binder series.

[19] Minute, Chiefs of Staff Committee COS 116 (48), 20 August 1948. CAB 106/834.

[20] Cable, Chief of Staff to MacArthur, 10 December 1948. MacArthur Memorial, RG9, blue binder series.

[21] Letter, Blamey to Robertson, 12 July 1948. AWM PR85/355. Blamey papers. Reply, 24 July 1948, *ibid. See also* letter, Gascoigne to Dening, 9 October 1948. FO371/69935, which comments at length on Blamey's views on the occupation; Hetherington, *Blamey*, 392-3.

[22] Letter, Robertson to Northcott, 25 October 1946. Northcott papers, MSS1431/18.

[23] Letter, Robertson to Northcott, 28 March 1947. Northcott papers, MSS1431/19.

[24] *South China Morning Post,* 14 January 1948.

[25] Green, *Memories of Occupied Japan,* 151.

[26] *Sydney Morning Herald,* 5 April 1948.

[27] 'Why General hid his face', *Sydney Morning Herald,* 1 April 1948.

[28] [Melbourne] *Age,* 16 April 1948.

[29] 'A General meets the Press. Our Army in Japan', *New Zealand Listener,* 13 February 1948.

[30] 'Big Job Well Done by BCOF in Japan', *Sydney Morning Herald,* 27 April 1948.

[31] Letter, Gascoigne to Dening, 27 April 1948. FO371/69817.

[32] 'Australia's Major Role in Japan Force', [Melbourne] *Age,* 28 May 1948. Minute, Dedman to Shedden, 3 June 1948; Sturdee to Robertson, 11 June; Robertson to Sturdee, 5 July; minute, Dedman to Chiefs of Staff, 13 September. CRS A816, 52/301/286.

[33] Letter, Robertson to Northcott, 13 August 1948. Northcott papers, MSS1431/19.

[34] 'Our Army has a big chance in Japan', [Sydney] *Sunday Telegraph,* 10 October 1948; 'Red Robbie — He grew up with Duntroon', [Sydney] *Daily Telegraph,* 26 February 1949.

[35] Letter, General Sir Arthur MacDonald, Assistant Adjutant General, Army Headquarters, to author, 9 April 1987.

[36] Rowell, *Full Circle,* 173.

[37] Letter, Colonel John Buckley, Assistant Secretary (Supply and Logistics) to author, 22 October 1987. Buckley was Sturdee's son-in-law, and thus was privy to much of the background to events at this time.

NOTES

[38] Letter, Colonel Geoff Hollings, personal assistant to Robertson 1953-54, to author, 10 March 1988.

[39] 'Call-up ballot is from Tatts' barrel', *Sydney Morning Herald,* 7 May 1966.

[40] Letter, Gascoigne to Dening, 1 April 1949; minute, Scarlett to Commonwealth Relations Office, 11 June 1949. FO371/76255.

[41] This was an Australian delegation led by the ALP's Mr Leslie Haylen. It spent one day visiting BCOF while in Japan.

[42] There are three unpublished accounts of these trips, written by Brigadier R. N. L. Hopkins, who accompanied Robertson on them. Copies in the author's possession, courtesy of Major General R. N. L. Hopkins.

[43] 'Band plays "Auld Lang Syne" as Gen Robertson ends Shikoku tour', *Sydney Morning Herald,* 25 October 1948.

[44] Letter, Gascoigne to Dening, 14 October 1948. FO371/69935.

[45] Dispatch 103/1948, 17 May 1948. CRS A1838, 481/1.

[46] Gascoigne to Bevin, annual review for 1948, 24 January 1949. FO371/76176. In a file note, a Foreign Office official minuted that 'the gloom induced by ... Gascoigne's summary ... is not much allayed by the knowledge that the prolonged military occupation is having precisely the results that we foresaw'.

[47] Minute, Robertson to Shedden, 24 March 1949. CRS A1838, 481/1.

[48] 'MacArthur's "kind to Japs" order poses dilemma', [Melbourne] *Herald,* 29 September 1949.

[49] Minute, McIntyre to Secretary, Department of External Affairs, 4 October 1949. CRS A1838, 481/1.

[50] Piggott, 'Occupying Japan', 116.

[51] Letter, Pink, Tokyo to Scarlett, Foreign Office, 25 June 1949. FO371/76216.

[52] Cabinet agendum 78, 24 March 1950. CRS A4639/ XM1.

[53] Circular airgram, State Department to Chiefs of Mission, 28 April 1950. *See also* cable, Department of the Army to MacArthur, 29 April 1950. MacArthur Memorial, RG9, blue binder series.

[54] 'Japan peace treaty hint', [Melbourne] *Age,* 3 April 1950.

[55] Robertson, unpublished MS, 102.

[56] 3rd Royal Australian Regiment War Diary, 8 June 1950. AWM 85.

[57] Letter, Robertson to Sir John Latham, 10 June 1950. ANL MS1009, 1/7682, Latham papers.

[58] Letter, Robertson to sister, 20 June 1950. Copy in the author's possession, courtesy of Mrs Nanette Clutterbuck of Perth, Western Australia.

[59] Minute, Scarlett to Cumming-Bruce, CRO, 11 June 1949. FO371/76255.

[60] Letter, Gascoigne to Robertson, 26 August 1952. Robertson papers.

[61] Buckley, *Occupation Diplomacy,* 188-9.

[62] 'Directive to the Commander-in-Chief, BCOF in Japan', March 1949. CRS A816, 19/323/36, part 6.

[63] Transcription of interview with General Edward M. Almond, 1975, section 4, 6. Almond papers, United States Army Military History Institute, Carlisle, Pennsylvania.

9   Robertson, BCOF and the Korean War: 1950-1951

[1] The Foreign Office files relating to the recommendation, originally held in FO371, have been destroyed.

[2] Minutes and signals, 26-28 June 1950, all at CRS A816, 58/301/174.

[3] Letter, Robertson to Jessie, 29 June 1950. Robertson papers.

[4] *Ibid.*

[5] Radio message, MacArthur to Robertson, 28 June 1950. MacArthur Memorial, RG9, messages, personal for various people.

[6] Minute, Chiefs of Staff Committee meeting, 3 July 1950. CRS A5954, box 1659.

[7] Cable, Chiefs of Staff to Robertson, 3 July 1950. CRS A2107, K1.07; minute, Chiefs of Staff Committee meeting, 10 July 1950. CRS A5954, box 1661.

[8] Defence Committee minute, 1950/89. CRS A5799.

[9] Cable, Robertson to Chiefs of Staff, 17 July 1950. CRS A5954, box 1661.

[10] Roy K. Flint, 'Task Force Smith and the 24th Division: Delay and Withdrawal, 5-19 July 1950', in Charles E. Heller and William A Stofft (eds), *America's First Battles 1776-1965,* Lawrence [Kansas], 1986.

[11] Cable, Rourke, Washington to Shedden, Melbourne, 31 July 1950. CRS A5954, box 1661.

[12] Defence Committee minute 137/1950, 17 August 1950. AWM 124, Records of the Joint Administrative Planning Committee 1949-51.

[13] Cable, Robertson to Chiefs of Staff, 4 August 1950. CRS A5954, box 1688.

[14] Cable, Robertson to Rowell, 31 August 1950. CRS A5954, box 1661.

[15] Robertson, second unpublished MS, 18.

[16] Cables Z3714 and Z3715, Robertson to Chiefs of Staff, 12 September 1950. CRS A816, 19/323/15, part 3.

[17] Signal, Robertson to Rowell, 27 August 1950. CRS A5954, box 1661.

[18] Cable, personal, Rowell to Slim, 31 August 1950. *Ibid.*

[19] Cable 43030 (MO2), Slim to Rowell, and 43032 (MO2) Slim to Rowell and Cassells, 4 September 1950. *Ibid.*

[20] Report, Joint Administrative Planning Committee, 29 September 1950. *Ibid.*

[21] Minute, Rowell to Shedden, 3 October 1950. CRS A5799, 1950/107.

[22] Cable, War Office to UK Military Mission, Washington and C-in-C BCOF, ? November 1950. CRS A2107, K14.2.

[23] I have dealt with the Commonwealth organisation during the Korean War at length elsewhere; see Jeffrey Grey, *The Commonwealth armies and the Korean War: An alliance study,* Manchester, 1988.

NOTES

[24] Cable, VQMG to Robertson, 28 November 1950. CRS A2107, K14.

[25] 'Brief for Commander-in-Chief: Reasons which prevent the reduction of BCOF', ? December 1950. AWM 114, 130/2/15.

[26] Robertson, second unpublished MS, 16.

[27] Cable, Chiefs of Staff to Tedder, Head, British Joint Services Mission, Washington, 11 July 1950. AIR8/1608.

[28] Cable, Gascoigne to Foreign Office, 14 July 1950. PREM8/1175. When Robertson complained to Gascoigne about the appointment the latter was quick to assure him 'that he had nothing to do with [it] and apparently did NOT agree with it'. Cable, Robertson to Rowell, 27 August 1950. CRS A5954, box 1661.

[29] Minute, Foreign Office to Attlee, 20 July 1950. *Ibid.*

[30] Chiefs of Staff Committee minutes, COS (50) 116, 24 July 1950, COS (50) 117, 27 July 1950, COS (50) 119, 28 July 1950. AIR8/1608.

[31] Minute, Chief Liaison Officer, United Kingdom Services Liaison Staff to Chiefs of Staff, Melbourne, 23 October 1950. CRS A5799, 50/148.

[32] Minute, DWSH [?] to Attlee, 25 July 1950, and telegram, Commonwealth Relations Office to High Commission, Canberra, 26 July 1950. PREM8/1175.

[33] Cable, Cassels to Chiefs of Staff, London, 28 October 1950. FO371/84162.

[34] Robertson, second unpublished MS, 18.

[35] Anthony Farrar-Hockley, *The British Part in the Korean War: volume I: A Distant Obligation,* London, 1990, 323.

[36] Cable, Cassels to Chiefs of Staff, London, 26 October 1950. FO371/84162. The Australian Chiefs of Staff recorded in the minutes that 'the Defence Committee considered that the arrangement proposed by the United Kingdom Chiefs of Staff for their representation to the Commander-in-Chief of the United Nations forces was not in harmony with the established principles for cooperation in British Commonwealth defence. It was felt, however, that the wishes of the United Kingdom Chiefs of Staff should be acceded to and it was decided, with regret, to accept their amendment.'

[37] Letter, Liesching, Commonwealth Relations Office to E. J. Williams, High Commissioner, Canberra, 18 November 1950. FO371/84162.

[38] Letter, Williams to Liesching, 29 November 1950. *Ibid.*

[39] Robertson, second unpublished MS, 17.

[40] Bouchier, report 9 October 1950. FO371/84069.

[41] Bouchier, report 21 August 1950. FO371/84160.

[42] Robertson, second unpublished MS, 17.

[43] Minute, Scott to Dixon and Strang, 19 October 1950. FO371/84108.

[44] Letter, Clutton to Scott, 24 April 1951. FO371/92656. Bouchier himself noted that 'since MacArthur left here it has become more difficult for me to gain access to Ridgway and his top operational staff'. Bouchier, report 13 June 1951. FO371/92740.

[45] Letter, Clutton to Scott, 10 April 1951. FO371/92814.

46 'No action likely here on "Robbie"', [Melbourne] Sun, 20 April 1951; *Nippon Times,* 20 April 1951.

47 Letter, Ministry of Defence to Scott, Foreign Office, 20 April 1951. FO371/92816.

48 I Corps after-action summary, office of the acting chief of staff, G3, 24 April 1951. Washington National Record Centre, Suitland, Maryland, RG407, Command Reports 1949-54, First Corps.

49 Robertson, second unpublished MS, 31.

50 JAPC report 19/1951, 26 July 1951. AWM 124.

51 Minute, New Zealand Joint Services' Representative to Shedden, 13 August 1951. CRS A5799, 1951/120; *see also* cable, Australian High Commissioner, Wellington to Department of External Affairs, 16 August 1951; and minute, A.S. Brown to Menzies, 14 August 1951. CRS A462, 443/1/8, part 2.

52 Cable, VCIGS to Rowell, 28 August 1951. CRS A816, 52/301/319.

53 Cable, Rowell to VCIGS, 28 August 1951. *Ibid.*

54 Letter, Scott to Clutton, 28 September 1951; letter, Scott to Chiefs of Staff Secretariat, 29 September 1951. FO371/92835.

55 Letter, Clutton to Scott, 9 October 1951. FO371/92657.

56 See articles in the [Melbourne] *Sun,* 7, 20, 23, 24 November, [Melbourne] *Argus,* 15, 17 November, [Melbourne] *Herald,* 19 August.

57 Transcript of Radio Australia broadcast, 14 November 1951. FO371/92811. See also 'Australia owes a tremendous debt', *The Listening Post,* 31, 1, January 1952, 3-4.

10 The final years

1 Folder 1, item 14, Hetherington papers.

2 Diary, 10 October 1949. Item 10, Berryman papers.

3 'Notes on the appointment of the Chief of the General Staff' and letter, Berryman to Sir Eric Harrison, 29 November 1952. File 1.8, Berryman papers. 'The CIGS is appointed from a successful commander and not from a General serving in the War Office ... In Australia the opposite system was followed.'

4 Letter, Rowell to Berryman, 13 October 1949. File 7.11, Berryman papers.

5 Letter, Lieutenant General Sir Thomas Daly, to author, 7 May 1987.

6 'Notes on the defence problem 1951 by the Director-General of Recruiting', 21 February 1951. CRS A5954, box 1663.

7 *See,* for instance, memorandum, Major General Victor Stantke, GOC Queensland Line of Communications Area to Army Headquarters, 11 June 1946. CRS MP742/1, 240/1/3038.

8 'The post-war army — policy paper no 1', 6 March 1946. Copy in the author's possession.

9 Army Postwar Plan, March 1947, 2. CRS A816, 52/301/245.

10 Minute, McBride to Minister for the Army, Josiah Francis, 26 July 1951; cable, McBride to Robertson, 26 July 1951. CRS A5954, box 1663.

NOTES

[11] Cable, Robertson to McBride, 29 July 1951; cable, Shedden to Robertson, n.d. CRS A663, 0180/1/315.

[12] Minute, Shedden to acting Minister for Defence, 27 July 1950. CRS A5954, box 1663.

[13] Parliamentary question on notice, 26 September 1951. *Ibid.*

[14] Chapman, *Iven Mackay*, 305. Cable, Robertson to Minister for Defence, 21 October 1951; minute, Shedden to Minister, 26 October 1951. CRS A663, 0180/1/315.

[15] For example, [Melbourne] *Argus*, 17 November 1951. 'A colourful soldier in the spotlight', and '"Red Robbie" has a big new job'.

[16] Radio Australia broadcast, 30 November 1951, transcript. FO371/92799.

[17] Statement by the prime minister, 4 October 1951. CRS A663, 0180/1/315.

[18] 'Memorandum on the constitution of the recruiting campaign', n.d. CRS A663, 0180/2/397; *see also* chart of the recruiting organisation, CRS A5954, box 1663.

[19] *See* minutes on strengths of the services prepared by the Second Naval Member, Air Member for Personnel and the Adjutant General, November 1951. CRS A663, 0180/2/397; 'Notes on organisation of field force element of CMF', n.d. CRS A663, 0156/1/215.

[20] Letter, Robertson to Shedden, 11 January 1952. CRS A663, 0156/1/215.

[21] Letter, Robertson to McBride, 18 January 1952. CRS A663, 0180/1/315.

[22] Minute, CGS to Minister, 22 January 1952; see also note for Secretary [Shedden], 22 January 1952. CRS A5954, box 1663.

[23] Letter, Robertson to McBride, 24 January 1952. *Ibid.*

[24] 'General Robertson on Korea', *Stand-To*, June-July 1952, 25.

[25] 'Be strong — or we perish', [Melbourne] *Sun*, 9 August 1952.

[26] Letter, McBride to Robertson, 7 January 1953. CRS A663, 0180/1/315.

[27] Letter, Hollings to author, 10 March 1988.

[28] For example, letters, Rowell to Robertson, 13 July, 25 August 1953. Robertson papers.

[29] Letter, Rowell to Robertson, 5 November 1953. Copy in file 1.8, Berryman papers.

[30] Letter, Rowell to Robertson, 19 July 1954. Robertson papers.

[31] For example, *Herald*, 22, 29 October, 6 December, *Sun*, 23 October, 1 November, *Argus*, 23, 26, 30 October, *Age*, 26 October, 7 December 1954.

[32] *Bulletin*, 4 May 1960.

[33] *Sydney Morning Herald*, 29 April 1960.

[34] [Adelaide] *News*, 29 April 1960.

11 'Red Robbie': a summation.

[1] R. G. Hodge, 'In Defence of "Red Robbie"', *Bulletin*, 27 July 1960.

[2] Letter, Elliott to D. M. Horner, 10 July 1974. I am grateful to David Horner for a copy of this letter.

[3] Colonel C. W. T Kyngdon, Deputy Assistant Quartermaster General, 1st Australian Armoured Division, in Warren Perry, *The Naval and Military Club, Melbourne: a history of its first hundred years 1881-1981,* Melbourne, 1981, 264.

[4] Notebook 27, Long papers.

[5] Annual Confidential Report, Lieutenant L. R. Greville, 30 June 1950. I am grateful to my uncle, Brigadier L. R. Greville, for a copy of this report.

[6] Letter, Colonel C. W. T. Kyngdon to author, 16 June 1990.

[7] Observer, in 'Architect of the New Army', *Bulletin,* 29 June 1960.

[8] Letter, Major General R. N. L. Hopkins to author, 16 October 1989.

[9] Letter, *ibid.,* 1 October 1989.

[10] [Melbourne] *Sun,* 24 April 1960.

[11] Stephen J. Harris, *Canadian Brass: The Making of a Professional Army, 1860-1939,* Toronto, 1988.

INDEX

Abbott, C.L., 70, 73
Adachi, General Hatazo, 118, 119
Allen, Major General A.S., 76, 78, 85, 115
Antill, Lieutenant Colonel J.M., 8, 13, 20, 26
Australian army
    Administrative and Instructional Staff, xiv, 62, 66
    Australian Instructional Corps, xiv, 69
    Australian Regular Army, xiv, xvi, 167, 175
    Citizen Military Forces, xiv, xvi, 49-50, 51-4, 60-1, 67, 167
    demobilisation in SWPA, 119-20
    First AIF, xiv, xvii, 48-9,
    Interim Army, xiv, 166-67
    mechanisation of the army, 106-07, 111-12
    Permanent Military Forces, xiv, 51, 52
    postwar army, 125-26, 166-68; strength of, 198, 199
    Second AIF, 67; shortcomings, 76-77, 81; training, 95-96; unit commanders, 80-81
    Staff Corps, xiv, 21-22, 51, 52, 56-57; appointments to AIF, 73-74; Squires Report and, 67-69

Bardia, 81-83
Berryman, Lieutenant General Sir Frank, 57, 83, 93, 104, 114, 116, 125
    on Robertson, 119
Blamey, Field Marshal Sir Thomas, 67
    commands 2nd AIF, 74
    criticisms of, 116-17
    postwar army and, 122, 167
    relations with Robertson, 92-93, 97, 99, 111, 113
    relations with Savige, 79
    'revolt of the generals', 103-05
    visits BCOF, 167-68
Bouchier, Air Vice Marshal Cecil Arthur, 184-88, 192
Brazier, Lieutenant Colonel N.M., 7, 8, 10, 12
brigades:
    34th Australian Infantry Brigade, 131; indiscipline, 141-42; reduction of, 165-66
    3rd Light Horse Brigade, 7, 9
    9th New Zealand Infantry Brigade, 131, 139

INDEX

British Commonwealth Occupation Force (BCOF); *see also*: Robertson; MacArthur; Northcott; Northcott/MacArthur agreement; occupation policy, Japan:
    appointments in, 129
    area of responsibility, 130-31, 151-52, 156, 165
    assessment of, 176-78, 191-92
    Australian views on, 154, 162, 164
    British withdrawal, 146, 150-56 *passim*, 157
    command of, 126, 131-32, 158
    conditions, 135-37, 138-40, 141-43
    disarming of Japanese and, 134-35
    final withdrawal of, 175-76
    forces for, 127-28, 130-31
    Foreign Office attitudes, 134, 145, 154, 155-56, 192
    fraternisation, 140, 173-75
    in US command structure, 129-30
    Indian withdrawal, 146, 153-54
    Korean War and, 180-84 *passim*
    manpower, 155, 165-66
    military government, 136
    New Zealand policy towards, 164-65
    role, 134-35, 144
    venereal disease, 138-40

Cassels, Major General A.J.H., 186, 189
Chambers, Cyril, 141-43 *passim*
Cowan, Major General D.T., 133

Darwin Mobile Force, 69, 70-72 *passim*
divisions:
    1st Cavalry Division, 102-03, 106
    1st Motor Division, 103
    1st Australian Armoured Division, 103, 105, 107-12 *passim*
    5th Division, 117-18
    6th Division, 74, 76-77, 121; command of, 116, 118-119; losses in Libya, 92
    British Indian Division (Brindiv):
        despatch, 129, 133; role in Japan, 135
    Yeomanry Mounted Division, 37-43 *passim*

Eichelberger, Lieutenant General Robert L., 129, 137, 141, 151, 159-60

Gairdner, Lieutenant General Sir Charles:
    attitudes, 157-59
    career, 147-48
    clashes with Robertson, 146, 148-50, 157-58, 158-59, 163
    duties, 158-59
    on MacArthur, 147-48, 152
    prime minister's representative, 134
    removal, 163-64
Gallipoli, 10-19 *passim*
Gascoigne, Sir Alvary ('Joe'), 143, 158
    relations with Robertson, 146, 154, 157-58, 170
    on Gairdner, 149-50, 184

INDEX

on the occupation, 173

Herring, Lieutenant General Sir Edmund ('Ned'), 78, 103, 105
Hopkins, Brigadier R.N.L., 51, 62,
    in Japan, 131, 171-73
Hughes, Colonel F.G., 7, 13, 47

Joint Chiefs of Staff in Australia (JCOSA), 129, 130, 134, 138-39, 140, 143, 149, 151, 153, 155, 156, 162

light horse, 7, 8-9, 26, 28-29
Lloyd, Major General C.E.M., 100, 169-70
Long, Gavin, 51, 97
    on postwar army, 115
    on Robertson, 93, 108-109, 110, 111, 206-207

MacArthur, General of the Army, Douglas:
    appointment as SCAP, 128
    BCOF and, 166
    British policies and, 134
    command in Japan, 129
    dismissal, 188
    fraternisation, 140
    Korean War and, 180
    on brothels, 139
    relations with British, 146-48
    Robertson and, 149
Magdhaba, 29-34 *passim*
Mackay, Lieutenant General Sir Iven, 86, 91, 92, 199
    commands 6th Division, 76
    GOC-in-C Home Forces, 101
    Tobruk plan and, 85

Northcott, Lieutenant General John, 57, 107, 114
    as C-in-C, BCOF, 126, 130, 133
    returns to Australia, 136, 137
Northcott/MacArthur agreement, 129-31, 134

occupation policy, Japan, 127-29; *see also* BCOF; MacArthur; Robertson:
    American views on, 127-28
    British views on, 134, 153-54, 166
    Commonwealth role in, 127-28, 156-57
    function, 134-35, 144

Rafa, 34-35
'revolt of the generals', 103-05
Robertson, Jessie, 27, 54, 118
    marriage, 6
    death, 202
    difficulties with, 207-08
Robertson, Lieutenant General Sir Horace:
    career, xvii

INDEX

Youth:
  at RMC Duntroon, 3-5; birth, 3; marriage, 6; schooling, 3
First World War:
  as GSO III, 37; at Magdhaba, 30-4; August offensive, 12-13; awarded DSO, 33-4, 35; commands B Squadron, 10th ALH, 21, 25, 26; DAAG, AIF, 44; decorations, 44; embarks for Gallipoli, 10-11; Hill 60 battle, 13-16; joins 10th ALH, 6-7; joins Yeomanry Mounted Division, 37-38; posted to Delta Force, 43; posted to Force in Egypt, 43-44; repatriated 1919, 44, 47; service with Yeomanry Mounted Division, 38-43; wounded, 19
Interwar:
  attends Staff College, 49, 54-59; Chief Instructor, Small Arms School, 60-61; Commandant 7MD, 69, 70-74 *passim*; courses in England, 59-60; DMA at Duntroon, 63-64, 66; Inspector-General's Branch, 61-62; interwar frustrations, 53-54; Murdoch and, 67; posted to 2 MD, 63; publications, 63-65; relegated, 62-63; service in 3 MD, 47
Second World War:
  attack on Tobruk, 83-89; attitude to postwar army, 122; Bardia, 81-83; command of 19th Brigade, 74, 73-79 *passim*; commands 1st Armoured Division, 105, 106, 107-12; commands 1st Cavalry Division, 102-04, 106; commands AIF Reinforcement Depot, 94-99; commands III Corps, 113-14, 116; demobilisation 1945, 119-20; departs for Middle East, 77; falls out with Blamey, 92-93; GOC 5th Division, 116-18; GOC 6th Division, 118; GOC Southern Command, 121; hospitalised 1941: 93-94, 1944: 114-15; medical problems, 43, 94, 114-15; Menzies' comment on, 92; moves to III Corps, 110-11, 112-14; pursuit of the Italians, 89-92; relations with Gordon Bennett, 112-13; relations with Savige, 83, 90-92; relations with unit commanders, 79-80, 89-90, 94; replaces Northcott 1941, 107; returns to Australia 1941, 99-100; reviews RMC, 114-15; 'revolt of the generals', 103-05; style of command, 113-14; takes Adachi's surrender, 118-19; trains 19th Brigade, 77-78
BCOF:
  appointment of CGS 1949, 171, 195-96; arrives in Japan, 137; as C-in-C BCFK, 183-184; attends CIGS exercises, 162-63; British views on, 157-58, 183-84; Cassels on, 186; Chifley's concerns re BCOF, 138; command of BCOF, 133; criticism of, 142, 168-70; dismissal of MacArthur, 188; early problems in Japan, 141-43; Gascoigne on, 154; Japanese war guilt, 140; knighted, 176-77, 179; Macmahon Ball on, 137, 143; New Zealand views on, 189; New Zealand withdrawal, 164-65; on MacArthur, 180; outbreak of the Korean War, 179, 180-81; postwar promotion, 125-26; relations with Bouchier, 184-88; relations with Cowan, 133; relations with Gairdner, 146, 148-50, 152-53, 158-59; relations with Gascoigne, 176-77; removal of Gairdner, 163-64; responds to critics, 170; selection as C-in-C BCOF, 126; tours his command, 171-73; UK Chiefs of Staff and, 184-86, 186-87, 188; UN Command and, 181; withdrawal of forces, 153-55
Later years:
  appointed GOC Southern Command, 201; clashes with Rowell, 201; contemporaries' judgements, 205-06, 207-08; death, 202-04; Director General of Recruiting, 190, 196-201 *passim*; Hetherington on, 195; memoirs, 210; on postwar army, 175-76; recalled to Australia, 190-91, 198; retires, 201-02
Rowell, Lieutenant General S.F., 74, 97, 116, 125
  as CGS, 171, 195-96, 200

BCFK and, 182-83, 186
DCGS, 101
interwar army, 53, 57
on Northcott, 137
on Robertson, 136-37
'revolt of the generals', 105
Royal Military College Duntroon:
First World War and, 5-6, 19, 21-22, 36, 43, 45
foundation, 3-4
interwar, 63, 66
reviewed, 114-15
Royston, Brigadier J.R., 26, 31, 33

Savige, Lieutenant General Sir Stanley:
commands 17th Brigade, 76, 78
on postwar army, 122
Robertson and, 83, 90-92
shortcomings, 115
Small Arms School, Randwick, 59, 60-61
Squires, Lieutenant General E.K., 68-69
Stevens, Major General J.E.S., 80, 116, 118
Sturdee, Lieutenant General Sir Vernon, 51, 99, 119, 130, 171
as postwar CGS, 125
selects Robertson for Japan, 126

Tobruk, 83-89 *passim*
Italian losses, 88
Todd, Major T.J., 12, 17, 20, 23, 31, 33, 35

units:
10th Australian Light Horse Regiment, 7, 9, 12-13, 14-16, 20, 22, 23, 26-27

Vasey, Major General George, 51, 57, 83, 93, 94, 103, 114
on appointments to 2nd AIF, 74-75, 77, 78
on Robertson, 116, 230n

Wilmot, Chester, 86
on Robertson, 93

For EU product safety concerns, contact us at Calle de José Abascal, 56–1°,
28003 Madrid, Spain or eugpsr@cambridge.org.

www.ingramcontent.com/pod-product-compliance
Lightning Source LLC
LaVergne TN
LVHW010338260326
834688LV00036B/776